DEFENDING PROFESSIONALISM

DEFENDING PROFESSIONALISM

A Resource for Librarians, Information Specialists, Knowledge Managers, and Archivists

BILL CROWLEY, EDITOR

LIBRARIES UNLIMITED

AN IMPRINT OF ABC-CLIO, LLC
Santa Barbara, California • Denver, Colorado • Oxford, England

Library of Congress Cataloging-in-Publication Data

Defending professionalism : a resource for librarians, information specialists, knowledge managers, and archivists / Bill Crowley, editor.

      pages cm

  Includes bibliographical references and index.

  ISBN 978-1-59884-869-4 (pbk.) — ISBN 978-1-59884-870-0 (ebook)

1. Libraries and society. 2. Library education. 3. Librarians—Professional ethics.
4. Information scientists—Training of. 5. Information scientists—Professional ethics.
6. Knowledge workers—Training of. 7. Knowledge workers—Professional ethics.
8. Archivists—Training of. 9. Archivists—Professional ethics. I. Crowley, William A.,
1949–editor of compilation.

  Z716.4D43 2012

  020.92—dc23   2012006410

ISBN: 978-1-59884-869-4
EISBN: 978-1-59884-870-0

16 15 14 13 12   1 2 3 4 5

This book is also available on the World Wide Web as an eBook.
Visit www.abc-clio.com for details.

Libraries Unlimited
An Imprint of ABC-CLIO, LLC

ABC-CLIO, LLC
130 Cremona Drive, P.O. Box 1911
Santa Barbara, California 93116-1911

This book is printed on acid-free paper ∞

Manufactured in the United States of America

CONTENTS

INTRODUCTION: HOW DID WE GET INTO THIS DILEMMA IN THE FIRST PLACE?

Bill Crowley
Dominican University

PROFESSIONALISM BEFORE, DURING, AND "AFTER" THE GREAT RECESSION: TALES OF THREE NATIONS

Britain

In January 2011, news media reported on the projected closings of "a third of all Britain's libraries" or a total of more than 1,300 public library outlets. Proportionate layoffs of British librarians and other staff were also predicted. These draconian reductions were announced in response to a decrease of six and a half billion pounds in the funds distributed to local authorities by the British coalition government headed by Conservative Prime Minister David Cameron (Boniface 2011). From the perspective of the public library community and many library users, this slashing of funding for libraries, librarians, and other staff was and is an ill-considered, unthinking, and much too rapid reaction by local officials whose knee-jerk response failed to evaluate the worth of the library and other programs before taking action.

Canada

Serious Canadian problems of library funding exist, a number of which preceded the current world financial crisis and are indicative of a long-standing dilemma for professionalism. In a media release dated June 7, 2011, the Canadian Library Association (CLA) reported on yet more school library and teacher-librarian (school librarian) reductions. CLA stressed that in some Canadian school systems "no professional staffing exists" to provide quality library service. In its documentation of specific librarian losses at the provincial level, CLA described the elimination of additional teacher-librarian positions in British Columbia and stressed the remarkable fact that Manitoba has "lost approximately 60% of its teacher-librarians" since the 1980s (Canadian Library Association 2011).

A similar reduction in the number of professional teacher-librarians in the more populated Canadian province of Ontario was reported by People for Education in its 2011 Annual School Survey. During the 2010–11 school year, only "56% of elementary schools" employed a teacher-librarian, and then mostly on a part-time basis. This represented a massive reduction in the total number of teacher-librarians since the 1997–98 school year when 80 percent of Ontario's elementary schools, their students and teachers, benefited from the work of professional librarians in the delivery of school library services (People for Education 2011).

United States

Since the 2007 multinational financial implosion, increasing numbers of experienced and newly graduated American library, information, knowledge, and archival professionals have endured the bitter experience of job loss or the inability to secure a beginning professional position. The fear of being one budget decision away from the unemployment line is now commonplace for many professionals. In many instances, American public, academic, and school libraries have borne a disproportionate share of the cutbacks made by state and local governments, universities, and school systems (American Library Association 2011).

As analyzed in the American Library Association's *The State of America's Libraries, 2011*:

- in 2010, U.S mayors found local public libraries preferred targets for cutbacks in budgets and programs. "*The main target was maintenance and services at parks and gardens (41 percent), with local libraries close behind at 39 percent*" (12; italics added);
- high poverty areas saw "significant declines" in spending for school libraries (23); and
- 3 out of 10 (30%) university libraries that reported budget cuts planned to reduce funds spent on staffing (29).

Although officially over, having commenced in the United States in December 2007 and "concluded" in June 2009 (National Bureau of Economic Research 2011), the effects of The Great Recession are yet felt on a daily basis. Above-average unemployment, lowered government revenues, and spiraling requests for assistance now constitute the ongoing crisis of the day-to-day. Worse, according to a recent analysis contained in *Facing Facts: Public Attitudes and Fiscal Realities in Five Stressed States*, many states are facing additional budget gaps in upcoming years (Pew Center on the States and the Public Policy Institute of California 2010, 4–5). Such gaps will inevitably limit the availability of state dollars for the support of library, information knowledge, and archival professionals and other employees in state-assisted public libraries, public schools, and higher education institutions, which, in time, will cause library and information personnel reductions within state governments themselves.

Analyses of present-day patterns of deprofessionalization have been insightful and useful both as problem indicators and descriptions of areas for remedial action (Oder 2009, 2010). These include "skills versus education" analyses focused on the development of electronic reference and information skills by lesser-paid staff without a relevant professional education (Rubin 2010, 261).

In the context of financial restraints and the revelation that many library and information programs have failed to develop a clientele willing to strongly advocate for their services, it appears fighting battles over professionalism in a limited resource environment is likely to extend into the foreseeable future. At least one official source, the British government, expects the consequences of the current economic breakdown to last a decade (Winnett 2009). Consequently, efforts to understand and counter threats to professional status will need to simultaneously address both the immediate crisis and its longer term causes.

In following the urging of Keith Michael Fiels, Executive Director of the American Library Association (ALA), to beat "plowshares into swords" and strongly resist personnel reductions, program cutbacks, and building closings, it would be self-defeating not to address the fundamental reasons why "the library is the first to be cut or is disproportionately cut, regarded as a 'nonessential' service" (Fiels 2009, 8) when academic, community, or school funding becomes constrained or reduced.

A FOREWARNING FROM THE EDITOR

The author of this introduction, who is also the editor of *Defending Professionalism: A Resource for Librarians, Information Specialists, Knowledge Managers and Archivists*, feels obligated to express regret in advance to readers who might become offended by claims that some of their actions, even those taken with the best of intentions, contribute to undermining professionalism and lessening the quality of American, Canadian, and British library, information, knowledge, and archival services. In truth, the consequences of such actions, whether intended or unintended, are at times incredibly destructive to the potential benefits provided by appropriately educated professionals. As such, they must be discussed and understood so that they can be reversed or at least mitigated.

SYMBOLS AND GENERALITIES OR "THE PROBLEM OF DEFINING THE PROBLEM"

Even sympathetic readers of *Defending Professionalism* may well object to some aspect of the problem definition, particularly as it is played out in differing British, Canadian, and American environments. Borders are more than lines on a map. They can also indicate the existence of different ways of thinking. It is not for naught that the BBC stressed George Bernard Shaw's sage remark "that the US and the UK are 'two nations divided by a common language'" (BBC News 2001). Interchanges between Canada and America are a bit more understandable, with the exception that the French context of Quebec requires a more Gallic mindset. Unfortunately, this editor's five years of French, of which four were spent studying with the De La Salle Christian Brothers, have been sadly diminished through lack of use.

Readers of *Defending Professionalism* will soon discover the compounding factor in thrashing out what really is the problem of maintaining and enhancing professional status. It is the simple matter of different points of view. Librarians, information specialists, knowledge managers, archivists, trustees, academic administrators, local officials, and others will bring a broad spectrum of life experiences and preexisting opinions to a reading of this work. Our different life experiences function to provide us with diverse ways of looking at the same facts. This brings into play a cultural truth that we ignore at our peril—"symbols and generalities unite while details divide." It is likely that a clear majority of readers will agree that there is a serious predicament involving the employment and retention of professionals in our libraries, corporations, schools, and universities. The impasse with discussing the "dilemma of deprofessionalization" begins when we try to define exactly what the problem really is.

Matters of nuance aside, readers are also likely to be divided over the value of the solutions proposed by the individual chapter authors and the volume editor. Nevertheless, because no worthwhile examination of the problem of professional status is possible without a definition (Crowley 2005), one will be provided.

DEFINING THE DEPROFESSIONALISM PROBLEM

In the case in point, library and information *deprofessionalization* usually involves the elimination or downgrading of the status of professionally educated librarians, information specialists, knowledge managers, and archivists through their replacement, in whole or in part, with less-educated staff or volunteers, or, following the so-called McDonaldization approach, where work is transferred to eager or uneager customers who save the organization money by meeting their own needs (Crowley 2001, 570–73).

A sudden deprofessionalization, often undertaken in response to financial limitations, generally indicates that directors or program heads have not been doing the job of ensuring that work that can be defined as *nonprofessional* is replaced with new duties of a more professional nature on an ongoing basis. Professional time is a scarce resource and regularized assessments are of paramount importance, particularly in the nonprofit or government sectors of library, information, knowledge, and archival services, which are notoriously under-resourced. Effective managers in such organizations predictably have a lengthy list of what else could be done if they only had more professionals and other staff. If such a list is missing or not utilized to rewrite position descriptions whenever technology or other causes suggest that certain duties are no longer professional—and that certain professionals now have time for more appropriate work—it is a telling indicator of the problematic quality of the director or manager responsible. Here it should be stressed that there are times when changes in professional responsibilities require more than a simple reassignment. They may necessitate additional formal and informal training and education and a manager's recollection that effectiveness in mastering new assignments generally develops in the form of the well-known learning curve and improves over a period of time.

Inasmuch as budget restrictions have persistently limited the number of professionals employed in a given library or other organization, managers have always been forced to prioritize where the expertise of their professionals will be most valuable in providing services and addressing community or organizational problems. Such diligence has been most successful when the managers and professionals involved are addressing needs identified as priorities through a consistent marketing effort. Of late, problems have tended to arise when funding becomes limited and professionalism that has been wrongly applied is redefined as professionalism that is not needed.

APPRAISING THE VALUE OF DEFENDING PROFESSIONALISM

Arguably, the chapter authors of *Defending Professionalism*, writing from a variety of North American perspectives, have set forth a spectrum of visions, blending historic sources of public and organizational support with emerging technical and marketing approaches to refashioning and reinforcing contemporary library, information, knowledge, and archival professionalism. This reality means that readers who might be academic librarians can find inspiration for defending their professionalism in a chapter primarily concerned with corporate information and knowledge management. Similarly, public librarians might find that the chapters dealing with academic environments are enormously helpful in safeguarding professionalism in their local communities. In the opinion of the editor, there are gems in nearly every chapter that can be of help to all librarians, information specialists, knowledge managers, and archivists who find themselves called upon to justify the value of their professional status.

Readers of this work are asked to consider several significant points in drawing upon the valuable cross-disciplinary and cross-boundary contributions that make up this work. First, in virtually all documented human history, *perceptions* of the worth of anything, including libraries, have inevitably proven more influential with decision makers than the actual *facts* of the matter. This priority was again restated in *Perceptions of Libraries, 2010: Context and Community: A Report to the OCLC Membership,* where it was stressed by the researchers involved that "perception predicts tomorrow's reality" (De Rosa et al. 2011, 2).

The second point, discussed by Sharon Begley in an August 16, 2010, *Newsweek* column titled "The Limits of Reason," addresses the believability of the evidence presented to advance or dispute a point. According to Begley, "we tend to look harder for flaws in a study when we don't agree with its conclusions and are more critical of evidence that undermines our point of view" (2010, 24). In short, we tend to agree with those who agree with us.

The third important point is that the perfectionist who demands that every assertion contained in this chapter and elsewhere in *Defending Professionalism* must be accompanied by a mountain of irrefutable facts is going to be gravely disappointed. Few human developments share the specificity and reliability of the boiling point of fresh water at sea level at a given outside temperature and humidity. The author, a cultural pragmatist, believes "that 'truths' are always more or less provisional and must be continually tested in a variety of contexts" (Crowley 2005, 202). As such, he will ask the reader to keep the following questions in mind when reading this and any other chapter in *Defending Professionalism*:

1. Does/do the chapter author/authors provide the reader with a greater understanding of the relevant values of local, academic, school, organizational, or other service cultures that either support or undermine the professionalism of the librarian, information specialist, knowledge manager, or archivist?
2. Do the solutions offered in a given chapter for sustaining professionalism make sense for the relevant aspects of library and information science (LIS) and their service cultures?
3. Does the reader envision better approaches for sustaining professionalism than those offered in a given chapter or in the book as a whole? If so, how would the reader propose to act on implementing those approaches?

LATE TO THE TABLE?

Prior to the last several decades, library, information, knowledge, and archival professionals benefited from historic patterns of public and organizational appreciation for their well-rendered services. The result was an unfortunate level of satisfaction at being seen by communities and organizations as a valuable human resource. The value of these professionals was seldom doubted in public, even if dollars for their employment were always less than sufficient. This regularity of public praise for professional expertise had the unfortunate effect of masking the increasingly urgent need to undertake effective campaigns of personal and organizational marketing.

It is only of late, when the massive deprofessionalization of professional positions has underscored for many the folly of taking one's "market" and "reputation" for granted, that the relative lack of human and textual resources to bolster the value of professional expertise became evident. This was the critical time when the chapter authors of *Defending Professionalism* volunteered to fill the gap. With apologies to any Canadian and British readers (and a first-rate Canadian author) who might possibly be offended by the borrowing of the words of the Englishman who inspired America before becoming a true citizen of the world, the chapter authors proved to be the furthest thing possible from the "summer" and "sunshine" (Paine 1776) leaders who benefited from professionalism but did and do little or nothing to defend it. Drawing on their well-earned knowledge of their library, information, knowledge, or archival contexts, these authors, like Thomas Paine, "know our situation well, and can see the way out of it" (1776).

In addition to this editor's heartfelt appreciation for the work of each chapter author, I would like to offer particular thanks to two thoughtful professionals. During the period in which the book was written, I was able to benefit from the fortuitous circumstances that brought Maria Otero-Boisvert, a well-recognized academic librarian, to Dominican University's Graduate School of Library and Information Science. Once at Dominican, in addition to her studies, Maria officially worked as my research assistant, cowrote a chapter, and volunteered to serve as a most-effective "second reader" for several of the other chapters before leaving for additional study.

Here, I would also like to take the opportunity to thank my spouse, Theresa Van Gundy Crowley, a multitalented professional in her own right, who also served as an irreplaceable sounding board and critic for a number of the ideas that did—and did not—find their way into my own chapters.

As volume editor, I naturally take responsibility for any instances where the work of the chapter authors might have failed to match their normally outstanding quality.

REFERENCES

American Library Association. 2011. *The State of America's Libraries: A Report from the American Library Association*. Chicago, IL: American Library Association. Accessed June 19, 2011. http://www.ala.org/ala/newspresscenter/mediapresscenter/ameri caslibraries2011/index.cfm.

BBC News. 2001. "Divided by English" (July 19). Accessed July 7, 2011. http://news. bbc.co.uk/2/hi/uk_news/1445564.stm.

Begley, Sharon. 2010. "The Limits of Reason." *Newsweek* (August 16): 24. Accessed June 6, 2011. http://www.newsweek.com/2010/08/05/the-limits-of-reason.html.

Boniface, Susie. 2011. "A Third of All Britain's Libraries to Close in ConDem Cuts." *Sunday Mirror* (January 23). Accessed February 23, 2011. http://www.mirror.co.uk/

news/top-stories/2011/01/23/a-third-of-all-britain-s-libraries-to-close-in-con
dem-cuts-115875-22868062/.

Canadian Library Association. 2011. "Canadian School Librarians and Libraries under Siege." Accessed June 19, 2011. http://www.cla.ca/AM/Template.cfm?Section= Home&TEMPLATE=/CM/ContentDisplay.cfm&CONTENTID=11410.

Crowley, Bill. 2001. "Tacit Knowledge, Tacit Ignorance, and the Future of Academic Librarianship." *College and Research Libraries* 62(5): 565-84. Accessed July 7, 2011. http://crl.acrl.org/content/62/6/565.full.pdf.

Crowley, Bill. 2005. *Spanning the Theory-Practice Divide in Library and Information Science.* Lanham, MD: Scarecrow Press.

De Rosa, Cathy, Joanne Cantrell, Matthew Carlson, Margaret Gallagher, Janet Hawk, Charlotte Sturtz, Brad Gauder, Diane Cellentani, Tam Dalrymple, and Lawrence J. Olszewski. 2011. *Perceptions of Libraries, 2010: Context and Community: A Report to the OCLC Membership.* Dublin, OH: OCLC. Accessed February 26, 2011. http:// www.oclc.org/reports/2010perceptions/2010perceptions_all.pdf.

Fiels, Keith Michael. 2009. "ALA Executive Director's Message: In Tough Economic Times." *American Libraries* (March): 8.

National Bureau of Economic Research. 2011. "The NBER's Business Cycle Dating Procedure: Frequently Asked Questions." Accessed February 27. http://www.nber.org/ cycles/recessions_faq.html.

Oder, Norman. 2009. "MLS: Hire Ground?" *Library Journal* (June 1), 44-46. Accessed February 25, 2012. http://www.libraryjournal.com/article/CA6660920.html.

Oder, Norman. 2010. "LSSI Controversy in Santa Clarita, CA Makes New York Times Front Page (Updated)." *LJ Insider* (September 28). Accessed February 25, 2012. http://blog.libraryjournal.com/ljinsider/2010/09/28/lssi-controversy-in-santa-clarita-ca-makes-new-york-times-front-page-but-much-is-missing/.

Paine, Thomas. 1776. *The Crisis.* Accessed August 3, 2011. http://www.ushistory.org/ paine/crisis/c-01.htm.

People for Education. 2011. "School Libraries and Information Literacy." In *2011 Annual School Survey.* Accessed June 19, 2011. http://www.peopleforeducation.com/ schoollibraryreport2011.pdf.

Pew Center on the States and Public Policy Institute of California. 2010. *Facing Facts: Public Attitudes and Fiscal Realities in Five Stressed States.* Washington, DC: Pew Center on the States and San Francisco, CA: Public Policy Institute of California. Accessed July 5, 2011. http://www.pewcenteronthestates.org/uploadedFiles/PCS_PPIC.pdf.

Rubin, Richard E. 2010. *Foundations of Library and Information Science.* 3rd ed. New York: Neal Schuman.

Winnett, Robert. 2009. "Britain's Banking Crisis May Last for Almost a Decade." *Telegraph* (January 20). Accessed June 19, 2011. http://www.telegraph.co.uk/finance/news-bysector/banksandfinance/4298934/Britains-banking-crisis-may-last-for-almost-a-decade.html.

1

WHY ARE WE TRASHING THE PROFESSIONALISM OF LIBRARIANS, INFORMATION SPECIALISTS, KNOWLEDGE MANAGERS, AND ARCHIVISTS?

Bill Crowley
Dominican University

AN ILLINOIS DEPROFESSIONALIZATION STORY

In fall 2010 the author was in the audience for a discussion of librarian profession-alism arising out of a presentation on director-board relations by an Illinois public library trustee. After talking about various library matters from a board member's perspective, the trustee described how her library's director had proposed to the full board of trustees that the title "librarian" no longer be limited to holders of master's degrees from programs accredited by the American Library Association (ALA). According to the trustee, the library director defended her proposal to expand use of the title "librarian" on the grounds that the public already views all adult library personnel as "librarians," and it simply wasn't worthwhile to main-tain a distinction between those with a master's degree from a program accredited by the ALA and those who lack the professional education symbolized by the degree.

Over this trustee's opposition, the members of the public library's board of trustees approved their library director's proposal to undermine the value of her own professional education.

Discussion of the Illinois Precedent

Shortly after this trustee's presentation, I discussed the director's proposal and subsequent board approval with a former library director who possessed both the accredited master's degree and a Master of Business Administration (MBA) from a nationally ranked program. In the course of this conversation, it became clear to both of us that the public library head in question, by convincing the board to remove the required professional credential for recognition as a librarian, had also left herself open to being replaced by someone who might not have a master's de-gree from an ALA-accredited program but who did possess an MBA degree. This would be achievable if the matter of professional credentials and regulations for state aid was successfully finessed.

As our discussion continued the former director added,

> I strongly disagree with the idea of running a library with only an MBA, but someone else might try to make the case. In my own business program we were taught that a good executive with an MBA could manage any organization, whether public or private, and satisfy the customer, expand market share, and maximize return on investment. If you don't believe that being a professional in a library requires a specialized knowledge and service philosophy, then your position is just a job and the library is just another organization. And organizations are what MBAs are trained to run.

IDENTIFYING ILLUSIONS AND UNDERSTANDING THE PROFESSIONALISM PROBLEM

Readers who support library, information, knowledge, and archival professionalism may find this chapter's discussion of the barriers to be overcome as somewhat off-putting. It is only to be expected. As someone who helped organize statewide lobbying campaigns that accomplished what some doubters saw as unachievable—defeating a sitting Indiana Speaker of the House on a vote on his bill in his own chamber—I can assure such readers that initial doubts are more or less inevitable even when impossible things are later achieved (Crowley 1994).

Promoters of the employment of appropriately educated professionals as a positive good for communities and organizations will inevitably think first of the obstacles to be overcome as they analyze what needs to be done and develop plans to do it. Many such promoters do not understand the reality that a past history of ineffective marketing has put them in the situation where professionals actually have to remind, or even inform, potential allies of the true value to them of library, information, knowledge, and archival professionalism. Nonetheless, devising ways to promote such professionalism is one of the primary problems to be addressed. Professional associations, programs of professional education, employers, as well as customers, users, patrons, and other decision makers, all have their own priorities. The value of our professionalism may not presently be at the top of their lists unless we help make it so.

Like all problems to be solved, this apparent lack of positive engagement of others with the "professionalism issue" must be defined and analyzed before solutions can be developed. In consequence, much of this chapter deals with this seemingly simple question: *Why don't potential partners, even the most obvious allies and those most affected, make library, information, knowledge, or archival professionalism a critically important priority?*

SUPPORTERS AND OPPONENTS OF PROFESSIONALISM

In Canada and the United States, and to a lesser extent in Great Britain, the professional status of librarians, information specialists, knowledge managers, and archivists has customarily been created, defined, and supported—or undermined—through interactions among and within the following groups:

I. Professional associations, which often helped bring about the initial availability of appropriate professional education;
II. Universities providing such professional education;

III. Professionals and students seeking to become professionals;

IV. Employers who hire, in part, on the basis of an appropriate education, defined in law, regulation, or policy, often adding the further requirement of relevant experience; and

  V. Funders, customers, patrons, and users and other decision makers within geographical or organizational (academic, corporate, government, school) communities who accord professional recognition and/or support only to those they see as acting "professionally" to advance their interests.

The influence of the preceding sectors on the education and employment of librarians, information specialists, knowledge managers, and archivists has been substantial, if varying by the profession. Much of this disparity in commitment is due to historic differences in the origins and priorities of these professions, as well as the revolutionary effects of the increased availability of information in electronic formats, particularly since the mid-1990s explosion of the Internet.

Formal library professional education in a higher education program can be traced to 1887 and the creation of the "library economy" program at Columbia College (Crowley 2008, 52). *Information science* as a term and field developed from the mid-1950s and was taught, under various names, in ALA-accredited and other academic programs (Crowley 2008, 63–65). Although methods to standardize archival practice proliferated since 1900, it was not until the 1970s that the Society of American Archivists (2011a) issued "the first of a series of guidelines for graduate archival education." *Knowledge management* as a professional practice only crystallized "in the mid-1990s" (Koenig and Srikantaiah 2000, 23).

With the reminder to the reader that disagreement increases when analysis moves from generalities to specifics, I believe that exploring how five critical sectors impact professionalism—professional associations, university education programs, professionals and students, employers, and funders/customers/users/patrons/other decision makers—is crucial to any discussion of how professions are supported or undermined. As such, the impact of each sector will be addressed in this chapter.

I. Professional Associations and Professionalism

Only a selected number of library, information, knowledge, and archival associations are directly involved with the initial professional education of their members. For example, organizational sponsorship of a particular form of basic professional education doesn't seem to be a fundamental issue for the American Society for Information Science and Technology (ASIS&T) because this organization openly claims a membership that includes "information specialists from such fields as computer science, linguistics, management, librarianship, engineering, law, medicine, chemistry, and education" (American Society for Information Science and Technology 2011) who are united by a shared interest in information. Similarly, the Knowledge Management Professional Society (KMPro), which views itself as the premier international organization for knowledge management (KM) professionals, sees university-level KM education as more theoretical than job related and does not certify higher education programs. Instead, it stresses the value of its own continuing education and certification programs (Knowledge Management Professional Society 2011). For its part, the Society of American Archivists (2011b) calls attention to the reality that "individuals can prepare for a career in archives through a variety of educational programs."

Other associations, such as the American Association of Law Libraries, Medical Library Association, and Special Libraries Association, have a greater interest in a relevant type of initial professional education, particularly one provided through a program accredited by the American Library Association. Given these realities, this discussion will focus on the body that accredits a broad spectrum of library, information, knowledge, and archival education—the American Library Association or ALA.

The American Library Association (ALA)

In the area of professionalism, the ALA is to be commended for committing decades of time and resources to accrediting "library and information studies" programs at the master's degree level. It is a system, with all its problems, that attempts to provide some level of quality control. However, ALA's organizational culture, which includes disputes over the value of such professional education, has made it impossible for the association to take a leadership role in protecting library, information, knowledge, and archival professionalism. Effective public campaigns can be both lengthy and costly, and ALA's allegiance to professionalism effectively stops with the award of the master's degree. The association does not provide the resources necessary to promote the value of its own graduates to potential employers and the general public. In analyzing the formal support for librarian professionalism of ALA, Richard E. Rubin termed it "strong but not unequivocal" and noted that ALA "does not, for example, insist that all professional librarians possess a master's degree from an accredited program" (2010, 99).

For all intents and purposes, ALA's history in accrediting professional education can be dated to 1924 when the association created the Board of Education for Librarianship. In so doing, it joined newer and more historic professions in efforts to replace the traditional apprenticeship system for preparing professionals with a systematized course of study (Crowley 2008, 52). On the other hand, the 1972 claim of library historian Phyllis Dain that "graduation from college and then an academic library school to qualify for supervisory or professional positions" was "virtually mandatory" (1972, 331–32) never did, and still does not, describe conditions in many American and Canadian libraries, particularly in rural areas. In U.S. rural libraries serving populations of 2,500 or fewer people, only about 14 percent or so of "librarians" possess the master's degree from an ALA-accredited program (Flatley and Wyman 2009, 33). Despite the contested status and incomplete reach of educated professionalism, the fact that ALA accredits leading Canadian and American programs offering library, information, knowledge management, and archival education at the master's degree level is a positive cross-border commitment that is worthy of emulation in an increasingly globalized world.

Two ALA divisions have demonstrated more positive, if somewhat differing, ways of supporting the concept of suitable professional education. The Association of College and Research Libraries (ACRL), a division of ALA, has endorsed the master's degree from ALA-accredited programs as the appropriate credential for academic librarians (Association of College and Research Libraries 2011). However, ACRL has yet to effectively address the ramifications for professionalism of academic libraries hiring librarians on the basis of a subject PhD and an apprenticeship system (Crowley 2004). In the midst of a period of financial constraints, it would not be a rational strategy for ACRL, or any organization dominated by professional academic librarians, to avoid addressing the "PhD versus MLS librarian issue" on the theory that it will go away even if no one does anything about it.

Additionally, ALA is a member of the National Council for Accreditation of Teacher Education (NCATE). One of ALA's divisions, the American Association of School Librarians (AASL), officially believes that an appropriate education for school library professionals can also be delivered if the program is accredited by the NCATE, using standards developed by AASL itself (American Association of School Librarians 2011). Such an approach undoubtedly strengthens the professional competencies of school librarians, who might otherwise be educated in more problematic programs accredited only by state education agencies. It may even function to increase the number of ALA dues-paying members.

ALA cannot effectively defend professionalism because its membership is not solely composed of professionals possessing an endorsed credential. It does not operate as a union in the fashion of the American Federation of Teachers or National Education Association. Rather, it enrolls as members library employees of all types and educations, as well as a wide range of individuals and organizations supportive of its somewhat contradictory aims, historically described as, "the object of the American Library Association shall be to promote library service and librarianship" (American Library Association 2011a).

These aims have an obvious priority ranking, perhaps unavoidable under the circumstances. Nevertheless, the reluctance of ALA to support appropriately educated professionals as a priority in its *2015 Strategic Plan* demonstrates that the association's support for the graduates of its own accredited programs may have gone from a secondary priority to an even lower status. A recent release announcing the plan, communication aimed at influencing the media to publicize the ALA document, proclaims a "vision" that "ALA builds a world where libraries, both physical and virtual, are central to lifelong discovery and learning and everyone is a library user" (American Library Association 2010a). In the appendix to the actual plan, this is referred to in the currently fashionable phrase as ALA's "Big Audacious Goal" (American Library Association 2010b, 7).

A world where everyone is a "library user" is, of course, a magnificent vision for librarians and library supporters. And just how is this world going to be created? One of the basic rules of advocacy, learned long ago while I served as a Public Relations Representative for the New York Public Library, is that your vision of what should be must include what you really want people to know about your organization. Nowhere in this critically important document is there a firm commitment to the specific aim of promoting the value to customers, users, employers, and funding sources of professionals with a master's degree from an ALA-accredited program.

Another demonstration that ALA's internal contradictions make it a poor resource for defending library, information, knowledge, and archival professionalism can be found in the comparative failure of its underfunded companion association, the American Library Association-Allied Professional Association (ALA-APA). Ironically, APA-ALA was specifically created to "promote the mutual professional interests of librarians and other library workers," but it has had limited success in advancing a positive professionalism message. Ever since its founding in the 2001–2002 period, ALA-APA has been operating on limited allotments of money and personnel. While it has launched commendable efforts to promote voluntary certification at professional and paraprofessional levels, it has been unable to make substantial progress in its proclaimed effort "to improve the salaries and status of librarians and other library workers" (American Library Association, Allied Professional Association 2011).

The ALA-APA director's position now seems to be a part-time job, and the organization owes ALA about $240,000, money that the association is clearly determined to recoup (Casey 2011). Because ALA seemingly prioritizes recapturing the lent dollars over supporting the value of professionals educated in its own accredited-programs, I believe that ALA-APA will have even less capacity to assert a commitment to appropriately educated professionalism anytime in the foreseeable future.

Despite one's disappointment with ALA's unwillingness to support educated professionalism through effective advocacy, it is important not to see this state of affairs as a moral failure. Researchers have long pointed out that the association is "a highly bureaucratized environment" (Molz and Dain 1999, 181), and any reasonably competent sociologist knows that the first rule of a bureaucracy is its own survival. With ALA, support for the professionalism of librarians, information specialists, knowledge managers, and archivists educated in its own accredited programs stops when a degree from one of its accredited programs is awarded.

This lack of activism for professionalism on the national stage impacts advocacy for professionalism at state and local levels. The aversion of ALA, the oldest and premier national library association, to strongly advocate for the employment and retention of the graduates of its own programs makes the efforts of all others that much more difficult. ALA and its chapters do not collectively function to defend professionalism, and thus, there is no centralized direction for state and local associations to make the case for hiring graduates of ALA-accredited programs. Without doubt, the battles over professionalism would be easier to fight on national, state, and local levels if ALA had emulated the New Jersey Library Association and its commitment to "Work with trustees, administrators and commissioners to affirm the value of the professional library degree (MLS, MLIS)" (New Jersey Library Association 2009).

My own research and conversations with several knowledgeable Canadian librarians suggest that support at the level of national and provincial associations for library, information, knowledge, and archival professionalism is every bit as problematic as it is in the United States. Once again, support effectively stops with the award of the degree from a Canadian ALA-accredited program. However, activism is not entirely absent in America's northern neighbor. Just as the United States has the New Jersey Library Association, Canada has the smaller, and resource-challenged, Concerned Librarians of British Columbia (2011), self-defined as "An advocacy group of Canadian librarians formed in 2004 whose goal is to heighten awareness on current issues as they pertain to the profession."

The professionalism problems now being faced in Britain are even more substantial than described in Crowley's *Renewing Professional Librarianship* (2008). As in past years, Britain seems to represent the worst case scenario for those who believe in and support the value of professionally educated librarians, information specialists, knowledge managers, and archivists, particularly those in not-for-profit and government sectors. Readers who need updates on the accumulating accounts of libraries being closed and librarians and staff members being made redundant (British for laid off) need only repair to the *Public Library News* website to view the latest body count (http://www.publiclibrariesnews.com/).

II. Universities Providing Professional Education

The Core Ideology of the Former ALA–Accredited Library Programs

Contemporary ALA-accredited programs operate with the vision that libraries of all types are simply information providers and components of a national information infrastructure (Crowley 2008). This reality represents a dramatic transformation of the purposes that originally brought such programs into existence.

To borrow and adapt the terminology used in the ALA's *Strategic Plan 2011–2015*, the ALA-accredited programs, like other organizations, operate on a *core ideology* that, when analyzed, reveals a hard-to-change "identity." This core ideology has two elements. The first element is the organization's *core purpose* or "reason for being," and the second element consists of the *core values* or the "essential and enduring principles" that direct an organization as it develops its organizational culture and chooses the direction it will take (American Library Association 2010a, 2).

Prior to the transformation from library to information education, the *core purpose* of ALA-accredited programs was library-related, particularly idealistic, and aimed at advancing humanity's development through educating librarians for professional work supporting variations of lifelong learning in academic, public, school, and special (corporate, government, medical, etc.) libraries. It was also a practitioner-oriented learning environment that reflected the mainstream American view that a truly valuable education is one that "most directly deals with practical problems" (Holmes and Rhoads Holmes 2002, 16).

In the former library education programs, experience as a library practitioner was esteemed and often a tacit, if not formal, requirement for appointment as a faculty member in an ALA-accredited program. The *core values* of these programs can be summarized as the commitment of libraries and librarians to supporting individual and institutional achievement in the areas of education, information, and recreation (Leigh 1950). In middle decades of the 20th century, this commitment was still powered by the long-established "Library Faith." A secular creed, the "Library Faith" consisted of "a belief in the virtue of the printed word, especially of the book, the reading of which is held to be good in itself or from its reading flows that which is good" (Leigh 1950, 12).

In Robert D. Leigh's *The Public Library in the United States*, this "Library Faith" was described as a force that "sustained the men and women who have built and operated public, as well as university and research, libraries and the men [and women] of wealth and political position who have provided for their financial and legal support" (Leigh 1950, 12). Taken as a whole, this common library culture, education, and career path, based on a *core purpose* and *core values* shared by students and faculty alike, constituted what ALA would now term the *core ideology* of the former library education for the library profession (American Library Association 2010a, 2).

Information Ideology and Contemporary ALA–Accredited Programs

Spread of the more contemporary *core ideology* of information, an intellectual stance that prioritizes study of the information life cycle and meeting the research expectations of universities over teaching of practical techniques to library, information, knowledge, and archival students, was the most significant development within

ALA-accredited programs of the last half-century. Inasmuch as programs seeking to teach information courses without totally deleting library classes or having them taught by part-time or adjunct instructors often required adding additional faculty, the transformed ALA-accredited institutions sometimes expanded their income base through offering undergraduate degrees in information technology. This helped introduce a more businesslike approach to information, with programs seeing it more as an economic engine and less as a public good. Additionally, these programs added additional master's degrees or majors—and occasional PhDs—in varied information-relevant subjects. This expansion coincided with (a) the appeal to many faculty of responding to the economic and other possibilities offered by the developing information age and (b) a real concern, after several library schools were closed by their universities, that adaptation to the information age was essential for organizational survival (Crowley 2005).

The information *core ideology* supporting the transformed ALA-accredited programs included the *core purpose* of developing new information research and information theories, as well as educating for-profit and other information professionals for the information age. The *core values* driving these information programs asserted the inclusive nature of the information model, as well as its economic possibilities, and stressed that all libraries were primarily providers of information and, as such, that all library education is rightfully an information education. Such values required that all students in the transformed programs take the same foundational information courses and that students be encouraged to take advanced information classes in newer—and preferred—areas of information (Crowley 1999, 2008).

The Information Ideology and Mixed Support for Professionalism

Years after the information turn in ALA-accredited programs, it is clear that an information-centric definition of library and information science allows ALA-accredited programs to potentially teach any student with an interest in information in practically any context. Further, such an information orientation undoubtedly supports the corporate and research work of information science and knowledge management professionals. For these new and experienced professionals, a profession built on appropriate information or knowledge education is fundamentally defensible.

However, something happened to libraries and librarians on their way to the brave new information world. Of late, the perceived need for librarians and information specialists to serve as intermediaries between consumers seeking information and the information itself seems to have plummeted. The exploding use of social networks, Google, and Google-equivalents for obtaining information on a self-service basis means that the daily experiences of potential customers leaves many doubtful of the library's value as an information provider and the librarian's worth as an information intermediary. For the same reasons, local and academic officials are increasingly dubious about employing information specialists from ALA-accredited programs as public or not-for-profit competitors to Google. Their information expertise is increasingly seen as redundant and few have made the case for applying librarian information proficiency to defining and solving problems of literacy, reading, lifelong learning, and community building.

While ALA-accredited programs with an information orientation have benefited from a wider range of students and programs, their library-oriented graduates are finding that information know-how may be viewed as no better than the skill sets already possessed by K–12 teachers (Alper 2010), university faculty, students, and community members. Lacking a thorough grounding in identifying and solving problems through an education based on the former—and much broader—library triad of education, information, and recreation, these past and current graduates are increasingly being seen as expendable as the number of reference questions continues to decline.

Equally problematic is the reality that current "information" professors, well versed in theory, often lack the years of practical experience that enabled their "library" predecessors to be of assistance in defending professionalism in academic, public, school, and corporate environments. America, in particular, is a country with little use for theory without a useful purpose. Without practical experience, the same information theory orientation that assists faculty in achieving promotion and tenure in their universities can be a liability outside the campus environment when their prized theories run up against the more relevant, tacit knowledge of experienced practitioners (Crowley 2005). On the other hand, those knowledge management professors who have years of experience in corporate and research environments, in addition to their advanced educations, can be of enormous assistance in justifying the value of their students' professional educations in terms readily understood by their employers. When dealing with practitioners and managers, working experience in library, information, knowledge, or archival environments simply adds to a professor's credibility in making the case for professionalism.

The faculty authors of chapters in *Defending Professionalism* are examples of the benefits of combining relevant professional education and experience. Their life histories and research are of fundamental importance to this work. These faculty members are exceptions to the rule that, in the majority of instances, professors in ALA-accredited programs will not be taking leadership roles in the necessary and ongoing efforts to defend the worth of their own programs, master's degrees, and the value of the professionalism of their graduates. One challenge for the readers of this work, to be discussed further in the final chapter, is to demonstrate to many professors in ALA-accredited programs that their own self-interest demands steadfastness in defending professionalism.

The Absence of an Education in Effective Marketing and Advocacy

Regardless of where readers might stand on the information–library dispute, now complicated by knowledge management and informatics (information + electronics) education, the reality is that students, alums, employers, and funding sources can justifiably charge many ALA-accredited programs with a particularly grievous failure in instruction. We faculty have too often allowed students to earn their master's degrees without required marketing and advocacy courses. As a result, they frequently lack the personal marketing skills necessary for securing a professional position and the advocacy talents for retaining it. On a broader scale, these "educated professionals" too often cannot identify the problems that customers, patrons, and funding sources want solved and justify the value of their organization "solving" such problems to their funding sources. Lacking both knowledge and justification, they often are short of resources and are thus unable to demonstrate the value of their library, information, knowledge, or archival expertise.

By not requiring marketing and advocacy courses for all students as part of all our degrees, we faculty, collectively, have failed to equip graduates to respond to the crucial challenge described by Britain's Annie Mauger in her 2010 report on libraries for the Doncaster Metropolitan Borough Council. To slightly adapt Mauger's finding, "the library [information, knowledge, and archival] service must re-focus on the customer, not on the mechanics of customer services but on putting the customer at the heart of all decisions made about services" (Mauger 2010, 9).

In discerning and meeting customer needs, no better approach has been found than a solid marketing orientation. In securing the necessary resources to meet those needs, it is absolutely essential to advocate for the value of one's program and demonstrate how its services can advance the interests of funders and other decision makers.

III. Professionals and Students Seeking to Become Professionals

Blaming the Victim?

A few years after being hired as an assistant professor by Dominican University, I had an interesting discussion with an experienced professor before the start of the annual conference of ALISE, the Association for Library and Information Science Education. This instructor, long since gone from any ALA-accredited program, described an unusual approach to teaching a foundational course. At the start of the first class the instructor informed the students that if they were needy, if they saw the library as a refuge from the world and its problems, if they viewed library and information science as a field where they could earn a living without being required to advocate for resources by engaging in both internal and external politicking, then they ought to drop the course, ask for a refund, and leave the program. This instructor had considerable experience in libraries before earning a doctoral degree. Having seen libraries and related organizations become sanctuaries for professionals seeking to flee the world and its problems, the instructor viewed students with similar beliefs as a menace to their future employers.

I was recently reminded of this hardnosed approach to winnowing out introverted students while reading an article about a director who applies a similar method to hiring—Gerry Meek, Chief Executive Officer of the Calgary Public Library (Story 2010).

As described in the OCLC *Next Space* profile,

> Gerry [Meek] makes sure that advocacy is a lifestyle, not just a series of programs, at the Calgary Public Library in Alberta, Canada . . . Gerry's commitment to advocacy begins with whom he hires. By his estimate, 80 percent of librarians are introverts, 20 percent extroverts. He has filled his staff from that 20 percent, he claims! (Story 2010, 4)

Director Gerry Meek may ultimately prove to be erroneous in his extrovert–introvert calculations. As a student with a theater degree once stressed in one of my Dominican University courses, with proper training or experience, even the most introverted actors can adopt the personas of dynamic extroverts. Day after day, such actors can perform so well on the stage that even perceptive reviewers might swear that they have outgoing personalities. From personal experience, while working as a librarian at the New York Public Library, I can testify to regularly observing introverted library professionals performing as lively extroverts at busy reference desks, repeatedly balancing in-person questions with electronic queries. Admittedly, after retreating to the work room at the end of their shift, these librarians sometimes dropped precipitously into their office chairs, exhausted from yet another two-hour performance.

Building a Program on Extroverts—or to Hades with Myers–Briggs?

As suggested, Director Gerry Meek's division of librarians into 80 percent introverts and 20 percent extroverts may well be true in his context, or it may be falsified by candidates adopting an "extrovert persona." What is known is that there exists a variety of opinions on the validity of any division by personality. According to one sampling of the results of the Myers-Briggs Type Indicator (MBTI), the majority of librarians are introverts (Rubin 2004, 473–74). Alternatively, another study saw the testing of librarian personality types as flawed but found that different library and information specialties attract people with diverse characteristics (Rubin 2010, 106).

For this author, the issue as to whether professionals are naturally introverted or extraverted is trumped by their effectiveness—or ineffectiveness—in providing services and marketing themselves and their programs. In the more competitive environments faced by library, information, knowledge, and archival professionals, funding is simply harder to get. Introverts, as well as low-energy extroverts, regardless of their degrees, should not expect to encounter many positions where one can hide from the public. Increasingly, professional positions require demonstrated abilities with personal marketing (to secure the job) and a commitment to organizational marketing (to retain it).

In the final chapter I will address how students and alums can build up their marketing skills and advocacy approaches and develop the personal communication skills that are so often overlooked when ALA-accredited programs must concentrate on ensuring that students, at minimum, have at least the online social networking abilities of the average teen. Such e-skills are a necessary but far from a sufficient condition for success. Effectiveness in face-to-face (F2F) communication remains a critical necessity, at times *the* critical necessity. Consequently, even if students must lobby their programs for relevant personal communication, advocacy, and marketing courses, the result of such hands-on activism can only ensure that students are more effective advocates for themselves and their professionalism than might otherwise be suggested by any introverted Myers-Briggs "type."

Myers–Briggs Types

During several decades as a practitioner, manager, educator, and/or legislative committee chair in five states, it became clear to me that the Myers-Briggs Type Indicator (MBTI), which undoubtedly has value in therapeutic matters, too often becomes an excuse for inaction by those who view themselves as introverted. Although usually related in a more or less humorous matter, this author is a bit tired of hearing excuses at the level of directors or program heads (!), which predictably translate as, "I can't talk to that legislator, superintendent, or university president. I'm ISTJ (Introversion, Sensing, Thinking, Judging) or INTJ (Introversion, Intuitive, Thinking, Judging). I'm just too introverted to do that."

At a time when all professionals must become effective communicators, market-ers, and advocates, it is increasingly necessary for students, faculty, and employers to put Myers-Briggs in its place. We must cease ignoring the often demonstrated real-ity that, with sufficient time, energy, and support, people can adapt. Properly taught and supported, mentally healthy human beings can learn new behaviors at any age.

All graduates of ALA-accredited programs need to be provided by educators (during the preparation for their careers) and by employers (as those careers prog-ress) with the instruction and practice necessary to develop and maintain personal and organizational marketing, advocacy, and communication skills. In consequence, with the exception of establishing a baseline from which to measure progress, the correct reply to those who silently or publicly justify their inactivity through refer-ence to being an introverted Myers-Briggs type is "To Hades (or the more biblical *Gehenna*) with Myers-Briggs! Let's talk about appropriate training and support."

IV. Employers

An Alabama Story

A number of years ago I was attending one of the regular quarterly meetings of public library directors called by Anthony W. (Tony) Miele, Director of the Ala-bama Public Library Service. A Pennsylvanian business owner turned administrator of several Illinois libraries, and later an Alabama department head, Tony had a keen grasp of the give and take of practical politics. This understanding was why he used these meetings for more than providing relevant information and a forum for dis-cussion of pertinent issues. He also saw the quarterly director meetings as a means of building library solidarity in order to lessen the likelihood that any one library director would go to her or his state legislator to demand a change in library law, policy, or funding that might negatively impact other libraries in the state.

At this particular meeting the library directors were discussing the difficulties of designing library services that meet user needs while simultaneously responding to the political agendas of the elected officials who controlled the local dollars al-located for library budgets. One director had just mentioned that finding out the real aims of city or county politicians could be difficult because their reelections de-pended, in part, on the ability to meet a lot of demands with relatively little money.

"They can be a bit circuitous," she observed, demonstrating the hard-won wisdom of someone who had learned that negative political assessments made in public have a way of coming to the attention of those so evaluated. In response, from the back of the room, one of the newer library directors shouted a bit more directly, "And they're liars and crooks too!"

A general laughter greeted this remark, but a few members of the audience, whom I recognized as being significant players in the politics of their local com-munity, grimaced or shook their heads at the shouted criticism. After the meeting, I had the opportunity to discuss the matter with one of the more effective library politicians who shared her belief that the protesting library director was not likely to be particularly effective in securing the funds necessary to run a quality library.

Goo–Goo Library Directors and Effective Library Politicians

Depending on context, directors and managers of libraries, information centers, knowledge management centers, and archives, as well as their professional staff members, tend to be overwhelmingly female and Caucasian (Rubin 2010, 101–2). They also tend to be middle class, politically liberal, and lack engagement in the day-to-day operations of their communities or organizations. This is particularly so with academic, public, and school librarians. One rare conservative librarian, quoting a column by David Brooks containing research into political donations in the 2004 Bush–Kerry U.S. presidential election, reported that librarians contributed to the Democratic candidate John Kerry over the Republican candidate George Bush by a factor of 223 to 1. The corresponding ratio for university and college faculty, also generally considered to be liberal, was a much lower donation ratio of 11 to 1 in favor of Kerry (Durant 2005).

From the perspective of this library and information science educator, the real problem is certainly not the liberal political orientation of LIS personnel. The best professionals in the public sector understand their obligation to provide resources and programs for all political points of view and to develop the coalitions necessary to secure appropriate funding. Private sector professionals may well be the most expert at justifying human and financial resources because so many of their activities are judged by return on investment (ROI), otherwise known as their contribution to the organization's financial bottom line.

The true problem with a liberal political orientation is the fact that too many professionals in academic, public, and school libraries fall into the naive wing of what Americans have termed "goo-goos" or members of the "good government" movement. Historically, these individuals have cherished nonpartisan government supporting services on objective measures of value to communities, universities, schools, and other beneficiaries of tax-support. While this is an admirable ideal, it inevitably proves difficult to achieve and sustain. Even worse, these overly idealistic goo-goos also tend to view their professional colleagues who happen to be active in political matters as being somehow tainted, particularly in light of the backroom deals that are so often rumored and occasionally found with partisan political activity.

What political idealists, including those of the library, information, knowledge, and archival variety, have too often failed to understand is that funds and other resources are seldom allocated by governments and organizations on the basis of objective rankings of value. Rather, resources tend to be distributed to meet political or organizational priorities and to support whatever activities can be seen as advancing the careers or interests of those who control the money.

As suggested previously, there are directors and program heads that are quite savvy about demonstrating how their programs meet outstanding needs and advance the political or organizational priorities of those who have power over funding. Simple statistics suggest that most library or information managers are likely to be liberal in their political views. It is possible to be both liberal and effective, even in conservative communities and organizations. Every now and then I meet progressive librarians, information specialists, and archivists who inspire me with their political acumen. These practical idealists function as first-rate community or organizational politicians who are able to organize supporters and make obvious the value of their programs through relevance and performance. These are the same managers and directors who can convince suburban mayors, university presidents, school superintendents, or corporate CEOs that increasing support for their programs is in the senior managers' best interests. They are, in short, sensible idealists who are willing to "get their hands dirty" in order for their libraries, information/knowledge centers, and archives to achieve community or organizational goals.

The introduction addressed the evidence that ALA provided regarding the preference of mayors to cut American public libraries in greater proportion than anything other than maintenance and parks (American Library Association 2011b, 12). Such cutbacks are likely to be facilitated by one of two factors in play in many libraries. First, certain public libraries may be headed by extroverts who have grown complacent and have not implemented a sound marketing approach to identifying community needs and delivering appropriate programs and services that are prioritized by their funding sources and customers/patrons/users. Alternatively, these same libraries may be administered by introverts whose unwillingness or inability to effectively network is matched by a preference for meetings where they can (1) reassure themselves about the safety of their own jobs and (2) talk to each other about "inevitable cutbacks." Such cutbacks are never "inevitable" for programs that benefit funding sources. Instead of busying themselves in their offices with fruitless meetings, such leaders should have taken this "Politics 101" lesson to heart. Even now they should be implementing more productive connections with library funding sources and library customers, activities that demand either an outgoing personality or an effective introvert with an extravert persona but that might have prevented or limited such extraordinary funding reductions in the first place.

The public library sector is not the only area that suffers from either ineffective extroverts or introverts unable to adopt an outgoing persona. The overall fondness of many professionals for talking rather than performing will be further addressed in the final chapter. Here it will be noted that the preference of some librarians for meetings instead of taking effective actions has actually reached the point in higher education where planners at a major American university were publicly critical of their library and its response to a statewide financial crisis. In print and online, the university library was chastised for squandering "human resources in overly protracted discussion" when it chose "time consuming" meetings over needed action in the midst of a university-wide funding failure (Office of the Provost and Vice Chancellor for Academic Affairs 2010, 6).

Any thoughtful academic knows that deferring plant maintenance and cutting libraries are well known and relatively safe reductions for a university head to make in a time of financial crisis (Kerr 1995, 182). In consequence, it is just possible that this university library's endless series of meetings, justified as part of its New Service Model (NSM) program, might actually be a cagy strategy to defer otherwise inevitable reductions. Notwithstanding, academic libraries and librarians do not have a high priority on a research university campus (Crowley 2001). Unless library managers and other professional librarians have a history of successfully marketing the library's services to administrators and influential faculty, preferably including researchers with multiyear/multimillion dollar grants, they are not likely to be given the benefit of the doubt when demands for cuts from the central administration are intensified.

V. Funders, Customers, Patrons, Users, and Other Decision Makers

In publicizing the availability of a newer publication titled *Maximize the Potential of Your Public Library: A Report on the Innovative Ways Public Libraries Are Addressing Community Priorities* on its web page, the International City/County Management Association (ICMA) (2010) informed its members that they could "learn how public libraries can help local governments tackle critical community priorities such as economic development, public safety, environmental sustainability, cultural diversity, education, and literacy."

The first question that came to mind after reading the advertising copy for *Maximize the Potential of Your Public Library* (ICMA 2011) was, "Why does the International City/County Management Association have to tell its members about what their own public libraries are doing or not doing?" This was immediately followed by the question, "Are the public libraries informing local governments about the value of their programs of service?" Fortunately, the text of *Maximize the Potential of Your Public Library* provides a number of structural and attitudinal answers to these questions, answers that will be discussed in detail in chapter 12, "The 'Political Case' for Supporting the Value of Professional Education." At this point, it is sufficient to restate ICMA's overall and most problematic finding that "libraries can be their own worst enemy" (2011, 2). It really is true, they can.

FURTHER THOUGHTS ON ACADEMIC AND ARCHIVAL PROFESSIONALISM

A few years ago, I had just delivered a presentation at the annual conference of the Academic Library Association of Ohio (ALAO) where I attacked the yet fashionable idea of substituting a PhD and an apprenticeship in an academic library for earning the ALA-accredited master's degree. It is pernicious tactic sponsored by the Council on Library and Information Resources (CLIR) and represents one of the more unashamed attacks on professionalism by any library or information organization (Crowley 2004). The Ohio presentation proved controversial, and a number of supporters of this CLIR program in the audience had reacted angrily, rightly seeing my words as an attack on their professional judgment.

After an extended post-presentation discussion with both supporters and opponents of the "academic librarian without the professional degree" approach, I found a place to sit in the large room, which, if memory serves, housed both tables for distributing conference materials and a number of vendor exhibits. Temporarily secure from attacks by outraged academic librarians, I considered their remarks and thought about whether or not to insert certain ideas into the draft of what eventually became a published *Library Journal* article (Crowley 2004).

While thus engaged, my manuscript editing was interrupted twice. The first time was by a rather intense librarian who wanted to discuss the plight of a colleague in an eastern state. It seems that the director of a certain academic library had tried to convince the university administration that the library needed an archivist with electronic skills to oversee digitizing university archives deemed to be of considerable value to scholars. As related to me, the request for the digital collections archivist was turned down by the university administration on the basis that other units of the university had successfully used student assistants to digitize their own material. As a result, it was recommended that the academic library save the university's money and take the same cost-effective route. The subtext seemed to be that if a student could digitize, the operation certainly did not need to have its own librarian supervisor.

When asked to provide advice, I inquired if the support of the university's history department had been secured for the digital collection archivist request. I also asked if the university archives saw its holdings as teaching materials and actively encouraged historians to bring their students, even in freshman classes, to the archives for a hands-on session on using the raw material of the historical record.

"Does the history department, or for that matter, do the political science, sociology, and popular culture departments, see the university archives as essential to their own work?" I concluded. "Would their faculty and students benefit if certain material was online?"

Shortly afterwards, this librarian left with my business card in hand and the promise she would later bring me up to date on the proposed digital archives position (she never did). Not 10 minutes later, the director of a small academic library walked to my table. She had been intrigued by the suggestion made during my presentation that professionally educated academic librarians who themselves earned doctorates would benefit the library much more than imported subject specialists who lacked a library education and had failed to make a career in the fields or disciplines where they had earned their doctorate. Thus encouraged, she asked if the degree had to be a PhD or would a Doctor of Education (EdD) be sufficient. She would have to leave her directorship to earn the PhD but could study for an EdD part time with financial support provided by her college president. Knowing that both degrees would entitle her to be termed Doctor, and understanding from personal experience just how substantial are the financial and other difficulties one faces when giving up a senior library position for full-time PhD study, I informed the library director that part-time study for an EdD would be sufficient.

Present conditions in the academic world are nicely demonstrated by the two Ohio conference anecdotes. First, colleges and universities operating on business-inspired ROI (return on investment) strategies will opt for the least expensive approach (student assistants) to solving problems (migrating archives collections to digital form) when academic libraries lack sufficient influence to secure a more expensive, if higher quality, solution (digital collections archivist). Second, even at a time when the University of Phoenix and its for-profit counterparts are using armies of master's degree holding instructors to teach largely scripted classes, a doctorate can be most useful for academic librarians who already possess the professional master's degree from an ALA-accredited program. Academic librarians with PhDs but lacking library degrees are toxic for professional librarianship in the long run. However, it is usually problematic for an academic library dean to be the only one sitting around a university president or provost's table who cannot be addressed as Doctor. Whether academic librarians like it or not, that is how the game is played in leading university environments. A doctorate has been almost a necessity for respect in such institutions since America's first research psychiatrist attacked the practice more than a hundred years ago (James 2011).

PROFESSIONAL SUICIDE BY TRASHING THE PROFESSIONAL DEGREE—A SUMMING UP

In January 2005 Deborah Ginsberg and I published an article titled "Professional Values: Priceless" in *American Libraries*. Within this piece we used the expression "intracultural reciprocity" several times. By design, intracultural reciprocity is an ugly phrase and, we hoped, thereby more memorable. It is defined as "the changing, context-specific perceptions of mutual worth by participants in geographical, social, cultural, and other arenas" (Crowley and Ginsberg 2005, 53). To cite an example, corporate knowledge managers possess intracultural reciprocity when other professionals, such as product developers, marketing personnel, and corporate executives, see knowledge managers as the experts on securing, analyzing, and distributing valuable information or knowledge on the major issues being addressed by the corporation. The key here is that the knowledge managers value their own professionalism and, through strong and consistent effort, using effective marketing and successful performance, see it as a daily challenge to convince a critical mass of significant players in the organization to "buy into" and support their self definition as indispensable professionals. Their aim is to be seen as the human gold standard for securing, analyzing, and disseminating information and knowledge within the organization.

In a classic *Science* article titled "The Tragedy of the Commons"—cited thousands of times according to a July 16, 2011, Google search—Garrett Hardin argued that the early modern English commons, on which villagers collectively grazed their cattle, failed as a shared resource because those involved pursued personal advantage and overgrazed the commons in a not-unreasonable effort to increase their own gain. Hardin used the matter of the overgrazed commons as an example of how "the individual benefits as an individual from his [her] ability to deny the truth even though society as a whole, of which he [she] is a part, suffers" (Hardin 1968, 1244). The exact historical details and causes of problems with the commons are subject to debate. Nonetheless, the point Hardin made of a common responsibility to maintain a valuable and shared resource is fundamentally important.

If our shared resource of professionalism in library, information, knowledge, and archival contexts is marginalized and diluted, certain individuals will still prosper. However, they may do so through such truth-denying actions as refusing to require marketing and advocacy classes in ALA-accredited programs or deprofessionalizing subordinate librarians in academic or public libraries. The first instance undermines the practical effectiveness of the ALA-endorsed education, and the second devalues the professional educations that helped the errant librarian managers achieve their successes in the first place.

The title of this chapter, "Why Are We Trashing the Professionalism of Librarians, Information Specialists, Knowledge Managers, and Archivists?" was selected to point toward the reality that too often librarians, information specialists, knowledge managers, and archivists are acting out of an unreflective survival instinct that leads them to undermine the profession and professional education that facilitated their own success. Without diminishing personal responsibility for one's actions, it is possible that such managers did not receive the necessary guidance, support, and training, either in their professional educations or in the earlier part of their careers, on why and how to support professionalism, including the professionalism of those they supervise.

SECTOR LIMITATIONS ON SUPPORT FOR PROFESSIONALISM

The American Library Association (ALA) will not effectively advocate for professionalism because of concerns about alienating those without the master's degree from its own accredited programs. For their part, these same ALA-accredited programs do a miserable job of developing extrovert personas in their introverted students. They also fail to require both introverted and extroverted students alike to take mandatory marketing, advocacy, and communications courses.

Many students and alums do not accept their own obligation to market themselves and to market and advocate for their future or present organizations. Even where available, they fail to take marketing courses, advocacy workshops, or otherwise develop a full spectrum of effective communications abilities. Web-based skills are absolutely necessary, but all professionals must be able to communicate on the critical face-to-face level. Lacking this spectrum of skills, such professionals often remain unassertive, fail to understand what is needed, and do not provide or justify responsive and effective services to address those needs. In consequence, they and their organizations may lack a network of committed supporters willing to defend the value of their professionalism in troubled times.

It is an unfortunate reality that those who hire in library, information, knowledge, or archival organizations are too often more senior examples of the same problematic professionals who consistently fail in their obligation to effectively market, advocate, and communicate. They simply do not really care to know, will not understand, and will most likely fail to effectively address the true priorities of their funding sources, customers, patrons, and users. This is why their programs are the first to be cut in troubled financial times. For such managers, deprofessionalization of other librarians, information specialists, knowledge managers, and archivists is not a shared tragedy. It is merely another management strategy, a method of adjusting downwards taken by programs that have not made themselves into organizational or community priorities.

Ironically, funding sources, customers, patrons, users, and other direct or indirect decision makers may be the least culpable of all the sectors contributing to library, information, knowledge, and archival deprofessionalization. If a library informs its city government or academic administration that the services of professional librarians can be dispensed with, all executives who have not otherwise learned the value of such educated professionals would be judged foolish for not cutting costs by taking the library director or dean at her or his word. This is particularly so where the library has not come forward to assist community or university leaders in advancing their priority goals. The same analysis can be applied to professionalism in school libraries, as well as to corporate, governmental, or university archives, information centers, and knowledge management centers.

Fortunately, the necessary actions to support and advance professionalism are also practical and achievable. There need not be further loss of professionalism in British, Canadian, and American national, organizational, intellectual, and educational environments. This positive conviction is what drove the development of this book and motivated the chapter authors to come forward with pragmatic and useable strategies. The reader will find that the point will be made by a number of the chapter authors that the first and most necessary step is to stop undermining professionalism so that its benefits can again flow to those who know they need—or could learn to take advantage of—professional quality library, information, knowledge, or archival services.

It is best to end this chapter with the practical wisdom of the American humorist and commentator Will Rogers, who cautioned, "If you find yourself in a hole, stop digging" (California State Parks 2011). When it comes to the matter of professionalism, association executives, educators, students, employers, and funders have dug a very large hole, one whose size is sufficient to bury both individual careers and entire professions. It really is time for all who have benefited, or hope to benefit, from the existence of library, information, knowledge, and archival professionalism to understand that their individual careers will be more successful if we help each other climb out of this self-made chasm and begin rebuilding professionalism through a greater demonstration of its benefits to communities, organizations, and their leaders.

REFERENCES

Alper, Alex. 2010. "City's School Librarians on Borrowed Time." *The Brooklyn Ink* (December 15). Accessed July 16, 2011. http://thebrooklynink.com/2010/12/15/21865-citys-school-librarians-on-borrowed-time/.

American Association of School Librarians. 2011. "Some Frequently Asked Questions: Why Does ALA Belong to NCATE?" Accessed July 10. http://www.ala.org/ala/mgrps/divs/aasl/aasleducation/schoollibrary/faq.cfm.

American Library Association. 2010a. "A 2015 Strategic Plan Outlines Key Goals, Objectives for the Future." Accessed July 3, 2011. http://ala.org/ala/newspresscenter/news/pr.cfm?id=5932.

American Library Association. 2010b. *Strategic Plan: 2011–2015.* Accessed June 19, 2011. http://www.ala.org/ala/aboutala/missionhistory/plan/strategic%20plan%202015%20documents/strategic_plan_2.pdf.

American Library Association. 2011a. "Constitution: Article 2. Object." Accessed June 18. http://www.ala.org/ala/aboutala/governance/constitution/constitution.pdf.

American Library Association. 2011b. *The State of America's Libraries: A Report from the American Library Association.* Chicago, IL: American Library Association. Accessed June 19, 2011. http://www.ala.org/ala/newspresscenter/mediapresscenter/americaslibraries2011/index.cfm.

American Library Association, Allied Professional Association. 2011. Homepage. Accessed June 18. http://ala-apa.org/.

American Society for Information Science and Technology (ASIS&T). 2011. "About ASIS&T." Accessed July 3. http://www.asis.org/about.html.

Association of College and Research Libraries (ACRL). 2011. "Statement on the Certification and Licensing of Academic Librarians." Accessed July 3, 2011. http://www.ala.org/ala/mgrps/divs/acrl/standards/statementcertification.cfm.

California State Parks. 2011. "Will Rogers Legacy: Remembering That Old Cowboy." Compiled by Randall Young, Will Rogers historian. Accessed July 15. http://www.parks.ca.gov/?page_id=23998.

Casey, James B. 2011. "Notes from James Casey on the 2011 Annual Conference." *ALA Membership Blog.* Accessed February 26, 2012. http://americanlibrariesmagazine.org/ala-members-blog/notes-james-casey-2011-annual-conference.

Concerned Librarians of British Columbia. 2011. Homepage. Accessed July 12. http://concernedlibrarians.blogspot.com/.

Crowley, Bill. 1994. "Library Lobbying as a Way of Life." *Public Libraries* 33(2): 96–98.

Crowley, Bill. 1999. "The Control and Direction of Professional Education." *Journal of the American Society for Information Science* 50(12): 1127–35.

Crowley, Bill. 2001. "Tacit Knowledge, Tacit Ignorance, and the Future of Academic Librarianship." *College & Research Libraries* 62(5): 565–84. Accessed July 7, 2011. http://crl.acrl.org/content/62/6/565.full.pdf.

Crowley, Bill. 2004. "Just Another Field?" *Library Journal* (November 1): 44–46. Accessed July 10, 2011. http://www.libraryjournal.com/lj/ljinprintcurrentissue/872965-403/just_another_field.html.csp.

Crowley, Bill. 2005. *Spanning the Theory-Practice Divide in Library and Information Science.* Lanham, MD: Scarecrow Press.

Crowley, Bill. 2008. *Renewing Professional Librarianship: A Fundamental Rethinking.* A Beta Phi Mu Monograph. Westport, CT: Libraries Unlimited.

Crowley, Bill, and Deborah Ginsberg. 2005. "Professional Values: Priceless." *American Libraries* (January): 52–55.

Dain, Phyllis. 1972. *The New York Public Library: A History of Its Founding and Early Years.* New York: New York Public Library.

Durant, David. 2005. "The Loneliness of a Conservative Librarian." *The Chronicle of Higher Education* (September 30). Accessed July 6, 2011. http://chronicle.com/article/The-Loneliness-of-a/33191.

Flatley, Robert, and Andrea Wyman. 2009. "Changes in Rural Libraries and Librarianship: A Comparative Survey." *Public Library Quarterly* 28(1): 24–39.

Hardin, Garrett. 1968. "The Tragedy of the Commons." *Science* 162(3859): 1243–48. Accessed July 16, 2011. http://www.sciencemag.org/site/feature/misc/webfeat/sotp/pdfs/162–3859–1243.pdf.

Holmes, Lowell D., and Ellen Rhoads Holmes. 2002. "The American Cultural Configuration." In *Distant Mirrors: America as a Foreign Culture.* 3rd ed., ed., Philip R. De Vita and James D. Armstrong, 4–26. Australia: Wadsworth/Thomson Learning.

International City/County Management Association (ICMA). 2011. *Maximize the Potential of Your Public Library: A Report on the Innovative Ways Public Libraries Are Addressing Community Priorities.* Washington, DC: ICMA. Accessed July 13, 2011. http://icma.org/en/icma/knowledge_network/documents/kn/Document/302161/Maximize_the_Potential_of_Your_Public_Library.

James, William. 2011. "The Ph.D. Octopus." (First published in the *Harvard Monthly* of March 1903.) Accessed July 16. http://des.emory.edu/mfp/octopus.html.

Kerr, Clark. 1995. *The Uses of the University.* 4th ed. Cambridge, MA: Harvard University Press.

Knowledge Management Professional Society (KMPro). 2011. "KMPro—Our Purpose and History." Accessed July 3. http://www.kmpro.org/static.php?file=about_purpose.htm.

Koenig, Michael E. D., and T. Kanti Srikantaiah. 2000. "The Evolution of Knowledge Management." In *Knowledge Management for the Information Professional,* ed. T. Kanti Srikantaiah and Michael E. D. Koenig, 23–36. Medford, NJ: Information Today.

Leigh, Robert D. 1950. *The Public Library in the United States: The General Report of the Public Library Inquiry.* New York: Columbia University Press.

Mauger, Annie. 2010. *Better Libraries, Better Lives: A Review and Improvement Plan for Doncaster Metropolitan Borough Council.* Accessed July 4, 2011. http://www.whatdotheyknow.com/request/43674/response/111822/attach/4/Doncaster%20Libraries%20Review%20Final.pdf.

Molz, Redmond Kathleen, and Phyllis Dain. 1999. *Civic Space/Cyberspace: The American Public Library in the Information Age.* Cambridge, MA: MIT Press.

New Jersey Library Association. 2009. "New Jersey Library Association Strategic Plan." Accessed July 3, 2011. http://www.njla.org/statements/strategicplan.pdf.

Office of the Provost and Vice Chancellor for Academic Affairs. 2010. *Stewarding Excellence @ Illinois: University Library and Law Library: Final Report.* Urbana-Champaign: University of Illinois. Accessed July 7, 2011. http://oc.illinois.edu/budget/SEI_Library.pdf.

Rubin, Richard E. 2004. *Foundations of Library and Information Science.* 2nd ed. New York: Neal-Schuman.

Rubin, Richard E. 2010. *Foundations of Library and Information Science.* 3rd ed. New York: Neal-Schuman.

Society of American Archivists. 2011a "An Introduction to SAA." Accessed June 20. http://www2.archivists.org/about/introduction-to-saa.

Society of American Archivists. 2011b. "So You Want to Be an Archivist: An Overview of the Archives Profession." Accessed June 20. http://www2.archivists.org/profession.

Story, Tom. 2010. "The Ripple Effect: Part 2: Extending the Library's Circle of Influence." *Next Space,* no. 14: 4–10. Accessed July 6, 2011. http://www.oclc.org/nextspace/014/1.htm.

2

JUSTIFYING PROFESSIONAL EDUCATION IN A SELF-SERVICE WORLD

Rachel Rubin
Bexley Public Library, Ohio

Richard Rubin
Kent State University

The time has at last come when a librarian might, without assumption, speak of his occupation as a profession.

—Melvil Dewey, "The Profession"

I. INTRODUCTION

As information technologies ostensibly make it easier for individuals to locate information without assistance, libraries and librarians are increasingly challenged to verify their utility and value. Libraries have responded with numerous studies, using a variety of measurement tools, confirming their substantive and positive contribution to local economies, communities, and users. When assessing their impact, however, most of these studies have emphasized the institutional manifestation of the library: the library as building and collection. The direct contribution of the *librarian* to these outcomes has often been obscured. Although the library as physical place is certainly important, it is equally important to consider the contribution of the professional librarian as service provider and educator.

Since the early development of the profession in Canada and the United States, the library, not the librarian, has been the primary focus. We have the American *Library* Association, not the American Librarians Association; the Canadian *Library* Association, not the Canadian Librarians Association. The emphasis has been on the institution, rather than on the people who fulfill its mission. The impact of focusing on libraries rather than the professionals who work in them is not benign. It brings into question the importance of and the need for professional expertise and, by extension, the value of professional preparation and training. In today's current environment, this is a substantive issue that must be addressed.

II. THE DUTY OF LIBRARIES AND LIBRARIANS

Today's library administrators face numerous challenges from both fiscal and technological sources. In such stressful circumstances, the substantial commitment that librarians and libraries make to citizens, communities, and to society as a whole can be underestimated. The ALA characterized these commitments, expressed in its policy "Libraries: An American Value" (American Library Association 1999), as a "contract with the people we serve." The stipulations of this contract include the following:

- We defend the constitutional rights of all individuals, including children and teenagers, to use the library's resources and services;
- We value our nation's diversity and strive to reflect that diversity by providing a full spectrum of resources and services to the communities we serve;
- We affirm the responsibility and the right of all parents and guardians to guide their own children's use of the library and its resources and services;
- We connect people and ideas by helping each person select from and effectively use the library's resources;
- We protect each individual's privacy and confidentiality in the use of library resources and services;
- We protect the rights of individuals to express their opinions about library resources and services;
- We celebrate and preserve our democratic society by making available the widest possible range of viewpoints, opinions, and ideas so that all individuals have the opportunity to become lifelong learners, informed, literate, educated, and culturally enriched. (*ALA, Adopted by Council of the American Library Association, February 3, 1999.* Reprinted with permission.)

The "We" in these statements applies equally to the library as an institution and to the professional librarians who embody the library's ideals.

These ideals are rooted in the historical expectations of professional librarianship in North America. Since the emergence of the profession at the end of the 19th century, librarians have been prepared with a strong sense of their cultural and educational purpose. More than 130 years ago, Melvil Dewey emboldened and exhorted American librarians to undertake a major, albeit prescriptive, social responsibility. In the first issue of *American Library Journal* he maintained:

> [the librarian] must see that his library contains, as far as possible, the best books on the best subjects, regarding carefully the wants of his special community. Then, having the best books, he must create among his people, his pupils, a desire to read those books. He must put every facility in the way of readers, so that they shall be led on from good to better . . . Such a librarian will find enough who are ready to put themselves under his influence and direction, and, if competent and enthusiastic, he might soon largely shape the reading, and through it the thought of his whole community. (Dewey 1876, 5)

Although paternalistic to modern sensibilities, the implication that librarians should promote ideas, good reading habits, and play an essential role in the community remains consistent with 21st-century attitudes and expectations. It is a considerable responsibility requiring advanced education and training. Pierce Butler, nearly 75 years after Dewey, maintained the importance of the librarian's societal role by characterizing the significant responsibilities of the librarian:

The cultural motivation of librarianship is the promotion of wisdom in the individual and the community . . . to communicate, so far as possible, the whole of scholarship to the whole community. The librarian undertakes to supply literature on any and every subject to any and every citizen, for any and every purpose . . . [these actions], in the long run, will sharpen the understanding, judgment, and prudence of the readers and thus sustain and advance civilization. (Butler 1951, 246–47)

Today, we might express the librarian's commitments in somewhat less scholarly terms, but our passion for fulfilling the library's purpose persists: a strong focus on education, reading, and learning remains a consistent *raison d'etre*. At the same time, the breadth of our professional scope has expanded considerably. In addition to traditional print materials, we must also focus on digital books and resources; on innovative programming, especially for the young; and on providing access to knowledge in its many forms. From past to present, our obligations to individuals, society, and to democratic institutions remain central and deep. It is a challenging contract, and librarians must possess significant knowledge and training to fulfill it.

III. THE INTERNAL THREAT: ADMINISTRATIVE VS. PROFESSIONAL PERSPECTIVE

Today, there are numerous real and substantive threats to the fulfillment of our contract with the citizenry. Not all of them are external in origin: many have arisen as a result of administrative decision making and a fundamental difference in the perspectives of library administrators and librarians. More than three decades ago, Lynch (1978) characterized this bifurcated perspective as a clash of ends: administrators view efficiency as key to library function and survival, while professionals view effectiveness as essential. For administrators, performing library tasks with minimal staff and resources is the optimal condition. For professional librarians, providing the highest quality of service is critical. The librarian focuses on the purpose of the library, the administrator on the costs. Although in the real world, librarians and administrators care about both, they do not care about both equally.

No one questions the fact that significant fiscal challenges have placed great strains on library administrators. Because personnel expenses make up a larger percentage of a library budget than any other category, and many other categories are logistically difficult to cut, such as heating and lighting expenses, it is understandable that the personnel budget is especially vulnerable to reduction. It is tempting for a library director, then, to replace professional librarians with paraprofessionals, or to let professional openings linger unfilled, producing smaller staffs with a higher proportion of paraprofessionals. Unfortunately, this trend is increasing. The AFL-CIO Department for Professional Employees estimates that between 2002 and 2012, the number of librarians is expected to increase by only 10.1 percent, while the number of library technicians is expected to rise by 16.8 percent and library assistants by 21.5 percent (Eberhart 2006). Eberhart (2006) reported that "in a recent American Library Association Support Staff Interests Round Table survey of 212 library support staff, 73% stated that they are now performing tasks previously performed by Master's of library science librarians at their library" (Eberhart 2006, 9–10). Support staff are being asked to perform the tasks of librarians, but without the requisite training and education.

The effects of this substitution are significant and harmful to the institution. The library cannot fulfill its primary functions without an adequate supply of professionally educated librarians. It is ironic that the greatest threat to professional librarianship might come from inside the profession—a manifestation of administrative dominance over professional obligation. In an effort to achieve financial stability, library administrators too often sacrifice the significant value that librarians bring to the workplace, diminishing the contribution of the library to society as a whole. Upon reflection, this is not financially responsible at all. Sadly, because state and national library associations are often dominated at their leadership level by institutional and administrative perspectives, they often remain silent or faint-hearted in the face of this critical dilution of quality and purpose.

IV. THE EXTERNAL THREAT: THE INTERNET, SELF-SERVICE, AND THE LIBRARIAN

Although financial challenges might present the greatest pressure against maintaining a strong, professionally educated workforce, an equally cited rationale for reducing the number of professional librarians is that the world of information access has changed. The argument is that new technologies have created a seemingly self-sufficient world in which the expertise of the librarian is no longer needed. Indeed, some appear to believe that the librarian will go the way of the human appendix: an extraneous component, a vestigial organ. In this scenario, librarians are not needed because technology supplants the added value that librarians once delivered. To be fair, there is some evidence for this perspective. For example, Dinkins and Ryan's (2010) research at an academic library found that only 7.4 percent of questions asked at the reference desk required a referral to a professional librarian, and only 11 percent of all questions asked potentially required a professional to answer them.

There is no doubt that in some real sense the world has changed. Traditionally, librarians have always provided individuals with information access and organization. Now that vast stores of information are available in many forms and can be delivered directly into offices, homes, and hand-held devices, librarianship is, in many ways, being transformed. The Internet has affected how information is delivered both inside and outside the library. People's expectations about the knowledge and skills required to locate information have dramatically changed. Many people believe that they simply need access to an Internet connection and a Web browser—no human intermediary needed, and certainly not a librarian! This was a central inference of the 2003 OCLC publication *The 2003 OCLC Environmental Scan: Pattern Recognition* (De Rosa, Dempsey, and Wilson 2004), which noted that information seekers were demanding more and more of what the Internet could provide: a self-service environment. OCLC characterized the resulting evolution in information seeking as "Self-Service: moving to self-sufficiency" (De Rosa, Dempsey, and Wilson 2004, 5).

It is clear that the Internet gives people more control over their information seeking than was possible in the past. Today's reality harkens back to the 1940s when Vanever Bush proposed MEMEX, a one-size-fits-all information storage and retrieval machine (Bush 1945). As people become proficient online and as search engines improve at locating information, is the librarian truly becoming obsolete? And if the Internet makes librarians obsolete, what about the library?

We should not infer from the OCLC findings that librarians or libraries are on a path toward extinction. The truth, however humbling, is that people have never perceived the library as the primary source when they have an information need. One study in the 1980s (Chen and Hernon 1982), for example, revealed that less than 3 percent even considered the public library as a potential source of information. As troubling as this might appear, it is not surprising. Convenience has *always* dominated the search for information. In the past, people were most likely to seek information from a friend, neighbor, or coworker. Then as now, only after these informal searches fail to provide the desired information do people usually think of institutional sources for help. (In reality, if most of the public thought of the library as the first or primary source of information, libraries would long ago have been overwhelmed.) Today, the Internet is certainly as convenient as a friend or neighbor and, in that sense, serves as an alternative for the more informal aspects of information seeking. People have always been primarily self-service information seekers, but the fact that people use the Internet in no way implies that librarians are less necessary or that people will not use libraries. To the contrary, a study by the OCLC found that people who obtain information from librarians are equally satisfied with it as with the information from the Internet, which can be read as a positive indicator of the library's persistence as a desirable and reliable information source (De Rosa et al. 2005).

In fact, some have argued that the Internet has actually increased the importance of librarians. Today, public librarians help thousands of individuals efficiently navigate, select, and evaluate information from myriad unfiltered sources on the Internet, ranging from health and government to careers and self-help. Librarians, serving as knowledgeable ambassadors of digital content, can find information faster than ever before and help ensure the authority of the information provided.

Although some information seekers might be satisfied with less than authoritative and accurate information, it is pernicious to accept this as an institutional standard: good enough is not good enough. Our professional standards do not permit us the latitude of accepting poor information for good. It is, moreover, our obligation to respect individuals' intelligence and our civic duty to promote an informed public. In fact, the Internet has increased the ability of professional librarians to provide high-quality information at very low cost. It is ironic that at the very moment we can provide greatest access to the most accurate information, the public is actually satisfied with quite modest levels of performance. It is perhaps more disheartening that too many library administrators accept a mediocre standard of performance as well.

Nearly 25 years ago, Robert Taylor (1986) proposed an information retrieval system as a metaphor for the library. In doing so, he repeatedly emphasized the role of the librarian as a critical component, noting that librarians provide the "value-added" functions of "flexibility," "adaptability," and "interfacing" by being able to respond to the needs and abilities of each information seeker and by adapting search techniques and methods to the information being sought (Taylor 1986). In the information-seeking world, the librarian continues to serve as a critical "interpreter" of the system.

Despite this commendable virtue, librarians must resist being characterized and judged solely on their ability to answer questions. Crowley and others have repeatedly warned us that viewing librarianship through the lens of information provision is myopic and fraught with unhappy consequences. By narrowing our profession to a technology-based, information-oriented search service, we inappropriately focus on one parochial, albeit important, aspect of our profession (Crowley 2008). By focusing on such a narrow definition of *practice* we are in danger of forgetting *why* we practice. Crowley has correctly observed that "Librarians are not defined by their tools. We use tools in our mission to help others in their lifelong learning endeavors" (Crowley 2007, 5).

Our true strength lies in our historical, philosophical, theoretical, and research-based understanding of knowledge and its production, organization, and dissemination. When applied during critical activities, such as materials selection and evaluation, collection development, knowledge organization, programming, information giving, and strategic planning, the true value of the profession is revealed. It is here that essential democratic concepts like privacy, open access, and intellectual freedom become manifest. In a world in which it is becoming more and more difficult to determine truth from fiction, fact from "spin," the librarian's function is placed in high relief. As Alkan (2008) warned,

> In order to stand truly firm against opposing arguments, librarians must understand the historical background of the book, library, librarian, and the profession . . . and focus once more on the meaning, value, and purpose of all these, as well as on the role of mediator between those who need information and the sources of information. (6)

The fewer the front-line staff with such knowledge and skills, the greater the peril to our institutions and to an open society. Put simply, there is a critical difference between a teacher and a teacher's aide, a nurse and a nurse's aide, and a librarian and a library assistant.

Many library administrators continue to place value on the knowledge and skills of professionally educated librarians. When faced with economic or other pressures, these administrators struggle to find what they hope to be a middle ground, balancing professional and paraprofessional staff. For example, they might place degreed staff in management, administration, and collection development, while designating paraprofessionals to provide public service. On its surface, this appears to be a good compromise: collection and policy decisions are still made by degreed staff, and responding to patron requests for information (only a small amount of which might be "reference" questions) is handled by proactive and service-oriented paraprofessionals. However, this arrangement has a fundamental flaw. What might appear to be simple questions or quotidian requests for materials or information often implicate deeper and more difficult issues. A case in point is the recent situation in Kentucky when the circulation staff refused to check out a graphic novel to an 11-year-old girl (Barack 2009). Such instances of restriction of materials or self-censorship at the point of service by library staff occur more often than we would like to admit. Professional librarians, in accordance with numerous ALA policies, affirm "the responsibility and the right of all parents and guardians to guide their own children's use of the library and its resources and services" (American Library Association 1999). Librarians in public service areas model and reinforce such essential values. Administrators must make a commitment to hiring and retaining professionally educated staff on the front lines. The Internet has revolutionized information retrieval, but it cannot institutionalize the notions of intellectual freedom, open access, or privacy. That requires an organization imbued with the professional values of librarianship and the persistent presence of professionally educated front-line librarians.

V. NOBLE ENDS

Despite decades of elucidation, librarianship is often confounded with numerous other activities that occur in libraries. It is important, therefore, to reexamine and affirm the historical roots of the North American librarian, lest we forget that these roots nourish us and keep us upright on a firm foundation.

Librarians have been part of the American and Canadian educational and cultural tradition for more than 200 years. Before the last quarter of the 19th century, the professional preparation of librarians involved little more than on-the-job training or, at most, a brief apprenticeship. By the late 1800s, however, as professions such as medicine, law, social work, teaching, and nursing emerged, librarianship took its place among the fields where a recognized body of expertise was required to fulfill the profession's purpose. All of the newly evolving professions arose, in part, as a counterbalance to the excesses of the industrial age (Winter 1988). Their purpose was altruistic and service-oriented, intended to improve the lot of the citizenry rather than to make money. It is not surprising, then, that Melvil Dewey in 1876 referred to librarianship as a *calling* when that term applied as much to the clergy. Dewey exhorted librarians to "stand side by side with the preachers and teachers" and reassured them that they now had officially joined the ranks of the professions (Dewey 1876, 5).

The 19th century was also the time when the concept of civic good was instantiated institutionally. Major civic initiatives such as public education, municipal water and light, safety forces, and public health programs were being created throughout Canada and the United States. The motivations of these municipal institutions and the helping professions were similar: to make the world or community a better place rather than to produce more products and profit. Despite the many decades that have passed, these public institutions and professions remain altruistic (some more than others).

Librarianship as a public good is not an anachronism. The obligation of librarians to use their powers to serve society and its citizenry has not diminished: it is an *idée fixe* of the profession. Although libraries do, indeed, have to consider the marketplace, such as adopting some of the marketing practices of bookstores, the library itself is not a business—it is a public service; its librarians are not retail clerks, they are a public instrumentality. The purpose of the efficient and effective use of funds is not profit, but a social end.

Many people become librarians because they want to belong to a profession whose members share a common sense of purpose and values. Librarians' "core values" are articulated by the ALA as access, confidentiality/privacy, democracy, diversity, education and lifelong learning, intellectual freedom, preservation, the public good, professionalism, service, and social responsibility (American Library Association 2004). These are not just words employed as a form of public relations; they are reifications of the principles by which library professionals live. To ignore these fundamental values would render our profession without a compass. In such circumstances, it is inevitable that we would lose our way. We must be careful not to succumb to the fate described by Danton nearly 80 years ago: "There is . . . far too much hit-or-miss, trial-and-error library practice, but even this . . . is not so pernicious as the carrying out of procedures without a clear consciousness of their purpose and a synoptic understanding of ends and aims" (Danton 1934, 545).

We would do well to remember that librarians protect the accumulated knowledge of our times and serve those who desire to understand that knowledge. Librarians are the guardians of open access and the defenders of the people's right to congregate, discourse, and dissent. Perhaps the fact that librarians and library administrators seem at times tentative about asserting these values speaks to the critical importance not just of library and information science education, but of even more rigorous library and information science education.

VI. DON'T CALL IT A COMEBACK

Recently an article appeared on CNN.com titled "Humans vs. Automated Search: Why People Power Is Cool Again" (Cashmore 2011). The author reports on the increasingly common perception that search algorithms are imperfect and that human intervention might be the solution: "curation is the new search" one cited pundit declares. While the report highlighted the importance of a human intermediary between knowledge seeker and body of knowledge, it also gives pause. Cool "again"? The "new" search? Librarians were not mentioned once in this article. Yet librarians have been quietly curating, defining search parameters, creating metadata, constructing information architecture, and providing the added value of human intervention for centuries. Every once in a while, librarians are rediscovered for their value and briefly recognized for their achievements, only to be taken for granted and forgotten again. Murray and Tschernitz (2004), in their article about the effect of the Internet on reference inquiries, suggested that "an additional issue in this increasingly electronic age is that people might reject technology and seek more face to face contact" (Murray and Tschernitz 2004, 85). Although it is unlikely that most people will wholly reject technology, today's information seekers need more help with more complex transactions: librarians find themselves spending even more time with patrons because of the user's desire "to interact with another person" (85). The human element remains an essential aspect of most information seeking.

VII. TEN VERY, VERY, IMPORTANT THINGS WE LEARNED IN LIBRARY SCHOOL: A PERSONAL REFLECTION

Numerous articles by library practitioners often comment on the many aspects of librarianship that are *not* taught in library school. These articles often explicitly state or imply that library schools teach students the wrong things; some have even suggested that a person does not really need formal, graduate-level education in library science. Despite the spuriousness of their claims, these articles are seldom refuted. In this case, however, the authors must take strong exception to such facile inferences. As co-authors with more than 30 years separating our dates of library school graduation, we contend that there were numerous, common aspects of our library education that helped us to achieve a shared professional identity, linking each of us with our historical roots. These are the enduring elements that are central to our profession and should be highly valued by employers with a commitment to high quality library service.

1. The importance of the library in a democratic society
2. An abiding commitment to the education and nurturance of young people
3. A deep dedication to intellectual freedom
4. An enduring commitment to protect the privacy of library users
5. An understanding of how knowledge is organized and a commitment to organize knowledge so that all individuals can access and learn from it
6. An understanding of how to find and evaluate information for our library users
7. An enduring belief in the preservation of our cultural heritage: our literature, art, film, and music
8. An abiding commitment to reading, learning, and their value to all
9. A commitment to serve the community, its institutions, and the public good
10. An obligation to provide the highest level of service to all

These essential threads were woven throughout our professional education and became an integrated and integral part of our identity as librarians. Achieving the professional degree brought with it a commitment to excellence in service, deep and abiding. Because both American and Canadian library programs have long been accredited by the American Library Association in a unique, collaborative effort, this fundamental commitment has shaped librarianship on both sides of our shared border.

We might indeed be in an age of "self-service" or "self-sufficiency," but this should not be confused with an age of isolation. Librarians have always been natural and constant partners to those who independently seek new ideas and knowledge of all types. While changes in technologies and information gathering techniques have affected the "how" of librarianship, our central purpose, our contract with the citizenry, remains the same. It is the "why" that makes librarianship the human face of a remarkable and enduring institution.

REFERENCES

Alkan, Nazli. 2008. "The Importance and Influence of Philosophical Thinking for Librarians." *Library Philosophy and Practice* 10 (September): 1–15.

American Library Association. 1999. *Libraries: An American Value.* Chicago: American Library Association.

American Library Association. 2004. *Core Values of Librarianship.* Chicago: American Library Association.

Barack, Lauren. 2009. "KY Library Relocates Graphic Novels after Staffers Fired." *School Library Journal.* Accessed February 2, 2011. http://www.libraryjournal.com/slj/articlescensorship/858412–341/ky_library_relocates_graphic_novels.html.csp.

Bush, Vanever. 1945. "As We Might Think." *Atlantic Monthly* 176 (July): 101–8.

Butler, Pierce. 1951. "Librarianship as a Profession." *Library Quarterly* 21 (October): 235–47.

Cashmore, Pete. 2011. "Humans vs. Automated Search: Why People Power Is Cool Again." Accessed February 2, 2011. http://articles.cnn.com/2011–01–13/tech/people.power.cashmore_1_google-popular-search-terms-search-results?_s=PM:TECH.

Chen, Ching-Chih, and Peter Hernon. 1982. *Information Seeking: Assessing and Anticipating User Needs.* New York: Neal-Schuman.

Crowley, Bill. 2007. "Don't Let Google and the Pennypinchers Get You Down: Defending (or Redefining) Libraries and Librarianship in the Age of Technology." Presentation at the British Columbia Library Association 2007 Conference, April 21, 2007, Burnaby, British Columbia.

Crowley, Bill. 2008. *Renewing Professional Librarianship: A Fundamental Rethinking.* Westport, CT: Libraries Unlimited.

Danton, J. Periam. 1934. "Plea for a Philosophy of Librarianship." *The Library Quarterly* 4 (October): 527–51.

De Rosa, Cathy, Lorcan Dempsey, and Alane Wilson. 2004. *The 2003 OCLC Environmental Scan: Pattern Recognition: A Report to the OCLC Membership.* Dublin, OH: OCLC.

De Rosa, Cathy, Joanne Cantrell, Diane Cellentani, Janet Hawk, Lillie Jenkins, and Alane Wilson. 2005. *Perceptions of Libraries and Information Resources: A Report to the OCLC Membership.* Dublin, OH: OCLC.

Dewey, Melvil. 1876. "The Profession." *Library Journal* 114 (June 15, 1989): 5.

Dinkins, Debbi, and Susan M. Ryan. 2010. "Measuring Referrals: The Use of Paraprofessionals at the Reference Desk." *Journal of Academic Librarianship* 36: 279–86.

Eberhart, George M. 2006. *The Whole Library Handbook.* Chicago: American Library Association.

Lynch, Beverly. 1978. "Libraries as Bureaucracies." *Library Trends* 26 (winter): 259–67.

Murray, Janet, and Cindy Tschernitz. 2004. "The Internet Myth: Emerging Trends in Reference Enquiries." *Australasian Public Libraries and Information Services* 17: 80–88.

Taylor, Robert. 1986. *Value-Added Processes in Information Systems.* Norwood, NJ: Ablex.

Winter, Michael F. 1988. *The Culture and Control of Expertise: Toward a Sociological Understanding of Librarianship.* Westport, CT: Greenwood.

3

YOUTH SERVICES IN PUBLIC LIBRARIES: A RETURN TO BELLIGERENCE

Janice M. Del Negro
Dominican University

Librarians who serve children make a regular investment in every corner of our community, bolstering our collective intellect with the insight that lives between the pages of a book. If we are cute or quaint or sweet, it is only incidentally. By trade we are strong and fearless and indefatigable. We are united in our commitment to seeing young people for who they are, young temporarily and people forever, and in that recognition promising to secure and protect their access to knowledge, freely, without judgment, and trusting that they will share that access, in turn, with another generation. Wisdom and empathy, integrity and wonder; these are the things of story. And librarians are the stewards of story. We sow the seeds of curiosity and reap the fruits of enlightenment, and we do so by knowing children and knowing stories and knowing how to bring them together.

—Thom Barthelmess, President, Association for Library
Services to Children, 2009–2010

THE STORY FROM THE OUTSIDE

From the outside the story appears grim. Contemporary urban—and rural—legend, perpetuated by shallow media investigation and the commercial heralding of the death of the book, posits a public library children's room that is a warehouse for random books and other resources. Bloggers, tweeters, and friends of friends, often those who have not utilized a public library in some time, tell the story of a ghost library of dusty shelves, old computers, and ratty paperbacks, a deserted space in which the traffic is minimal, services undermined by the mistaken belief that all desirable information and literary materials are available online. The children and families that used to come to the library for programming no longer do so because of the wide availability of digital entertainment. Government and other funding agencies, including some public library administrators, tighten expenditures at their institutions by eliminating professional librarian positions, often beginning with the youth services librarian because an MLIS degree is not required to read books to preschoolers. The short-sighted deprofessionalization of these positions means that libraries can be staffed by interchangeable clerks, materials ordered based on best-seller statistics and patron demand, and self-service checkout utilized to eliminate the need for interaction between patrons and library staff. Technology is ubiquitous, making public libraries and the accessibility they provide unnecessary for both individual quality of life and the greater common good. This meta-legend library, lacking professional librarians and subsequent professional direction, cannot help but fail to justify its worth to its community, and the doors close with little protest, saving money for the local taxpayers, or at least the local funding body.

THE STORY FROM THE INSIDE

The story from the inside, however, is an entirely different one. The successful children's room in a contemporary public library is a constantly changing environment in which children at all developmental levels (and their parents, teachers, and caregivers) engage in transliteracy-related activities that help prepare them to live and thrive in an information-driven society. Storytimes, reading, information seeking, social interaction, and other traditional activities of the child library patron are being accomplished across media platforms. The integration of technology with traditional library services allows an abundance of learning opportunities and provides multiple media through which the youth services librarians can communicate with their patrons and their community. Traffic is hectic, circulation is high, and in-house use of technology and other resources keeps the room humming. Outreach and in-house programming focuses on educating children about critical thinking so they can not only navigate the Internet but evaluate the information they find there. School visits to the library and librarian visits to schools and other community agencies, face-to-face and virtual, build a web of support for these activities. Youth services programming, integrated with the whole-library advocacy and marketing plan, guarantees the children's room, and the library, a high profile in the community. A director who advocates for Youth Services ensures that the public library is seen as an integral part of the community infrastructure, promoting literacy, leveling the educational playing field, and identifying and delivering library services that meet a community's recognized—and sometimes unrecognized—needs.

The difference between these two stories is found in the cast of characters; the second story has a hero, a credentialed youth services librarian committed to the ethics of professional librarianship and library advocacy; the first story does not.

STORY ONE, THE HISTORICAL VERSION

There is a fair amount of hyperbole in contemporary professional and popular media regarding the undervaluing of public libraries, especially as relates to the technological murder of the book. This is unsurprising, given the general undervaluing of books and libraries throughout the history of public libraries in the United States. Equally unsurprising is the undervaluing of youth services librarianship, that arena of public library services that has historically been considered women's work (Harris 1993, 874).

What is surprising, however, is that anyone is surprised by these most recent developments. The undervaluing of public libraries and youth services in public libraries in particular, is hardly a new phenomenon. Public libraries have long had to defend their role to funding bodies, which often do not recognize the foundational role libraries play in communities, as well as to those community members who are not library users. For a profession dedicated to transparent access to information, librarians have done a poor job communicating what they do and why librarians do what they do to the communities they serve and the bodies that fund them. Worthwhile services designed to meet the identified needs of library communities are not only poorly marketed to intended recipients, but also the reasons for those services are sometimes poorly understood by those who deliver them. Successful advocacy demands a deep understanding of the transformational role libraries and library services play in the life of a community and in the individual lives of patrons (De Rosa and Johnson 2008).

Within the greater American public library movement of the 19th and 20th centuries, services to children emerged as a dynamic force, promoted and supported by the women who created those services (Vandergrift 1996) and by the library directors, male and female, who embraced the challenge of serving whole communities. In the final decades of the 19th century, library services to youth were recognized by the American Library Association (ALA), culminating in the formation of the Section for Library Work with Children, which had its first meeting in 1901. During the first half of the 20th century, the Section for Library Work with Children evolved through several names and organizational changes into its current incarnation, the Association for Library Service to Children (ALSC), a division of the ALA. Ever since the women of the ALA carved youth services as a specialty from public librarianship in general, youth services professionals have been defending their patrons, budgets, spaces, and collections, while, not incidentally, attracting male youth services librarians to their ranks. Youth services librarians have fought and continue to fight, often successfully, for their place at the professional, administrative, and political table.

In his classic study of public libraries in the 1940s, Robert Leigh called public library services to children "an impressive achievement . . . Not only are the children's librarians expert but also in the community they are recognized as such . . . Thus children's rooms and children's librarians have been the classic success in the public library" (Leigh 1950, 99–100). However, the lengthy histories of public librarianship in the United States do not necessarily recognize the integral part that youth services plays in public libraries (Jenkins 2000, 103–4), nor have youth services librarians been particularly adept at promoting their own worth (Anderson 1987).

In 1949 Frances Clarke Sayers delivered a speech on being a youth services librarian titled "The Belligerent Profession," in which she stated,

> I would have us belligerent first within the ranks of our own profession. We have never, in my opinion, stood our ground firmly enough and declared what our peculiar, unique function was to be, and held to it and accomplished it . . . this enduring faith in reading books, to know them and make them useful has somehow been lost—not, I feel, because we are of lesser stature than our predecessors but because, perhaps, there have been such pressures, such multitudinous forces at work upon the culture of our generation— economic, political, mechanical, and inventive—and the joyous obligation to read and to induce others to read seemed too simple a function in a world

where everything and everybody were being mechanized, organized, industrialized, streamlined, geared for action in two wars, emotionally adjusted
for depression, progressively educated, and made socially conscious. (Sayers
1965, 29)

Sayers was referring not only to the importance of reader's advisory and the
promotion of literature and literacy, but to the perception of the youth service
librarian as the expert in the field of literature for youth, with true professional understanding of youth services' unofficial credo, "the right book for the right child
at the right time" (Jenkins 1996, 816). This deceptively simple phrase requires encyclopedic knowledge of the literature for and about children, encyclopedic knowledge of child development, and encyclopedic knowledge of individual patrons. In
a very real sense this phrase encapsulates the current Competencies for Librarians
Serving Children in Public Libraries from ALSC.

Effectively educated, MLIS-credentialed youth services librarians are firmly
focused on the promotion of reading and literacy in their communities as well
as access to information and technology. The technological access to text currently enjoyed by today's readers may be something entirely different by the time
this book goes to press. The contemporary credentialed youth services librarian
is trained to function across literacy platforms, to use multiple texts and media
formats to unite youth with literature, information and one another through individual, social, and technological connections. The contemporary youth services
librarian is the liaison between traditional and emerging literacies.

The foremothers of youth services in public libraries—including such women as
Caroline Maria Hewins (1846–1926), Mary Wright Plummer (1856–1916), Lutie
Stearns (1866–1943), Alice Jordan (1870–1960), Anne Carroll Moore (1871–
1961), Frances Jenkins Olcott (1871–1963), Effie Louise Power (1873–1969),
and others—essentially constructed their own profession and, with it, their own
professional culture. In her component of the bifurcated article developed with
Christine Jenkins, Betsy Hearne stressed, "Our foremothers were doers, and they
did literature. They were the genesis of an entire industry born of *their* industry"
(Hearne and Jenkins 1999, 537). Notable in this statement is the word "literature," not "books"—format is not the issue, access is.

PROFESSIONALISM AND LIBRARIANSHIP

Professionalism in general is characterized by mastery of a specific body of knowledge, autonomy and control of one's work and how one's work is performed,
motivation focused on intrinsic rewards and interests of patrons (which take precedence over the professional's self interest), commitment to the profession as a
career and to the service objectives of the organization for which one works, sense
of community and collegiality with others in the profession, some sense of accountability, and a commitment to the professional and ethical standards of the profession according to an established code of ethics (Abbott 1998; Litwin 2009). There
is increasing recognition that professionalism is limited in its application unless it
is supported by a professional or employing organization. In the particular case of
youth services librarianship, there was early and growing support for its objectives
and methods. As noted by Hearne in the composite Hearne-Jenkins examination
of the professional women of early children's librarianship, "Their grail was not just

information or even knowledge, but the enrichment of experience through whole reading, the kind of reading that engulfs the heart as well as engaging the head . . . and ultimately shapes a lifetime" (Hearne and Jenkins 1999, 538). This belief in the transformative possibilities of literature and libraries is part and parcel of what current research indicates is necessary for the long-term support and funding of public libraries (De Rosa and Johnson 2008).

Public librarianship in the United States, both historical and contemporary, is replete with visionary leaders who believe youth services librarianship to be a profession demanding of professional commitment epitomized by the attainment of the advanced MLS/MLIS degree. Professional youth services librarians are characterized by mastery of the body of literature for youth and command of the most effective ways of connecting youth to that literature. These professionals are committed to designing and developing collections and services in response to the specific needs of not only unique individuals but unique communities of patrons, and to the sharing of expertise throughout the profession for the greater good of the patrons and communities served. Motivated by the inherent value of connecting youth to literature and information whatever the format, professional youth services librarians thoroughly understand and affirm the ethics and values of the library profession, including youth's right to read, right to privacy, and right to social and educational well-being.

The credentialed youth services librarian must demonstrate that she or he is the unifying force among myriad disciplines, the individual who views the flotsam and jetsam of information within the larger contextual sea, and the professional who makes the connections between bits and bytes of information in order to turn them into knowledge. The multidisciplinary nature of a Library and Information Science education provides the tools necessary to teach critical thinking skills to youth within the real-world context of information overload. Youth services librarianship is the metadiscipline for all things children (Sujin Huggins, personal e-mail, March 14, 2011).

When Dorothy Anderson surveyed library directors about the skills necessary to be a children's librarian in 1987, the responding directors demanded children's librarians "who are compassionate, committed, and competent, and who will consciously target services toward the new [immigrant] populations" (Anderson 1987, 409). This description demands levels of expertise that include knowledge of the library client base, awareness of cultural diversity, and commitment to the ideals and core values of the public library (American Library Association 2011b). These ideals are communicated in effective graduate library and information science education in order to provide an understanding of not only the *how* of youth services but the *why*, creating credentialed youth services librarians that understand the practical application of theory.

In 2004, library directors queried on the skills necessary for a new children's librarian put forth the desire for a youth services librarian who had both the knowledge of the literature and the knowledge of the technology used to access and promote it (Adkins and Esser 2004, 17–18).

Recent works on youth services librarianship (Cerny, Markey, and Williams 2006; Walter 2010) have recognized the need for clearer understanding and communication of the role and purpose of the professional youth services librarian. In *Outstanding Library Services to Children: Putting the Core Competencies to Work* (a companion to the ALSC *Core Competencies for Librarians Serving Children in Public Libraries*), authors Cerny, Markey, and Williams (2006) examine each competency, explain its importance in the arena of best practices, and present a philosophy of service based on the necessary skills for building "an exemplary children's department in . . . public libraries" (vi). This title delineates the myriad skills necessary for effective youth services librarians, skills that go substantially beyond the capabilities of on-the-job and in-service training. Active advocacy, administration and management, networking, public speaking, communication across media platforms, as well as mastery of the body of literature and information specifically designed for youth are only some of the areas in which youth services librarians must be proficient.

Virginia Walter postulated a set of emerging issues that encompass expanding the information role of library services to youth (including the education of youth regarding seeking and evaluating information), leveraging community partnerships and collaborations, and promoting a global perspective in library services. Walter states that "today's children are citizens of the world, not just our own country, and . . . they deserve to have library services that reflect the interconnectedness of the world in which they live" (Walter 2010, 53).

DEPROFESSIONALIZATION: A SHORT-SIGHTED SOLUTION

The move toward deprofessionalization of librarians has a relatively long history (Litwin 2009). A move toward deprofessionalizing librarian positions in public libraries may have resulted from financial strain, but the move toward deprofessionalizing youth services librarians has certainly been assisted by a lack of understanding regarding the role of the credentialed youth service librarian. Youth services librarians are familiar with comments that unthinkingly belittle their work: "Oh, you're a children's librarian? How nice to play with children and read books all day!" How often have librarians been blind-sided by those who are, at best, surprised that an MLIS is necessary for youth services librarians working with children? Or that librarians are necessary at all because all information is freely available on the net? While the ALA's Core Competences of Librarianship define the knowledge to be possessed by all persons graduating from an ALA-accredited master's programs in library and information studies, the association does not categorically state the necessity for the professional degree in order to be a professional librarian, although some divisions within ALA specifically do so.

While the Young Adult Library Services Association (YALSA) does not address the required education of young adult librarians in its competencies (YALSA 2010), the ALSC competencies for children's librarians state: "The policy of this organization is that a master's degree in Library and Information Science from an ALA-accredited graduate school is the appropriate professional degree for the librarian serving children in the public library, but ALSC expects the same standards applied to paraprofessional staff." These otherwise excellent competencies include a blurring of the professional line that weakens the stance on what defines professional librarianship (Association for Library Services to Children 2009).

This is not to say that there are not tremendously talented paraprofessionals working in youth services, with the expertise gained through hard-won experience and on the job training, or that some youth services librarians with master's degrees in library and information science should not look for other work. What needs to be emphasized here is that the authority of the professional librarian, the authority of the profession of librarianship, is weakened by this nod to the worthy anomaly; an emphasis on the complexity and quality of the expertise expected from youth services in public libraries would have better supported and protected the recommendation and authority of the degreed youth services librarian. Without such a standard, the issue of professionalism becomes more difficult for hiring bodies and Human Resources Departments, as personnel can be hired for reasons not including the professional degree.

To say that a paraprofessional without a master's degree has the same level of education, and the benefits therefrom, as a librarian with a master's degree is, very simply, inaccurate. Librarians compromise daily on the realities of public service working within particular public library systems; the profession of librarianship cannot compromise on the ideal. All who work for the public library should be aware of its history and mission in the community. Talented paraprofessionals must be encouraged to pursue the professional degree, with both time and money. Those paraprofessionals who do not pursue an advanced degree must have access to a ladder for advancement, tied to continuing education, to senior paraprofessional positions.

That being said, the ALSC Core Competencies are specific and distinct, expressly requiring a graduate level degree and an extensive roster of expertise: knowledge of client groups, administrative and management skills, communication skills, knowledge of materials, user and reference services, programming skills, advocacy, public relations and networking skills, professionalism and professional development, and technology. A close examination of each of these criteria reveals a need not only for mastering particular specific skills, but for mastery of the underlying professional theory, historical, contemporary, and developing, that supports those skills.

A measure of a profession's development is the understanding of the values that govern its practice. Librarianship requires not only professional competence but ethical judgment. The need for ethical awareness has grown as the practice of librarianship has become more diverse, roles and services more complex, and information technologies faster and more pervasive (Preer 2008, xiii, xiv).

The argument for professionalism is supported by the professional organization as a whole, which accredits graduate schools of library and information science. The ALA Committee on Accreditation develops and formulates standards of education for library and information studies, in an effort to ensure that Accreditation standards reflect the needs and core values of the profession (American Library Association 2011a). Those professional standards, inextricably linked to the professional degree, demand a theoretical understanding of and commitment to issues such as access, confidentiality and privacy, democracy, diversity, education and lifelong learning, intellectual freedom, preservation, the public good, professionalism, service, and social responsibility.

At its core, youth services librarianship values those ethics that are the hallmark of professional librarianship cutting across all areas of specialization: providing service, ensuring access to information, avoiding conflicts of interest, and protecting patron confidentiality (Preer 2008, xiv).

DIGITAL DISPARITY

Public libraries responded to the rise of the world wide web in the 1990s with an unparalleled rush to keep up with rapidly introduced, quickly evolving technological advances. As a result, public libraries often strained their budgets and trimmed their professional staffs in an effort to afford the technology that would soon be ubiquitous, at least in households that could afford it.

The emerging availability of less expensive e-book readers, the misguided assumption that everything is or soon will be available online, and the popular belief that everyone has access to the Internet reinforces the impression that the traditional print book and the activities associated with it are very soon to be, if they are not already, obsolete. These unsupported claims are being used to make sweeping statements about the futures of publishing, books, reading, and libraries. Examination from a broader, more informed perspective reveals a reality that is far from the seamless, independent, technologically enhanced utopia promoted in the popular techno-media. Research puts the lie to the oft-repeated but unsupported idea that all American citizens have equal access to the technology that connects them to available digital resources. The digital divide is now an economic one, with a growing distance between those with personal access to recent technology and those without that access (Hilbert 2010; Jansen 2010; Lowery 2011; Nielsen 2006; Smith 2010; U.S. Census Bureau 2011). Even given access to technology, the magnitude of available information demands a level of critical thinking not all children have the opportunity to achieve. A prescient statement by Melvil Dewey in 1926 must again be restated: libraries do not warehouse books but support learning, the development of knowledge, and access to information in all its myriad forms (Dewey 1876; Preer 2008, 9).

The public library serves the common good; the youth services public librarian serves the common good of children, parents, teachers, and other caretakers everywhere. Beneficial technology has moved the library beyond its own physical boundaries and precipitated the development of libraries without walls dedicated to the common good, the global community, and the individual advancement of patrons. The public library is the access point for those aspiring to be educated, informed individuals in a democratic society, and the youth services librarian is the individual that provides both access and instruction to the nation's youngest citizens.

The growing need for skilled employees with strong critical thinking skills is morphing into a demand for transliterate individuals able to read, write, interpret, evaluate, and communicate across an array of traditional and technological platforms, from orality to print to digital media (Andretta 2009; Thomas et al. 2007). The definition of *transliteracy* and the stated range of platforms must expand to include *cultural literacy* as well. Access to technology cannot be separated from the discussion of literature, literacy, and reading in a global library environment.

In the results of the 2009 Programme for International Student Assessment (PISA) study of 15-year-old students, the United States ranked only average in reading literacy and science literacy among the industrialized nations examined. American mathematics literacy scores were even below average (Fleischman et al. 2010). Arguably, "average" or "below average" will not be sufficient for success in the 21st century's heightened competitive environments. In the United States, the number of children in poverty increased 28 percent between 2000–2009; more than 60 percent of fourth, eighth, and twelfth grade students in public schools are doing math below grade level (Children's Defense Fund 2011). Reading and literacy statistics show a nation of children who cannot read at grade level. Thirty-seven percent of American fourth graders fail basic skills tests in reading, and that percentage is higher in low-income families and ethnic minorities. Young children entering kindergarten and first grade vary greatly in their attainment of the early skills that provide the basis for later literacy (West 2000, West, Flanagan, and Reaney 2000).

Public libraries are part of the educational and social infrastructure that will address these issues. Communities may get the public libraries they deserve, but many communities are often unaware of the level of service they should expect from their local libraries and, by extension, from their local youth services librarians. The strongest possible recommendation is that professional youth services librarians be very good at explaining what it is they do, how and why they do it, and what it is worth to the communities they serve.

Children, regardless of the economic or social situations into which they are born, need and deserve protection and safety, recreation, intellectual stimulation, access to the technology of the day, developmentally appropriate resources, literacy support, strong cultural understanding, and a personal and national identity (UNICEF 1990). These values are long-standing in Canadian and American librarianship, and carefully designed library programs for youth can and do support the success of these future adult citizens. Resource-specific library programming, when properly marketed to and understood by a service community and its leadership, can be a unifying force that crosses political lines.

In order to demonstrate the worth of youth services librarianship to their service communities, to ensure support from both administrative and government entities, youth services librarians must first provide services that are seen as irreplaceable, not only by individual patrons, but by administrators and funding bodies. This does not mean a tremendous influx of new money; what it does mean is a tremendous amount of professional authority over collections, programs, and outreach. It also means that youth services librarians must become advocates for their cause and draw others into advocacy with them. Youth services librarians and their allies must market the worth of their services to critical stakeholders. Failure to do this effectively has left youth services librarianship open to elimination based on the ever narrowing idea of return on financial investment (ROI), corporate criterion that emphasizes cost and not value. This approach is problematic in that it does not consider the unquantifiable benefits of quality library services; it is also problematic because recent research does not support this approach when advocating for library funding and other support. The OCLC report, funded by the Bill and Melinda Gates Foundation, argues strongly for alternate strategies for both advocacy and success, stating that library funding and support is driven not by demographics but by voters' attitudes toward and perceptions of their public libraries. Those attitudes include the perception of "passionate librarians" involved in their communities, the belief that the library is a transformational force in people's lives, and the understanding that the public library provides a return on emotional investment (ROEI) that includes both psychological and intellectual rewards to its users (Crowley 2010; De Rosa and Johnson 2008). These perceptions, combined with research that indicates that early use of the library as a child is an indicator of library use as an adult (Bird 2002; Powell, Taylor, and McMillen 1984), supports youth services librarianship, long rooted in these very attitudes, as a vital asset to the public library's unambiguous relevancy in a changing information environment.

The successful public library children's room cannot function without a professional, credentialed youth services librarian and expect to achieve the high profile necessary for community and financial support. Recent management literature recognizes the synthesis of traits necessary to be an effective leader: the ability to lead with purpose, to form coalitions united behind a common goal, and to create sustainable change (Ellsworth 2002; Goleman 2004; Goleman, Boyatzis, and McKee 2002). The credentialed youth service librarian is trained to take a leadership position in the library's service community, with a robust aggregate of abilities that includes practical management and programming skills combined with the emotional intelligence to serve a wide variety of patron needs.

That the missions of individual public libraries vary from community to community is not at issue here; what is at issue is the professional obligation, mission, and standing of the youth services librarian in the public library in general. The youth services librarian must be positioned for the greater good of the community, mastering a spectrum of knowledge, expertise, and ethics that is rooted in the discipline of Library and Information Science. Both ALSC and YALSA competencies reference, directly and indirectly, these principles. The achievement of a master's degree in library and information science is a personal and professional commitment to the core ethics and values of the library profession: access, confidentiality, democracy, diversity, education and lifelong learning, intellectual freedom, preservation, the public good, service, and social responsibility (American Library Association 2011b).

Professional credentials indicate a conscious allegiance to the standards and values of the profession and help position the individual for the multiple roles the professional librarian plays in the public sphere. Advisory and literary expertise is only one facet of professional youth services librarians; properly credentialed youth services librarians move easily among their roles of literacy and literature expert, lifelong learning facilitator, architect and interior designer, public relations advocate, department and staff manager, lobbyist, performer, and community leader. In a concrete, powerfully symbolic way, graduate credentials are a personal and professional commitment to the core ethics and values of the library profession, which are now more critical than ever.

CELEBRATE. MOTIVATE. PERPETUATE.

The public library does that which no other community agency even begins to attempt. The public library connects patrons to literature (of all types, in all formats), promotes literacy and learning, and provides concrete evidence of a community's commitment to the importance of lifelong learning in an informed democracy. Public libraries—and their administrative and funding boards—have failed to respond effectively to uninformed media that insist that libraries are obsolete, that books no longer matter, or, as Steve Jobs so remarkably stated, nobody reads (Markoff 2008). The public library response to this campaign of misinformation has been inadequate and has allowed outsiders, who see technology as an end instead of a means, to tell the library story. The perpetual public library, that agency that will have heft and clout in its community, is still Ranganathan's constantly evolving organism (Ranganathan 1931), a fusion of tradition and technology that can flexibly respond to the evolution of reading (in whatever format) and the changing needs of its community. The perpetual public library is firmly rooted in its traditional service role even as it embraces the technological change that helps it achieve its constantly evolving mission. Professional librarians must vehemently, vocally, and virtually reclaim and fortify their areas of literary and advisory expertise. Youth services librarians must solidly establish, with internal and external stakeholders, their valuable contributions as the community's expert resource for all things related to children, learning, and literacy. Celebrate the literature, motivate the reader, and perpetuate libraries and their essential services. Youth services librarians must, in effect, become extraordinarily effective marketers for the institution that delivers incomparably beneficial services to the most valuable resource of any American, British, or Canadian community—its youth.

REFERENCES

Abbott, Andrew. 1998. "Professionalism and the Future of Librarianship." *Library Trends* 46(3): 430.

Adkins, Denice, and Linda Esser. 2004. "Literature and Technology Skills for Entry-level Children's Librarians: What Employers Want." *Children and Libraries* 2(3): 14–21.

American Library Association. 2011a. *Committee on Accreditation Strategic Plan 2005–2010.* Accessed July 26. http://www.ala.org/ala/aboutala/offices/accreditation/coa/COAstrategicplan2005.pdf.

American Library Association. 2011b. *Core Values of Librarianship.* Accessed July 22. http://www.ala.org/ala/aboutala/governance/policymanual/updatedpolicymanual/section2/40corevalues.cfm.

Anderson, Dorothy J. 1987. "From Idealism to Realism: Library Directors and Children's Services." *Library Trends* 35(3): 393–412.

Andretta, Susie. 2009. "Transliteracy: Take a Walk on the Wild Side." 75th International Federation of Library Associations and Institutions (IFLA) General Conference and Council, World Library and Information Congress, August. Accessed July 26, 2011. www.ifla.org/files/hq/papers/ifla75/94-andretta-en.pdf.

Association for Library Services to Children. 2009. *Competencies for Librarians Serving Children in Public Libraries.* American Library Association. Accessed: July 26, 2011. http://www.ala.org/ala/mgrps/divs/alsc/edcareers/alsccorecomps/ALA_print_layout_1_506107_506107.cfm.

Barthelmess, Thom. 2009. "Sixty-Second Speech." *ALAConnect* (August 26). Accessed: July 26, 2011. http://connect.ala.org/node/81153.

Bird, Bern. 2002. "Solving the Mystery: Children's Librarianship and How to Nurture It." *Australasian Public Libraries and Information Services* 15(1): 14–23.

Cerny, Rosanne, Penny Markey, and Amanda Williams. 2006. *Outstanding Library Service to Children: Putting the Core Competencies to Work.* Chicago: American Library Association.

Children's Defense Fund. 2011. *State of America's Children 2011 Report.* Children's Defense Fund. Accessed July 26, 2011. http://www.childrensdefense.org/child-research-data-publications/state-of-americas-children-2011.

Crowley, Bill. 2010. "Know Your ROEI: Emotional Investment in Service Delivery Can Return Lifelong Benefits." *Library Journal* (February 15): 34–35. Accessed July 26, 2011. http://www.libraryjournal.com/article/CA6718541.html.

De Rosa, Cathy, and Jenny Johnson. 2008. *From Awareness to Funding: A Study of Library Support in America.* Dublin, OH: OCLC. Accessed March 17, 2009. http://www.oclc.org/reports/funding/fullreport.pdf.

Dewey, Melvil. 1876. "The Profession." *American Library Journal* 1(1): 56.

Ellsworth, Richard R. 2002. *Leading with Purpose: The New Corporate Realities.* Stanford, CA: Stanford Business Books.

Fleischman, Howard L., Paul J. Hopstock, Marisa P. Pelczar, and Brooke E. Shelley. 2010. *Highlights From PISA 2009: Performance of U.S. 15-Year-Old Students in*

Reading, Mathematics, and Science Literacy in an International Context. Washington, DC: National Center for Education Statistics, Institute of Education Sciences, U.S. Department of Education. Accessed February 28, 2012. http://nces.ed.gov/pubs2011/2011004.pdf.

Goleman, Daniel. 2004. "What Makes a Leader?" *The Best of Harvard Business Review* (January): 1–11. Reprinted from 1998. Accessed February 28, 2012. http://bizedgegroup.com/Articles/040507%20What%20makes%20a%20Leader.pdf.

Goleman, Daniel, Richard E. Boyatzis, and Annie McKee. 2002. *Primal Leadership: Realizing the Power of Emotional Intelligence.* Boston, MA: Harvard Business Press.

Harris, Roma M. 1993. "Gender, Power, and the Dangerous Pursuit of Professionalism." *American Libraries* (October): 874.

Hearne, Betsy, and Christine Jenkins. 1999. "Sacred Texts: What Our Foremothers Left Us in the Way of Psalms, Proverbs, Precepts, and Practices." *Horn Book* 75(5): 536–58. (Hearne 536–47; Jenkins 547–58).

Hilbert, Martin. 2010. "The Manifold Definitions of the Digital Divide and Their Diverse Implications for Policy Responsibility." *38th Research Conference on Communication, Information, and Internet Policy. Telecommunications Policy Research Conference* (October). Accessed July 26, 2011. http://www.tprcweb.com/images/stories/2010%20papers/Hilbert%20manifold%20Digital%20Divide.pdf.

Jansen, Jim. 2010. "Use of the Internet in Higher-income Households." *Pew Internet and American Life Project* (November 24). Accessed July 26, 2011. http://pewinternet.org/reports/2010/better-off-households/overview.aspx.

Jenkins, Christine. 1996. "Women of the American Library Association, Youth Services and Professional Jurisdiction: Of Nightingales, Newberies, Realism, and Right Books, 1937–1945." *Library Trends* 44(4): 813–39.

Jenkins, Christine. 2000. "The History of Youth Services Librarianship: A Review of the Research Literature." *Libraries and Culture* 35(1): 103–39.

Leigh, Robert D. 1950. *The Public Library in the United States: The General Report of the Public Library Inquiry.* New York: Columbia University Press.

Litwin, Rory. 2009. "The Library Paraprofessional Movement and the Deprofessionalization of Librarianship." *Progressive Librarian* 33(Summer): 43–60.

Lowery, George. 2011 "Who Should Solve the Digital Divide?" PhysOrg.com (March 30). Accessed July 26, 2011. http://www.physorg.com/news/2011–03-digital.html.

Markoff, John. 2008. "The Passion of Steve Jobs." *New York Times,* January 15. Accessed July 18, 2011. http://bits.blogs.nytimes.com/2008/01/15/the-passion-of-steve-jobs/.

Nielsen, Jakob. 2006. "Digital Divide: The Three Stages." *Jakob Nielsen's Alertbox* (November 20). Accessed July 26, 2011. http://www.useit.com/alertbox/digital-divide.html.

Powell, Ronald R., Margaret T. Taylor, and David L. McMillen. 1984. "Childhood Socialization: Its Effect on Adult Library Use and Adult Reading." *Library Quarterly* 54(3): 245–64.

Preer, Jean. 2008. *Library Ethics.* Westport, CT: Libraries Unlimited.

Ranganathan, Shiyali Ramamrita. 1931. *The Five Laws of Library Science.* Madras: Madras Library Association.

Sayers, Frances Clarke. 1965. "The Belligerent Profession." In *Summoned by Books: Essays and Speeches by Frances Clarke Sayers,* ed. Frances Clarke Sayers and Marjeanne Jensen Blinn, 27–40. New York: Viking Press.

Smith, Aaron. 2010. "Home Broadband 2010." *Pew Internet and American Life Project* (August 11). Accessed July 26, 2011. http://www.pewinternet.org/reports/2010/home-broadband-2010.aspx.

Thomas, Sue, Chris Joseph, Jess Laccetti, Bruce Mason, Simon Mills, Simon Perril, and Kate Pullinger. 2007. "Transliteracy: Crossing Divides." *First Monday* 12(12).

Accessed July 26, 2011. http://www.uic.edu/htbin/cgiwrap/bin/ojs/index.php/fm/article/view/2060/1908.

UNICEF. 1990. *The Convention on the Rights of the Child.* Accessed July 22, 2011. http://www.unicef.org/crc/index_30160.html.

U.S. Census Bureau. 2011. "Section 24: Information and Communications." In *Statistical Abstract of the United States: 2011.* Accessed July 26, 2011. http://www.census.gov/prod/2011pubs/11statab/infocomm.pdf.

Vandergrift, Kay E. 1996. "Female Advocacy and Harmonious Voices: A History of Public Library Services and Publishing for Children in the United States." *Library Trends* 44(4): 683–718.

Walter, Virginia A. 2010. *Twenty-First Century Kids, Twenty-First Century Librarians.* Chicago: American Library Association.

West, Jerry. 2000. *America's Kindergarteners: Statistical Analysis Report.* With Kristin Denton and Elvira Germino-Hausken. Washington, DC: National Center for Education Statistics, U.S. Department of Education, Office of Educational Research and Improvement.

West, Jerry, Kristin Denton Flanagan, and Lizabeth M. Reaney. 2000. *The Kindergarten Year: Findings from the Early Childhood Longitudinal Study, Kindergarten Class of 1998–99.* Washington, DC: National Center for Education Statistics, U.S. Department of Education, Office of Educational Research and Improvement.

Young Adult Library Services Association. 2010. *YALSA's Competencies for Librarians Serving Youth: Young Adults Deserve the Best.* Chicago: American Library Association. Accessed July 26, 2011. http://www.ala.org/ala/mgrps/divs/yalsa/profdev/yadeservethebest_201.pdf.

4

WE BUILD COMMUNITIES THROUGH KNOWLEDGE: DEMONSTRATING THE VALUE OF THE PROFESSIONAL PUBLIC LIBRARIAN

Brenda Roberts
Bibliothèque d'Ottawa Public Library, Ontario

It's September. Thirty bright and eager six year olds have assembled in Sally Erskine's first-grade class. Ms. Erskine and her assistant proceed to hand out brightly colored netbooks to every student. Each one is slightly wider than a slim hard cover book and weighs about a pound. They're light and sturdy: coated with a washable rubber compound so they might even bounce if dropped. Each netbook has touchscreen technology and is fully loaded to run apps for eBooks, video, sound, and text processing. A wireless connection provides Internet access and social networking functionality while on school property. Each child is also provided with a thumb drive to store homework data.

During the course of the days and weeks that follow, Ms. Erskine's students will access a range of beautifully illustrated eBooks, developing their manual dexterity by "turning" the pages. When they succeed in tracing letters onto the screen to spell "CAT," a meow will be heard. When they do math or logic, Ms. Erskine will be able monitor their progress from her desk and step over when a little one-on one tutorial would be helpful. And so it will go, with increasing complexity—and in a range of colors because a different color netbook will be issued for each grade from 1 through 6—until the kids move into high school and receive netbooks that don't bounce. Here's the question: What are the odds that the kids in Sally Erskine's class will ever want to set foot in a bricks and mortar public library?

Don't answer the question as a librarian or branch manager, but instead, imagine yourself answering as the grownup iteration of one of Ms. Erskine's first graders. Now answer as a member of the tax-paying public. Now answer as a city politician looking for re-election in a cash-strapped economy.

Starting to feel a little uneasy?

I hope so, because that's the point of this chapter: the advent of eBooks underscores the necessity that librarians redefine and then strongly reassert our professional mission to the public. If public libraries are to retain their relevance, our mission must pivot on building communities through knowledge.[1] Professional librarianship is key to that goal and implies a pragmatic approach, one that combines mastery of information in all its forms with the hands-on commitment of a community organizer. As I will show, strong, successful public libraries and rigorous standards of professional librarianship go hand in hand.

PUBLIC LIBRARIANS AS CHANGE AGENTS

Everything in public libraries is in flux and always will be. Public librarians have no reliably firm foundation upon which to base librarianship. Instead, librarianship is practised within a shifting set of political, economic, and technological constraints and opportunities. In order to flourish, public libraries must therefore exemplify the values of adaptiveness, immediacy, and innovation. In order to thrive, public librarians must master the role of change agent. In order to practise the change agency that will keep public libraries a vital force for community building—and, not incidentally, to thereby retain reliable funding—libraries must embody a clear understanding that effective adaptation requires both top-down and bottom-up engagement. Specifically, librarians and branch managers must work together to resolve the top-down perspectives of municipal and administrative hierarchies with the bottom-up experiences of front-line staff and library users;[2] additionally, they must pull this off from a position marked by uncertainty, metaphorically building and maintaining a bridge from the middle of the river.

Fortunately, there's a methodological tool for that. It's called *pragmatism*.

PROFESSIONAL LIBRARIANSHIP AND PRAGMATISM

Pragmatism is a natural fit for public librarianship because it offers a coherent, common-sense approach to the infinite variety of decisions we are required to make.[3] Pragmatism advises us to replace actions based on absolute rules or abstractions with decisions based on outcomes we have evidence to believe will be workable in real life. Whether it's the truth of an idea or the validity of a policy, success is entirely defined by practical outcomes. For a pragmatist, the test is always: did it work; did it get the job done? Actions, in other words, will always speak louder than words.

In her 2008 paper "Rediscovering the Taproot," Patricia Shields makes a number of points about pragmatism and public policy that are directly applicable to public librarianship. She notes, for example, that "the goal is not to find eternal principles but rather to use an ongoing experimental process to develop plans for action that are evaluated in light of practical consequences" (Shields 2008, 206). We can see the application to public libraries when Shields goes on to say that the process of inquiry "usually contains an inherently social component—knowledge that is gained through inquiry is a social product of communities engaged in dialogue about common problems" (Shields 2008, 206). Shields then describes how classical pragmatism can be used to re-situate public policy. The four elements of pragmatism Shields uses—practicality, pluralism, participation, and process—may also be used to guide the practice of public librarianship.

Practicality: Truth Is What Works

A key tenet of pragmatism is the view that truth is not based on universal absolutes but emerges when thought and plans are joined to action. Applied to a practical problem, the test for the *truth* of a policy is therefore found in its outcomes. Put perhaps a little too simply, policymaking must be supported by experience.

How is this criterion to be applied to the work of public librarians? Let's take a hypothetical example of the decision-making process that informs the purchase of a new integrated library system (ILS) in a public library. The usual process involves managers of various departments consulting with each other and with their peers in other library systems, as well as with ILS vendors and local / municipal stakeholders who provide feedback related to the existing IT infrastructure. From a pragmatic perspective, however, a crucial part of the process is missing, one that can only result in a flawed outcome. None of the decision makers will actually use the prospective ILS on the front lines on a daily basis. This internal disconnect between the design of the ILS and its specific, on-the-ground application can result in costly decisions on many levels.

A pragmatic approach, on the other hand, would supplement existing decision-making inputs with a pilot project that provides actual end users with the opportunity to put the system through its paces in context over time. This approach has at least two immediate benefits. First, it would allow professional librarians to facilitate staff involvement in the decision-making process. Secondly, it would provide tangible evidence that could be used to leverage the library's bargaining position with the vendor. It should be noted that if the ILS vendor cannot provide an appropriate interface for testing by end users then, by definition, their product would not be considered for purchase.[4]

Pluralism: Strength in Diversity

One aspect of the "what works" criterion of truth is openness to a variety of problem-solving options from a variety of stakeholders. This fits nicely with the fact that pluralism and diversity have long been defining features of public librarianship. The wide range of disciplines that feed into public libraries through graduate schools of library studies is itself a robust resource and suggests a culture of librarianship that rejects perfectionism and celebrates diversity. Pluralism provides just the right preparation for navigating the increasingly diverse socioeconomic currents of the 21st century. An open attitude then makes the best use of a wide range of viewpoints, based as it is on the understanding that there is no single road to truth.

Let's apply these aspects of pragmatism to the challenge of eBooks. Much has been made of the fact that the increasing prevalence of eBooks will have dire impacts on the long-term viability of public libraries.[5] Rather than circling the wagons, however, pragmatic professional librarians see an opportunity for growth and community-building with the change this new format presents. These librarians will respond first by acting on the knowledge that different voices need to be heard and incorporated into the decision-making process. They would adopt a methodology that does not prejudge but rather listens with an open mind, synthesizes the most practicable lessons from each view, and then tests the outcomes with library users and staff.

Robert Darnton illustrates one possible outcome of this approach when he posits the development of a national digital library. As Darnton says in a recent *New York Review of Books* article, "Google demonstrated the possibility of transforming the intellectual riches of our libraries . . . into an electronic database that could be tapped by anyone, anywhere, at any time. Why not adapt its formula for success to the public good—a digital library composed of virtually all the books in our greatest research libraries, available free of charge to the entire citizenry, in fact, to everyone in the world?" (Darnton 2010). If Google's expertise contributes to the mission of building communities through knowledge, then pragmatic librarians will explore that option with an open-minded investigation. This aspect of pragmatism, in which assumptions and potential biases are continually reviewed and challenged, ensures that public libraries make the best use of constant change.

Participation: Building Collaborative Cultures Inside and Outside the Library

Participation is essential to the professional practice of librarians, both in their roles as internal bridges to frontline staff and as external liaisons with the public. In a broader context, librarians extend the collaborative role of the public library to the entire community. Shields cites a 2006 *Public Administration Review* issue devoted to collaboration and defines it as the "process of facilitating and operating in multi-organizational arrangements to solve problems . . . collaboration means to co-labour, to co-operate to achieve common goals working across boundaries in multi-sector relationships" (Shields 2008, 7). This definition is consistent with pragmatism's emphasis on communities of inquiry, even as it is inconsistent with top-down bureaucracies and operational silos. In a pragmatic model of public librarianship, collaboration supersedes the hierarchal corporate model. Mutual respect within the profession means that librarians who have chosen management roles would become allied with nonmanagement professional librarians. Hierarchies would give way to a collegial professional culture in which everyone shares the common mission of community building through knowledge. This model of collaboration is the best way to ensure a free-flow of innovative, creative solutions to the challenges we face.

Process: Action Supported by Evidence

Participation implies multiple points of view but need not result in cacophony. Rather, the pragmatic emphasis on process brings order to a diversity of views and interests and suggests that public libraries should become more like knowledge labs for the public good and less like bookstores, which simply give customers what they want. This point deserves some elaboration.

Pragmatism advances the notion that the most useful method to approach a problem is the process of inquiry. Internally, pragmatism would allow public libraries to function as communities of inquiry, with the understanding that the most robust growth is found in a risk-tolerant work environment. When librarians are focused on process rather than policy, they are not paralysed by fear of unintended consequences but are free to optimize opportunities.

Externally, pragmatism means that libraries facilitate public access to a wide variety of experts in the interests of furthering the public good. The content and mechanisms of inquiry are fluid, including everything from programs and databases to wikis, blogs, and workshops. The common element is that the conversation remains creative, flexible, and positive. In cases where solutions conflict, arguments for all views can be evaluated based on whether the outcomes contribute to stronger communities.

A PRAGMATIST CASE IN POINT

The pragmatic approach defined by practicality, participation, pluralism, and the process of inquiry provides an explicit framework for the practice of public librarianship. I speak from experience because this past year, while fostering one project, my library also successfully—albeit incidentally—piloted an experiment in pragmatic methodology.

Here's what happened.

As every librarian knows, a huge amount of the materials budget is tied up in electronic databases. At the same time, database use is chronically decreasing. A few years ago, an attempt was made to increase database use by creating a stewardship committee. The committee comprised about a dozen librarians from across the system. Each librarian was tasked with the role of go-to person for one subject area. In keeping with the traditional corporate committee model, an effort was made to engage librarians from all demographics and therefore included librarians from urban, suburban, and rural branches; librarians from various centralized services, including collection development, reference, and virtual library services; and librarians from three distinct pay grades and hierarchal ranks. With the first meeting, the committee fragmented into various interest groups. In a development repeated daily in public institutions across North America, internal political considerations undermined the best of intentions.

This outcome, however, was transformed into an opportunity when a senior manager informed librarians that Ontario's Ministry of Culture was calling for research proposals. Drawing on support from my manager and the City Librarian, I applied for funding with the objective of designing and testing a marketing protocol for electronic databases. This response reflects the adaptive element of pragmatism, while the project's research methodology illustrates the four aspects of pragmatism described previously.

First, the unworkable assumption in which a big problem is assumed to necessitate a big solution was rejected in favour of a more practical approach in which the multiplicity of subject databases was scaled back to focus on one database, with the criterion that it be a database that corresponds to the needs of the most rapidly growing segments of the community. Second, the corporate committee model was replaced by the software development approach in which a small group (in this case, three people) was charged with designing and implementing the protocol. This effectively reversed the work flow: a protocol (as hypothesis) was generated from inside the ranks, and management resources were called upon to help facilitate the research on an as-needed basis. Third, the project built a one-to-one communication approach with both to the project's internal clients (staff) and external clients (library patrons) into delivery of the project.

Finally, the study applied an experimental process in which all resources were dedicated to testing the value of the marketing protocol. Our goal was to use our funding to throw every conceivable resource at the problem of electronic database usage and then observe the results as objectively as possible. If the protocol moved usage upwards, it could then be adapted to other databases and used to increase usage in other subject areas. If the protocol failed to significantly increase usage, then a different set of adaptations would be generated. The goal of the project was to generate a product—the marketing protocol—and to do so in a distinctly pragmatic way. It was understood that failure was an option, in the sense that the "failure" of the project to increase usage (measured statistically) would be as instructive as its success.

The project is now complete and serves as a workable model of what Shields calls, "open-minded listening, talking, and sharing in a larger context of inquiry" (Shields 2008, 213). The protocol increased usage and will serve as a template for other databases going forward. The value of one-on-one engagement with the public and front-line staff was also clearly shown, underscoring the fact that merely providing access to databases that cost tens of thousands of dollars is not enough. Instructing staff and library members how to use a tool that could help to build better lives—in other words, building communities through knowledge—was the key to earning dividends on our database investment. Finally, underlying issues about statistical methodologies and fees also emerged in the process. Our recommendations addressed these issues as well, with the aim of strengthening the library's negotiating position with database vendors.

The project illustrates how a pragmatic approach best serves a wide range of public library interests. Not incidentally, standards of professional objectivity are a core element of the process. Let me expand on that.

In "Public Administration as Pragmatic, Democratic, and Objective," David Hildebrand points out that the pragmatist conception of democracy comprises two complementary parts. The first element is the communal basis, constituted by guidelines, laws, and policies. The second is the knowledge base defined by the collaborative process of inquiry in which a culture identifies, prioritizes, and resolves problems (Hildebrand 2008, 223). Communities form the substrate of life in a democracy. They, in turn, are nourished by their knowledge base. To develop this idea further, let's look more closely at the terms *community* and *knowledge* within the pragmatic approach.

Knowledge—defined by Hildebrand as "inquiry"—is the process communities use to solve problems and improve conditions. Inquiry assumes a *social* character when we appreciate that most major problems engage *groups* and not just individuals (Hildebrand 2008, 224). It is important to stress that the social dimension of inquiry is dynamic: outcomes are always provisional and require ongoing testing by experience.

It should be evident that these complementary aspects of democracy overlap with the public library's mission of building communities through knowledge. By extension, the ability to articulate and sustain professional objectivity becomes a core value of public librarianship. Therefore, as practitioners, librarians require a set of attributes that will facilitate objective judgement. Sceptical intelligence and autonomy, as opposed to reliance on external authority and policy, are two characteristics that come immediately to mind. In the public library, these attributes will mark the distinction between professional and nonprofessional tasks and responsibilities. In the pragmatic model of librarianship, objectivity informs professional practise, defined by Hildebrand as adherence to those habits that make inquiry an effective process (Hildebrand 2008, 225). Specifically, professional objectivity provides the assurance that library policies have been generated in a way that allows open verifiability of the process (Hildebrand 2008, 226). Professional practice sets the tone for both the internal dynamics of the library and external connections with the community, creating a sturdy basis for trust between all parties going forward.

THE NECESSITY OF *PROFESSIONAL* PUBLIC LIBRARIANSHIP

As we have seen, the building of strong communities through knowledge is well served by professional librarians working within a pragmatic approach. The values that define this professional standard are the keys to building trust and ensuring the continued growth of both librarianship and public libraries. Let's continue to develop this.

We can begin by applying our objectivity to the recognition that the public requirements of librarianship have changed drastically in the past two decades. It was once true that most questions asked of reference desk staff demanded the broad knowledge base of an undergraduate education supplemented by the specialized knowledge of reference tools and research methods gained with the MLS. However, with the advent of the Internet, user-friendly search engines such as Google, and reliable sources for subject overviews such as Wikipedia, all freely available online 24 hours a day, the number of queries requiring a master's degree has dropped precipitously. But this does not imply that the expertise is no longer required. Quite the opposite. It means that the expertise must be thoughtfully and effectively re-deployed. We all read *Library Journal,* so the claim that many public library administrators in North America have simply taken a bottom line, short-term approach and replaced highly trained professionals with paraprofessionals will come as no surprise. This strategy has come at a high cost to librarians and the communities we serve. The tacit implication that the two roles of professional librarian and paraprofessional are equivalent undermines librarianship even as it undercuts the perceived value of public libraries within the community.

In a recent paper on the deprofessionalization of librarianship, Rory Litwin (2009) draws on the work of sociologists Keith Roberts and Karen Donahue (2000) to articulate six defining factors of professionalism:

1. Mastery of specialized theory;
2. Autonomy and control of one's work and how that work is performed;
3. Motivation focusing on intrinsic rewards and on the interests of clients— which take precedence over professional's self-interests;
4. Commitment to the profession as a career and to the service objectives of the organization for which one works;
5. Sense of community and feelings of collegiality with others in the profession, and accountability to those colleagues; and
6. Self-monitoring and regulation by the profession of ethical and professional standards in keeping with a detailed code of ethics. (Litwin 2009, 6)

Let's be clear. These factors are rarely, if ever, either stipulated or implied in the tasks and responsibilities associated with library staff who do not hold an MLS; yet, as was discussed previously, these professional attributes are critical if we are to maintain the relevance and vigour of public libraries. At the risk of generalization, it should also be noted that because public librarians tend to be democratic and pluralistic by temperament, they find themselves vulnerable to the charge that by asserting their professionalism, they implicitly denigrate the valuable work of paraprofessionals. This unfounded assertion is often and all too easily used to short-circuit objections to creeping deprofessionalization. The hard fact is that librarians must be mindful of the threat posed by what Litwin refers to as the "paraprofessional movement." As a professional body, public librarians must have the courage to challenge the use (and misuse) of paraprofessionals in the public library, even as we redefine and assert our professional roles.

In a pragmatic model of public librarianship as I have described it, professional values are actively promoted. Why? The answer is simply because these professional attributes provide the most robust platform for building communities through knowledge. Quantitative research undertaken by the Online Computer Library Center (OCLC) backs this up with survey results that highlight the importance of professionalism in maintaining public support and funding for public libraries. Their 2008 report, *From Awareness to Funding: A Study of Library Support in America*, distilled eight key ingredients that drive public attitudes toward libraries. Patterns that emerge from the report connect professionalism and community building as essential components of reliable funding. Specifically, the public's perceptions of librarians in conjunction with their belief that the library is a transformative force in people's lives is directly related to the level of funding citizens are willing to support (De Rosa and Johnson 2008, 4–1).

Survey respondents also listed five attributes to describe the "passionate librarians" who inspire the most robust levels of community support. These librarians are

- True advocates for life-long learning;
- Passionate about making the library relevant;
- Knowledgeable about every aspect of the library;
- Well-educated; and
- Knowledgeable about the community. (De Rosa and Johnson 2008, 4–8)

A pattern is clearly evident here: these five attributes and the six attributes of professionalism show a remarkable degree of overlap. Taken together, this set of attributes may be taken as a recipe for the long-term viability of public libraries: "Voters who rate the librarian highly on the traits that comprise the 'passionate librarian' are more likely to say they would *definitely* vote yes for a library referendum, ballot initiative, or bond measure" (De Rosa and Johnson 2008, 4–9). Furthermore, when belief that the library is a transformational force in the community was positively correlated with funding support, the library was seen as a service that provides the emotional and intellectual rewards of *purposeful information*: "*The most likely library funding supporters do not view the library as a source of information, but rather as a source for transformation*" (De Rosa and Johnson 2008, 4–12/13, emphasis added). Clearly, the public understands that the best way for its local library to build community is not by merely providing *information* but by providing the means by which information is transformed into practical *knowledge*.

Perhaps now it may be frankly acknowledged why the information-centric model of the past six decades has not only failed to reinvigorate public libraries but may well have impeded our progress (Crowley 2005, 46). While both information and retail models have their uses, following those trends with nary a touch of sceptical pragmatism has often served to dilute professional standards even as it continues to divide the profession. As librarians, we need to remind ourselves that public libraries add value to information in hundreds of ways. It is libraries that provide the public space and resources necessary to help each and every citizen participate fully in the political, social, and cultural life of the community. It is librarians who not only ensure that citizens have equitable access to information but who also leverage taxpayer investment by providing the tools required to evaluate and use that knowledge to improve lives. My point here is that the value of public libraries has always been more a matter of advocacy than of information. Put simply, public libraries are a vital contributing factor to the growth of strong, healthy communities.

Come with me now for a glimpse of what a hypothetical public library driven by pragmatic principles would look like.

Our first impression of the library is the welcome desk. Distinct from both circulation and reference service points, it is staffed by library paraprofessionals as well as settlement workers and second year MLS/MLIS students. To provide an additional avenue for community engagement, the library makes good use of volunteers, including immigrants, retired citizens, and high school students fulfilling their community service requirements. Their roles range from running the second-hand bookstore to providing tutoring and guided tours.

Architecturally, the library is designed to reflect its function as a community knowledge resource and provides easy access to content in every format as well as venues for instruction. The lifecycle librarianship approach outlined by Bill Crowley (Crowley 2008a, 2008b) is evident throughout, with professional librarians designing and supervising a range of programs that provide cradle-to-grave resources for learning. Specialization is valued and provides continual professional development opportunities, thereby ensuring long and varied tenures for librarians. To imagine just one scenario, a librarian can start as a Teen/Young Adult specialist and then move to media and games. In-house training in project management would allow the librarian to develop management experience and may lead to promotion to collection management, where contract evaluation and negotiation skills could be honed. It should be noted that the opportunity to develop specializations and project management skills has an additional bonus for the library and the taxpayer in that it reduces the need for expensive external consulting. In this scenario, promotion to management remains a route to expanded responsibilities and professional challenge but is by no means the only path. This flexibility makes the public library an exciting place to work and attracts a rich pool of applicants.

The professional tone of the public library is ingrained, with job postings for librarians that require a combination of creative problem-solving aptitude along with rigorous academic achievement. The MLS from an ALA-accredited institution is non-negotiable and is not replaceable by a combination of work experience and other degrees or technical diplomas.

The pragmatic values of practicality, pluralism, participation, and process are woven into the culture of librarianship in this public library. Newly hired librarians are usually designated as L1 and normally focus on public service for their first three years of practice. As soon as they are hired, they become members of a New Librarians Forum[6] that meets quarterly and provides immediate professional networking opportunities and support. The core value of public service is underscored when the new librarian sees that every other librarian in the system, including IT, cataloguing, and collection development librarians, as well as branch managers, serves at least six hours per month on a public service desk. One of the few non-negotiable policies in the pragmatic public library, this ensures a commitment to service excellence based on consistent, direct contact with both the internal community of staff and colleagues and the external community the library serves.

After three years, librarians may apply for jobs at the senior (L2) level. L2 job descriptions include a range of specialized and centralized positions and are distinguished from L1 by the degree to which standards of professional practise are focused on community building. The best way to understand the distinction between L1 and L2 is to think of L2s as project management librarians. For example, each L2 is required to generate and manage at least one project per year and/or to publish or present to the profession at least once in every two-year period. L2 librarians are also expected to actively mentor new librarians as well as any paraprofessional who is interested in pursuing a career in librarianship. Unions play an important lobbying function in tandem with professional associations, so L2 librarians are expected to either participate as union members/shop stewards or to serve on professional association committees.

Every two years, all librarians are invited to submit proposals for funding pilot projects[7] that support the mission of building communities through knowledge. A panel that includes professional peers, a library board member, a community representative, and faculty from a graduate school of library science selects the best project. The winner is provided with sufficient financial resources and time over the course of a year to bring the idea to fruition. In return, he or she is required to publish or present the results to the profession and the community. Projects could include

- Outreach to adult high schools and vocational colleges to build literacy;
- Creation of a dedicated service point where library members can bring their devices, including video cameras, iPads, and PDAs, to receive one-on-one help[8];
- A pilot project in which Master of Social Work students work with librarians to build referral networks for the homeless and at-risk teens and to train staff on these issues; and
- Ongoing alliances with the municipal Public Health department to provide consumer health information to the public.

This internal competition for best projects ensures that every librarian is actively engaged in demonstrating the value of professional librarianship to the community on an on-going basis.

In 2005 Bill Crowley asked *Library Journal* readers what public libraries and public librarians can do to meet critical public needs and thereby safeguard their future (Crowley 2005, 46). I began this chapter by showing that the advent of eBooks in 2010 raised the stakes exponentially. But this challenge also presents public libraries with a golden opportunity to rededicate themselves to the mission of building communities through knowledge. The timing could not be better. OCLC's fifth report, *Perceptions of Libraries, 2010: Context and Community*, surveys the attitudes and habits of the emerging online information consumer and reports the widely held belief that our patrons see the library as an increasingly important community asset (De Rosa et al. 2011, 44). This, in my view, is a hopeful sign that individuals may be recognizing that community cohesiveness is connected to individual well-being. It bodes well for public libraries.

Ensuring a combination of common-sense pragmatism and the highest calibre of professionalism will allow us to pursue the mission of building communities through knowledge with boldness and vigour. As Harvard's Robert Darnton says,

"We have now reached a period of fluidity, uncertainty, and opportunity. Things have come undone and they can be put together in new ways, subordinating private profit to the public good and providing everyone with access to a commonwealth of culture" (Darnton 2010).

Professional librarians who have the courage and commitment to act as change agents are more crucial than ever to the success of public libraries. If we renew the culture of professional librarianship, graduating MLS students across North America will compete for positions in our public libraries, effectively reversing the prevailing view that public libraries are the option of last resort for a satisfying professional life. If we infuse professional librarianship with pragmatism, public librarians will become, to use James LaRue's metaphor, *visible leaders* who "link a bustling central hub to the community. They are readily available and highly expert . . . the visible librarian has a seat at the community decision-making table, actively clarifies choices, provides reputable and relevant information, and through every action, trumpets the unique contributions of the profession" (LaRue 2010).

Best of all, Sally Erskine's first graders will never run short of reasons to love (and support) the public library throughout their lives.

NOTES

1. This organizing principle of public librarianship is a pared down version of David Lankes' mission statement: "the mission of librarians is to improve society through facilitating knowledge creation in their communities" (Lankes 2011). The straightforward assertion that *public librarians build communities through knowledge* is meant to evoke the no-frills clarity of purpose and method that is a pragmatist trademark.

2. Aspects of change agency were developed by Carleton University's Professor Linda Duxbury in her "Change 101," an unpublished presentation to Ottawa Public Library (OPL) librarians, sponsored by OPL's Joint Professional Development Committee (October 1, 2010).

3. Readers who wish an overview of pragmatism that is both accessible and substantive should consult Christopher Hookway's description on the *Stanford Encyclopedia of Philosophy* website (http://palto.stanford.edu/).

4. Beta products, by the way, do not count.

5. See for example, the Chief Officers of State Library Agencies (COSLA) report (2010).

6. I owe this idea to one put into practice at the suggestion of the Ottawa Public Library's City Librarian, Barbara Clubb.

7. As far as I know, this idea, in its incarnation as the "Big Ideas Project," was first implemented at the Pickering Public Library in Ontario.

8. An example of the kind of innovation that can come from this approach may be found in the winner of the first Big Ideas Project. See Boncoglu (2010).

REFERENCES

Boncoglu, Kayhan. 2010. "Yes We Can: Tech Support as the Evolution of Reference." *OLA Magazine* 16(3): 20–21.

Chief Officers of State Library Agencies (COSLA). 2010. *COSLA: eBook Feasibility Study for Public Libraries.* Accessed December 15, 2010. http://www.cosla.org/documents/ COSLA2270_Report_Final1.pdf.

Crowley, Bill. 2005. "Save Professionalism." *Library Journal* 130(4): 46.

Crowley, Bill. 2008a. "Lifecycle Librarianship." *Library Journal* (April 1): 46–48.

Crowley, Bill. 2008b. *Renewing Professional Librarianship: A Fundamental Rethinking.* Westport CT: Libraries Unlimited.

Darnton, Robert. 2010. "The Library: Three Jeremiads." *New York Review of Books* (December 23). http://www.nybooks.com/articles/archives/2010/dec/23/library-three-jeremiads/.

De Rosa, Cathy, and Jenny Johnson. 2008. *From Awareness to Funding : A Study of Library Support in America: A Report to the OCLC Membership.* Dublin, OH: OCLC.

De Rosa, Cathy, Joanne Cantrell, Matthew Carlson, Margaret Gallagher, and Janet Hawk. 2011. *Perceptions of Libraries, 2010: Context and Community: A Report to the OCLC Membership.* Dublin, OH: OCLC.

Hildebrand, David. 2008. "Public Administration as Pragmatic, Democratic, and Objective." *Public Administration Review* 68(2): 222–29.

Lankes, R. David. 2011. *Atlas of New Librarianship.* Cambridge MA: MIT Press.

LaRue, James. 2010. "The Visibility and Invisibility of Librarians." *Library Journal* 135(19): 10. Accessed February 29, 2012. http://www.libraryjournal.com/lj/reviewsreference/887361-283/the_visibility_and_invisibility_of.html.csp.

Litwin, Rory. 2009. "The Library Paraprofessional Movement and the Deprofessionalization of Librarianship." *Progressive Librarian* 33(Summer/Fall): 43–60.

Roberts, Keith A., and Karen A. Donahue. 2000. "Professionalism: Bureaucratization and Deprofessionalization in the Academy." *Sociological Focus* 33(4): 365–83.

Shields, Patricia M. 2008. "Rediscovering the Taproot: Is Classical Pragmatism the Route to Renew Public Administration?" *Public Administration Review* (March/April): 205–21.

Stanford Encyclopedia of Philosophy. 2010. Accessed December 15. http://palto.stanford.edu/.

5

STRATEGIES AND ASPIRATIONS FOR DEFENDING SCHOOL LIBRARY PROFESSIONALISM

Don Hamerly
Dominican University

It's a mild January 2011 in Austin, Texas, and school librarians are three weeks into the spring semester, busily assisting teachers with upcoming research projects and planning for the dizzying pace of processing, programming, and instruction that the second half of any school year brings, when they receive two pieces of devastating news. First, the state legislature has proposed a budget that will gut library services statewide. Legislators stipulate a 99 percent reduction in spending on libraries and library services (Kelley 2011). Next, the local media reveal on Friday that the Austin Independent School District's board of trustees will meet the following Monday to consider letting go 537 employees, including 74 school librarians. A drop-everything e-mail campaign and a large turnout of supporters at the board meeting result in a bittersweet victory. The board decides to salvage 52 elementary school librarians but cuts 22 positions in the secondary schools (Heinauer 2011). Reactions to the cuts coalesce into a continuing advocacy effort to salvage the targeted positions.

WHAT'S NOT SHOCKING ABOUT THE NEWS?

More alarming than the news in Austin is just how un-news-like it really is. Nationwide, school librarians and school library programs are facing systematic reductions and deprofessionalizations. These drastic rollbacks continue despite 23 state studies conducted over 18 years that consistently demonstrate the positive correlation between quality school library programs with qualified school librarians and higher student achievement. In "The State of America's Libraries" (2011), the American Library Association (ALA) reports increases in library use and weekly workloads for school librarians from 2009 to 2010 in spite of decreases in funding in the majority of schools and no increases in the number of qualified school librarians. As the recession's impact on revenues continues to wreak havoc on state budgets, reports of deep cuts in education and of the dismantling of school libraries become common. They illustrate the range of effects that the cuts have on library programs, from reductions in library resources and services to the elimination of libraries altogether:

- In Boise, Idaho, library funding is "chopped," leaving school libraries with "a budget of zero" and no funding for new books or the renewal of subscriptions for magazines, newspapers, and online databases. Librarians worry that students may lose the fundamentals of reading ("No New Library Books" 2010).

- Reduced state funding for Pennsylvania libraries results in the loss of EBSCO online and prompts school librarians to wonder how they will fill the resulting gap in access to critical publications and journals (Moran 2010).

- Nearly half the 186 school librarians in Maryland's Prince George's district face elimination when school superintendent William Hite presents his 2012 budget, revised to close an $85.7 million shortfall (Staino 2011).

- New Jersey school librarian April Bunn laments "nightmare" state budget cuts, resulting in the elimination of all school librarians (including her) in some districts. In addition to the loss of services for students is the loss of quality school library programs where library school students can complete their practica (Bunn 2010).

- Marilyn Kulkurni, president of the Delaware School Library Media Association, checks off another two dozen librarians that districts have cut and replaced with teachers' aides (Kenney 2010).

- In spite of Oregon Quality Education Commission guidelines that specify library expenditures and the need for a certified school librarian on every campus, only 10 of 1,124 schools meet minimum commission requirements (Clark 2011).

- School library advocates in Utah worry that because most schools no longer have certified school librarians, many students will not be reading at grade level by the end of third grade (Park 2011).

- In Massachusetts the Bridgewater Raynham Educators Association, the local teachers union, files suit against district principals for replacing professional librarians with "proctors" and volunteers (Weinstein 2010).

- Nearly one-third of secondary schools in New York City have no school librarians, even though the State of New York requires that they do. One New York State Education Department insider remarks that the city's board of education ignores the law and does not buy into the need for a school library and librarian on every campus (Alper 2010).

- In Chicago 164 of the 600 schools in the city have no library. In Illinois significant cuts in education funding have resulted in a nearly 11 percent decrease in the number of school librarians since 2004 (Ahmed-Ullah 2010).

IS THERE ANY GOOD NEWS?

Covering program cuts and layoffs gets the attention that the media want from their consumers, more so than reporting on districts that value and support their employees, or on districts that heed advocacy efforts and keep programs and people in place. The public does occasionally read or hear a feature story on something positive happening in libraries, but the public's perception of libraries, and too often the perception that decision makers have about libraries, is subject to stories of anomalous occurrences in libraries. Will readers of the *Wall Street Journal* demand automated alternatives to school librarians after reading about the "robo-libraries" that have replaced public librarians in Hugo, Minnesota (Dougherty 2010)? How did *Houston Press* readers perceive school libraries after reading about a local principal who discarded nearly all the books in his high school library to make room for a coffee shop, ostensibly to impress the superintendent with a forward-thinking renovation (Downing 2010)?

Many school administrators *do* understand the value of school libraries, but their stories rarely make the popular press. The 2009 Idaho study, "How Idaho Librarians, Teachers, and Administrators Collaborate for Student Success," reveals the high value that school administrators place on library-related practices like flexible scheduling and librarians' involvement on school committees and in providing professional development. The Idaho study also includes comments from administrators, who describe their librarians as inspiring, as great assets, and as change agents for students (Idaho Commission for Libraries 2010; Lance, Rodney, and Schwarz 2010). Again, though, the state studies have had little influence on funding. Chris Lehmann (2007), principal of one of the top public high schools in the nation, the Science Leadership Academy in Philadelphia, wrote a supportive column for *School Library Journal* about the relevance of his librarian colleagues to learning in the 21st century. While the readers of *School Library Journal* surely appreciated the support, Lehmann was sermonizing the saved. Lehmann's frequent interviews in the Philadelphia press and his TEDxNYED talk did not feature his library, although his promotion of inquiry-based learning in a highly collaborative environment certainly implies a resource-rich library environment. School libraries did make the news in Philadelphia (Tales 2010) when the local teachers' union president called for mandated school libraries with adequate funding in every school, a refrain that the union had repeated "half a dozen times" to no effective action.

In response to the union president's call for school library reform in Philadelphia, the local "home and school association" president said that parents could bring awareness to the issue and spark change, but successful parental activism comes at a cost. The success of the "Spokane Moms" drew the greatest media attention to the plight of school libraries, but their success at securing funding for school libraries in Washington came at great sacrifice to the parents personally (Whelan 2008). In "The School Library Is the Link to Connecting with Parents," Michelle McGarry writes of her transformation from a parent who did not know what her children were missing without a qualified school librarian to a library school student and advocate for school libraries. She recalls a conversation with a friend, also a mother, about school librarian layoffs in Massachusetts. Her friend thought that if layoffs were inevitable, it was better to cut a librarian than a "real teacher" (McGarry 2009, 46). For McGarry her friend's reaction was evidence that school librarians need to change their image with parents. The limited success of advocacy efforts, often undertaken at great personal cost, indicates that the image of school librarians needs changing generally. In California, where years of budget crises have left fewer than 23 percent of schools with a librarian, hundreds more face dismissal in 2011. More of the state's districts will be left with no librarians at all, increasing the state's already dismal librarian-to-student ratio (Whelan 2011). In an effort to help preserve what remains of libraries in the state's schools, professional illustrators donated original art for use in a "Save California School Libraries" campaign

(Staino 2010). Illustrators have a stake in the campaign. Without qualified school librarians to vet and purchase their works, they face a diminished market.

WHAT IS NEEDED?

That school librarians and school library advocates have broadly and repeatedly brought the evidence borne out by the state studies to the attention of school administrators, boards of trustees, and legislators to little practical effect begs that school librarians reconsider advocacy efforts and retool strategies for better results. The good news is that school librarians may regain or secure their presence and professional status in schools if they adopt five strategies:

1. Reflect what decision makers value.
2. Support the capacity of school administrators to engage with evidence.
3. Increase their visibility as leaders and problem solvers.
4. Adopt an aspirational approach to professionalism.
5. Advocate for a qualified school librarian on every campus.

WHAT DO DECISION MAKERS VALUE?

Gary Walker reminds us that "the political culture is not an idea culture; it is a problem-solving culture" (Chapin Hall Center for Children at the University of Chicago 2005, 18). The quotation is from Walker's contributions to a 2004 conference to discuss how well social institutions serve young people as they make their way from adolescence to adulthood. Walker, who was then the president of Public/Private Ventures, a nonprofit organization that develops and evaluates programs that help improve lives in low-income communities, spoke about a "new phase" in social policy, a change from 40 years of morally inspired policymaking to utility-inspired policymaking. Policymakers place value on solving problems rather than merely describing them. They are pragmatists. The best advice for advocates and researchers is to tie concrete solutions for problems to issues that the public feels some responsibility to address, such as education. School library advocacy efforts have, for the past 15 years, been utility focused, offering abundant evidence to demonstrate that well-appointed and well-staffed school libraries help students read better and achieve at higher levels. As a result, libraries reduce the risk that students will drop out of school and contribute to "public problems" like unemployment and crime. At the time of this writing, however, policymakers seem to see more utility in doing away with school libraries than in supporting them. What must school librarians do to help decision makers see them as addressing problems rather than as problems to be addressed?

In *Renewing Professional Librarianship* Bill Crowley (2008b) ties the future of the library profession to its "capacity to demonstrate . . . responsiveness to the needs of its service communities [and] to identify and build upon the reasons why people, including community leaders and politicians, value their libraries and their librarians" (118). School library advocates have demonstrated how school libraries and school librarians respond to the needs of their learning communities by contributing to greater literacy and the social rewards that accompany it. School libraries also contribute to higher standardized test scores, the measures by which schools, and consequently school administrators and trustees, achieve status under state and federal education policy. Higher student test scores contribute to administrator job security. One would see improved literacy and increased test scores as valuable to school policymakers, as reasons to value school libraries, but somehow school library advocacy efforts have not achieved the outcomes desired. How can that be? As early as 1920 John Dewey warned about the difficulty faced when researchers presenting even the most rigorous scientific studies fail to appreciate fully the role of deeply held values (Dewey 1957, xxvi), such as the value principals and superintendents place on the services of the professional school librarian. Have advocates not successfully identified the reasons why, or even if, school policymakers value their school libraries and school librarians?

Ken Haycock (2011), in his Dominican University Graduate School of Library and Information Science 2011 Follett Lecture "Advocacy Revisited: New Insights Based on Research and Evidence," shared recent efforts to shift the focus of research from the effectiveness of advocacy efforts and groups to the decision makers that such efforts and groups target, to why and how decision makers make the choices they do. The public often sees advocacy efforts target decision makers in public, as in demonstrations at a state house, commentary from constituency groups at a city council meeting, or presentations at a school board meeting. Yet decision makers often do their work "in back rooms," away from public eyes and ears. Research suggests that public demands, entreaties, and messaging from stakeholders do not work unless decision makers already value the groups making them. So, what do decision makers respond to? What do they value?

Influence researcher Robert Cialdini uses the term *social validation* (or social proof) to describe the tendency decision makers (and people in general) have to value what others like them are doing (Haycock 2011). For school librarians, this makes benchmarking a valuable tactic in advocating for positions and programs. School library advocates may hold more sway with school administrators if they arm themselves with data on what neighboring and comparable districts and schools are doing. A thread on ISLMANET, the Illinois School Library Media Association's electronic discussion list, started when a school librarian in a prominent Illinois school district posted an email that asked to hear from neighboring school districts that had added librarian positions in the last three years. Her district was considering cuts, and she was looking for evidence to persuade her school board not to cut positions. Responses to the post indicated that four area districts had either maintained positions when librarians retired or had added positions. As of this writing, no librarians had been cut.

Decision makers also value agendas that support or connect with their own agendas (Haycock 2011). When decision makers recognize the legitimacy of an advocacy effort because it supports their own efforts and shares their values, the advocacy effort stands a chance of achieving its desired outcome. School library advocates can lose their focus on student achievement when they gaze too intently on outcomes or define successes in ways that school administrators with broader concerns choose happily to dismiss or overlook. In his editorial for the July 2007 *School Library Journal,* Brian Kenney shared his realization that "perceptions and portfolios are no longer enough" to convince principals to support their school librarians. Kenney's (2007) epiphany came at the end of a symposium that centered on the completion of a three-year study that looked at school librarians' successful collaborations with classroom teachers.

After symposium goers congratulated themselves on having facilitated successful collaborative projects that improved faculty collegiality and increased the status of the librarians and their services, an educational consultant responding to the study asked, "Shouldn't the point of collaboration be improvement in student learning?" Collaborative projects and advocacy efforts must focus on measurable outcomes that demonstrate improved learning rather than point to outputs that demonstrate library activities and the *perceived* learning outcomes that may result. When advocacy campaigns are so focused, they can achieve results.

Ohio Educational Library Media Association (OELMA) members realized increased funding to hire licensed school librarians in every district during a year of deep financial cuts in state funding by aligning their message with the aims of their then pro-education governor. Having faced years of cuts to school library positions, OELMA members knew they first had to create awareness, then advocate *not* for school librarians but for students and learning (Barack 2009). The success in Ohio culminated eight years of advocacy campaigning, which illustrates another quality that decision makers value: commitment. When advocates commit to an effort and remain consistent in their messaging, they may realize success. Haycock (2011) offers a definition for advocacy that the Ohio school library advocates understood and employed: *a planned, deliberate, sustained effort to develop understanding and support incrementally over time.*

Finally, decision makers tend to value those people whom they know and like, and they like passionate, extroverted librarians. As Bill Crowley (2010b) pointed out in an address to members of the Illinois School Library Media Association in October 2010, one of the most difficult hurdles for many school librarians to overcome is to exhibit an extroverted and passionate persona that does not come naturally. In his article "Data on the Instructional Role of the Library Media Specialist," Daniel Callison reviewed "positive and insightful testimonial examples" of Ohio, Wisconsin, and Indiana state studies and found comments in each study that imply "the library media specialist is the program. The personality, energy, ability, knowledge, and vision displayed by the professional are more powerful for promotion, advocacy, and instructional impact than any other resources, facilities or technologies" (Callison 2007, 58).

Unfortunately, many school administrators have had little exposure in their personal or professional lives to school librarians that exhibit the level of passion and energy that grab the attention of principals, superintendents, and trustees. School librarians have the ability, knowledge, and vision to run library programs that have positive impacts on students' learning, but they often lack the personality required to be powerful advocates. School administrators who have seen passionate, energetic librarians in action generally support their school libraries, and they look for passion and energy in the people they hire.

In her 2009 South Carolina study "Principals' Perceptions of School Librarians," Donna Shannon lists the "typical responses" principals supplied to an open-ended question asking what competencies they looked for in a new librarian besides the competencies from *Information Power* that the study questionnaire had provided them:

> The ability to utilize effective people skills. This is paramount!
> Must be an approachable, welcoming person.

Team player, works and gets along with faculty and staff.

Works congenially and collegially with faculty and staff. (Shannon 2009, 9)

The Shannon study found that while principals do value the sanctioned competencies expected of school librarians by the American Association of School Librarians (AASL) as expressed in *Information Power: Building Partnerships for Learning* and *Empowering Learners: Guidelines for School Library Media Programs*, they placed greater value on the potential of librarian candidates to work with everyone in the school and to love children and learning. Principals also targeted the personal interview as the most important indicator of whether they would hire someone, over certification, recommendations, and previous experience (Shannon 2009, 7).

School librarians can benefit from the advice provided to public librarians in the OCLC's 2008 report *From Awareness to Funding: A Study of Library Support in America* (De Rosa and Johnson 2008). Chapter 4 of the study, "Library Funding Support Is An Attitude, Not a Demographic," explores a number of issues that are relevant to discussions of the future of libraries and professional librarians. Perceptions of the librarian are highly related to support. "Passionate librarians" who are involved in the community make a difference. For school librarians, the learning community they serve extends beyond the students and faculty who visit the library's space to campus and district administrators, trustees, parents, and dispassionate taxpayers (De Rosa and Johnson 2008).

A 2008 Texas voter survey on libraries revealed that Texans, regardless of their political affiliations, overwhelmingly value their school libraries and support increased funding for them. Belief that the library is a transformational force in people's lives is directly related to their level of funding support (De Rosa and Johnson 2008, 4–1). School librarians must emphasize how their skills and services transform the learning culture on campus and the lives of students and families in the larger community.

Bill Crowley (2010b) drew on a spectrum of OCLC-sponsored research to reduce the key insights from the OCLC report *From Awareness to Funding: A Study of Library Support in America* (De Rosa and Johnson 2008) to these statements of crucial library problems:

- Emotional connections are critically important to developing "super supporters" of the library; therefore, library services should maximize ROEI (Return on Emotional Investment) to encourage users to develop a strong bond with their library, a bond that can be translated into support for budgets and services.

- The emotional connection of users with their libraries requires the dedication of "passionate librarians," whose fervor for assisting people in maximizing their benefits from the library can help socialize a significant number of lifelong and "passionate" library users.

- If people believe that the library "transforms" lives in positive directions, they are likely to become its strongest supporters, even if they are not frequent users of library services.

From Awareness to Funding also reports that attitudes and beliefs drive library funding behavior more so than demographics. Voters' perceptions of the role the library plays in their lives and in their communities are more important determinants of

their willingness to increase funding than their age, gender, race, political affiliation, life state, or income level (De Rosa and Johnson 2008, 4–1). Research needs
to determine if voters believe that school libraries play a positive role in their lives,
perhaps by playing a positive role in the lives of their children, and if contemporary
school librarianship is *emotional labor*, defined as "work performed by those whose
jobs involve a high degree of personal contact and who are expected to produce
an emotional state, such as pleasure, gratitude, or self-esteem in the people with
whom they deal" (Shockley-Zalabak 2006, 311).

In the context of emotional support for school libraries, Bill Crowley's emerging model of *lifecycle librarianship*, grounded in ROEI, underscores the need for
school librarians and their staff (if any), in collaboration with other librarians delivering services to potential, current, and former students, to develop long-term relationships with school administrators and trustees, teachers and staff, students and
parents, and other supportive members of the community (Crowley 2008a, 48).
ROEI "can be defined as a continuing emotional connection between users and
the libraries and professional librarians who provide the library services and programs that people deem vital to their lives. ROEI is also an essential component
of lifecycle librarianship, an approach to securing the future of libraries and professional librarians that is rooted in identifying and meeting priority community
needs for responsive services from 'the lapsit to the nursing home'" (Crowley
2010a, 34).

Lifecycle librarianship provides one way to think about developing and sustaining school administrators' and the learning community's appreciation of the value
of libraries and librarians in both good times and bad. Developing understanding
and support incrementally over time through a planned, deliberate, and sustained
effort requires of many librarians that they adopt the *persona* of an extrovert in
order to impress upon decision makers the value of effective library service in the
lives of learning community members. Research shows that school district administrators and trustees often need help interpreting and engaging with supportive
evidence, particularly when it comes in the form of scientific research. School librarians must also adopt the persona of an interpreter of research in order to help
decision makers better engage with evidence to help them solve the problem of
research.

WHAT DO DECISION MAKERS NEED TO BETTER ENGAGE WITH EVIDENCE?

In "What's the Evidence on Districts' Use of Evidence?" Coburn, Honig, and
Stein (in press) note that current education policies at the federal and state levels
demand that school district administrators use "evidence" to "ground their educational improvement efforts" (1). School administrators find this requirement difficult because often too much evidence of the wrong kind becomes available when
district officials need data that directly relate to pressing issues under consideration.
Too often officials have difficulty accessing available data, or they find conflicting
data, or data are too abstract or technical to be practical (4).

District officials also recognize the difference in the rapid pace of decision making and the much slower pace of research, so many decisions are made without
evidence. Even when evidence of the right kind is available at the right time, administrators "must still look for it, notice it, and attend to it—a set of processes called

'search'" (Coburn, Honig, and Stein, in press, 6). With the difficulties of search, administrators are likely to pay attention only to evidence that closely matches what they already know and expect (Coburn, Honig, and Stein, in press, 7). They are also likely to interpret, or make sense of, evidence that simplifies the complex. School librarians, by their education and practice, have skill in search and sense making that can make them valuable to their school and district administrators, but they must actively engage with and in research themselves and establish relationships with their administrators based on the ability to simplify complex research and present it in timely, discrete, and manageable parcels.

WHAT ROLES DO SCHOOL LIBRARIANS NEED TO PLAY?

In addition to understanding the role that evidence plays in shaping decision-makers' conceptions of issues, school librarians must understand what roles they must play to gain influence. James LaRue (2010, 1), in writing about the "continuum of librarian visibility" in public libraries, makes a case for public librarians' increasing their visibility that is salient for school librarians, as well. To make the shift from invisible to visible, librarians must make the shift from servants to leaders: "The visible librarian has a prominent seat at the community decision-making table, actively clarifies choices, provides reputable and relevant information, and through every action trumpets the unique contribution of the professional" (LaRue 2010, 3). For school librarians the "community table" may be in any of a number of settings throughout the learning community: campus- or district-level committees or teams, parent–teacher organizations, meetings of the board of trustees, or community activity meetings, such as weekly meetings of Kiwanis or the Rotary Club.

Ken Haycock (2011), too, advises that if librarians are to be leaders, they need to be at the table when problems are framed so they can help frame them. To do so successfully requires an understanding of what actions work to that end and what actions do not. "Talking library" does not, but talking literacy, economic development, or social justice does. For example, school librarians should relate at their various "tables" the results of the AASL *2010 School Libraries Count!* In an October 2010 press release, the AASL revealed that high-poverty school libraries showed a significantly greater decrease in collections than low-poverty school libraries from 2009 to 2010, creating unequal access to resources and information applications for students in high-poverty schools and decreasing their chances for success in and after school ("AASL Survey Results" 2010). Rather than report the statistic as a problem to be addressed, school librarians should tell the story of what happens, or better yet what does not happen, when schools fail students.

Both Crowley (2008b), in the third chapter of *Renewing Professional Librarianship*, "What's the Story?", and Haycock promote the power of story in advocating for libraries. Haycock tells of his encounter with James Carville, the political strategist, who admitted the importance of data but said visual images are crucial in efforts to influence decisions. School librarians must illustrate their stories. They must say, when districts cut library funding, students no longer need shades because their future is no longer bright.

School librarians must also illustrate for administrators what good library practice looks like. Brian Kenney, in an editorial column for *School Library Journal*, reminds us that many principals, teachers, and community members have never seen a good school library under the leadership of a good school librarian (Kenney 2006, 11).

Kenney volunteers at a Chicago school that has no library, helping teachers select reference and leisure-reading materials and advising them on appropriate sources for online content. He admits to a "subversive purpose" for his efforts, to demonstrate what good things *do not happen* when a school does not have a librarian.

With 37 states having adopted the new national Common Core State Standards, school librarians have a great opportunity to define their mission in terms that draw directly from the standards and tell the story of student learning. As one Illinois librarian put it after a workshop to explore the Common Core Standards (roughly paraphrased),

> What I see is an increasing emphasis on reading complex texts, including more nonfiction, for information and on information retrieval. How will any school do this effectively without a professional school librarian? The new standards require someone trained in the selection, organization, and promotion of materials. The new standards require someone trained to collaborate with teachers on information retrieval and reading for information. This is no time to cut professional staff, and it is certainly no time to cut clerical staff. If districts cut library clerical staff, then the trained professionals will be unable to do the work required by the adoption of the Common Core.

School librarians must help their administrators distinguish the apparent, recognizable work of the library from the valuable but less recognizable work that professionals do; that is, few administrators who have never seen a good library in action can distinguish what library clerical staff do from what a well-qualified professional librarian does. In order to help their administrators see professional, however, librarians must be willing to be professional.

WHAT DOES ASPIRATIONAL PROFESSIONALISM MEAN FOR SCHOOL LIBRARIANS?

Scour the various states' standards and guidelines for school libraries and school librarians. One is unlikely to find the word "professional" in them. The ALA Code of Ethics mentions "the profession" and "other professionals providing information services" but refers to its members as "librarians." In state guidelines one finds references to "the competent librarian" or "the effective librarian" or the "effective school library media program," but the word "professional," one must suppose, has only tacit meaning in the field of librarianship. Perhaps if the words "professional school librarian," which some might see as redundant, were expressed in our standards rather than implied, school librarians would not find themselves redundant in tough economic times. Rather, more school librarians might have an image of themselves as agents in a changing library landscape instead of victims of some relentless economic evolution (see Litwin 2009). To what ideal as a professional shall school librarians aspire if they are to secure their professional status?

Title 29, Section 152.12 of the United States Code ("Definitions" 2012) defines a professional employee as

> any employee engaged in work (i) **predominantly intellectual and varied** in character as opposed to routine mental, manual, mechanical, or physical work; (ii) involving the consistent exercise of **discretion and judgment** in

its performance; (iii) of such a character that the output produced or the result accomplished **cannot be standardized** in relation to a given period of time; (iv) requiring **knowledge of an advanced type in a field of science or learning** customarily acquired by a **prolonged course of specialized intellectual instruction and study in an institution of higher learning** or a hospital, as distinguished from a general academic education or from an apprenticeship or from training in the performance of routine mental, manual, or physical processes. (emphasis added)

Professional school librarians certainly fit the definition of professional employee as defined in the USC and have professional associations to look to—the ALA and AASL—for codes of ethics and standards for performance, but the associations do not make these codes and standards easy to access. Instead, they are tucked away deep online somewhere or in documents that librarians must purchase.

In their 2001 *Library Trends* article "Professionalism in Librarianship: Shifting the Focus from Malpractice to Good Practice," Randy Diamond and Martha Dragich offer a "blueprint for good practice" (396) that illustrates what "aspirational professionalism" looks like generally, outside the specific and, for some librarians, hidden codes and standards provided for the field. Because school librarians do not face censure under the nonenforceable codes of ethics that their professional associations prescribe, they must aspire to self-governance, professional knowledge, and shared values to "battle" for professional recognition (Diamond and Dragich 2001, 404). They must somehow balance the long-held values of the profession (think Ranganathan) with the need to reinvent themselves as information and user behaviors evolve in the networked society. When school librarians can market their aspirational professionalism to their building administrators, when principals recognize that the librarian's "invisible contract" (Crowley 2010b) demonstrates a passion and dedication to values that the principal shares, then school librarians can secure their professional status and gain influence.

Haycock (2011) warns that school librarians must avoid "inhibitors" to influence that may jeopardize their professional status: remaining within comfort zones or seeing opportunities to lead as outside their job descriptions; doubting their competencies and saying they cannot or do not know how to do something; believing that talking is influencing (not remembering that advocacy is a planned, sustained effort to develop understanding); refusing to address issues because they are too difficult or do not have a quick fix; or not learning whom to influence so not targeting their efforts, or targeting everyone with their efforts (the "spray and pray" approach). Finally, school librarians must resolve to sustain one particular advocacy effort at both the state and federal levels, to change their status in schools from legally optional to mandatory.

WHAT LEGISLATIVE EFFORT SHOULD NEVER DIE?

In his analysis of the 8th annual salary survey by *District Administration,* Alan Dessoff (2008) describes school librarians as "impassioned about their mission-to get children to read" but also as "the next-to-lowest level of auxiliary professional personnel in the ERS [Educational Research Service] salary survey" (4). Dessoff quotes Sara Kelly Johns, then president of the AASL and librarian at Lake Placid Middle-Senior High School in the Lake Placid (N.Y.) Central School District:

"The most frustrating thing for library administrators is that money gets allocated to mandates and libraries are not part of mandates." Still, she asserts, librarians are "a darned good investment because we play a lot of roles." A key role, says Joyce, is working with teachers—especially English teachers—"to motivate kids to want to read" (Dessoff 2008, 4). School library advocates can sustain no greater advocacy effort than to help lawmakers at the state and federal levels understand the need for legislation that would require every campus to have a qualified, professional school librarian to develop and maintain a quality school library program.

In her address to the New Jersey legislature in March 2010, Pat Massey, then president of the New Jersey Association of School Librarians, asked legislators to address, "over the long term," a "deficiency" in the law that does not require every school to have a library or certified librarian. In her closing remarks Massey said, "We know it is not the Legislature's intent to reduce support for school library programs. But, with so many mandated and fixed costs in their budgets, many school districts are forced to cut programs and services that impact directly on students." Massey (2010) illustrated for the legislators the result of losing library jobs and resources: diminished progress in literacy and student learning that would "hurt students and the State now and for years to come."

Efforts at the state level to mandate school librarians have had little luck, and efforts at the national level have stalled in committee twice with the SKILLs (Strengthening Kids' Interest in Learning and Libraries) Acts of 2007 and 2009. In spite of these setbacks, school library advocates should galvanize their campaigns for unified, sustained efforts at helping lawmakers understand the need for every child to have access to a school library and certified school librarian. Texas has taken an incremental approach in its effort to get school librarians on every campus. In 2011, House Bill 493 (Dutton) asked Texas legislators to recognize school librarians as teachers and pass legislation that would allow the Commissioner of Education to take into account the delivery of library services and the presence of a certified school librarian on school campuses as part of the process of accrediting school districts. If school benchmarks and rankings begin to suffer because of the lack of a quality school library program, school officials may begin to see the value in supporting mandates for school librarians. Remember, advocacy is incremental.

WHAT WORKS?

Recent research indicates that in order to garner support for libraries, professional librarians must reposition the library as a transformational force in the community (De Rosa and Johnson 2008, 4–12). The OCLC report from De Rosa and Johnson focuses on public libraries, but evidence exists to support the same strategy for school libraries. Callison (2007) analyzed the results of the Ohio state study to reveal that students and teachers identify the passionate, effective school librarian as "an educational change agent" that "transforms the learning environment" by responding to a "wide spectrum" of students' and teachers' needs (57).

School librarians must extend that agency beyond their libraries if they are to secure their professional status for themselves and for the field generally. Librarians must, in greater numbers than they do now, work with the leaders of their learning communities to demonstrate the value of their library programs as critical to the infrastructure of the school. Leaders include their building principals, of course, but also department chairs and team leaders; curriculum and technology directors on campuses and at central offices; district-level administrators; presidents of parent–teacher organizations; church leaders and businessmen; and school board trustees. But what strategies and tactics work best to wield that kind of influence?

School librarians must demonstrate that they are a good return on investment by focusing on the benefits they provide their learning communities rather than on the size of their collections or the types of technological tools they offer. Collections are important, but increasing literacy and student achievement is paramount. Providing access to online resources is important, but ensuring that students of all socioeconomic levels and intellectual abilities have *equal* access to resources and are equally equipped to use them knowledgeably and responsibly is crucial to democracy.

Ken Haycock (2011) offers some lessons from marketing research on how best to advocate. First, establish a clear and measurable objective. How will you know that your building principal recognizes that you are good ROI? Second, determine what tactics you will use. Will you build a coalition of support from among the faculty? Will you present a rational argument? Will you try an inspirational appeal by collecting qualitative and visual data from among the students? Third, consider what communication tool is most effective. Does your principal respond best to something written? to a brief face-to-face meeting? to a formal in-person report? What outcomes will you share? Not *outputs,* such as circulation statistics, but *outcomes.* Have reading scores improved because of collaborative planning with teachers? Have instances of Internet-related violations decreased in number and frequency because of library instruction on Internet safety?

The most effective way for school librarians to build support is to build trust. People in positions of authority value the people they trust, so librarians must first establish relationships with the people they want to have some influence with, then build trust over time. One builds trust the way one builds equity in anything else, by being committed to an effort and consistent in one's behaviors. School librarians historically hold public trust, which is one of the six pillars that David Armano (2011) outlines in "Pillars of the New Influence." Though written for business, Armano's blog post offers a model for school librarians to broaden support through the use of social media and social networks. School librarians can harness the power of digital social networking to build support for themselves and for their learning communities that can make them influential leaders in their communities. The other five of Armano's six pillars illustrate the power inherent in digital social networks: *reach,* or the ability of digital distribution platforms (think Facebook, Twitter, blogs) to reach multitudes of followers; *proximity,* or the ability of the individuals you reach to influence those close to them; *expertise,* or the ability to add value to a social system; *relevancy,* or the ability to have influence in a certain topical area; and *credibility,* or the ability to have influence within a certain community. School librarians must join their colleagues who are bolstering their local, face-to-face spheres of influence by harnessing the power of the network society.

WHAT'S THE LAST WORD?

The current crisis in school library funding and staffing is part of the general economic condition, which at this writing is beginning to improve. Facing legislative and administrative attempts to remove them from schools has offered school librarians an opportunity to reflect, retool, reposition, refocus, renew, relate, recruit, and research. The bad news is not over, but neither is the good. While many school librarians are facing layoffs, many more are building programs and collections and making great impacts in their communities.

It's March in Austin now and warm. Through their untiring efforts, school library advocates have secured all of the Austin Independent School District (AISD) librarian positions for this year, but all the library aides have been cut. Now the librarians are working to restore the educational technology department. The entire department was cut, even though it provides support and training in educational technology for the entire district. The librarians work hand-in-hand with them, so they do not want to lose them.

When asked what worked to secure all the librarian positions from cuts, one AISD librarian said it was the overwhelming support from parents and teachers who flooded the trustees' email boxes with messages titled "Support AISD Librarians." The board got so many email messages that they had a huge binder full of messages supporting the librarians. She added that the advocacy effort did not start just this year. For the last several years, Austin's school librarians have appeared in force at board meetings, signing up to speak and presenting the board with updates on their work. They have presented trustees with AISD Libraries calendars with photos of active teaching and the integration of technology in all levels of their libraries. In 2011 they presented the board with AISD Libraries T-shirts. "As sad and demoralized as we were," this librarian said, "we didn't stop fighting. Visibility was our goal. We were the little Whos in Whoville shouting 'we are here, we are here!' Untiring? We are tired, but how can we let down our guard? If we aren't vigilant and persistent, we might have to fight for the same positions next year." Like many of their advocacy fellows in many states, these school librarians know well that to defend their positions and professional status, their efforts must be planned, deliberate, sustained, incremental, and determined to develop an understanding of the important function they play in helping students learn and engage in an increasingly complex world.

NOTE

Thank you, Bill Crowley, for inviting me to write this chapter and for providing me material and mentoring to start (and complete) the process. To Shirley Lukenbill, thank you for inspiring me with your wisdom, energy, and Austin "updates." Thank you, Ken Haycock, first for agreeing to come to Dominican as the Follett Chair and then for being such a good friend and generous colleague. To Dean Susan Roman, Alexis Sarkisian, and Amy Killebrew, endless thanks for keeping the School Library Media Program at Dominican a model program. Finally, I thank all my fellow school librarians who have embraced a model of aspirational professionalism and sustain their efforts to provide quality school library services to all students in spite of great resistance. Keep the faith.

REFERENCES

"AASL Survey Results Show Lagging Economy Hit High Poverty Schools the Hardest."
        2010. American Library Association (October 13). Accessed March 1, 2012. http://
        www.ala.org/news/pr?id=5374.
Ahmed-Ullah, Noreen S. 2010. "In CPS, Library Void Goes Beyond One Sit-in." *Chicago
        Tribune* (October 26). Accessed March 1, 2012. http://articles.chicagotribune.

com/2010-10-26/news/ct-met-cps-libraries-20101025_1_elementary-schools-charter-schools-library-or-media-center.

Alper, Alex. 2010. "City's School Librarians on Borrowed Time." *The Brooklyn Ink* (December 15). Accessed March 1, 2012. http://thebrooklynink.com/2010/12/15/21865-citys-school-librarians-on-borrowed-time.

Armano, David. 2011. "Pillars of the New Influence." *Harvard Business Review*. Accessed March 1, 2012. http://blogs.hbr.org/cs/2011/01/the_six_pillars_of_the_new_inf.html#.

Barack, Lauren. 2009. "Ohio School Libraries May Net More Funding." *School Library Journal* (July 15). Accessed March 1, 2012. http://www.libraryjournal.com/slj/articlesfunding/857681–347/ohio_school_libraries_may_net.html.csp.

Bunn, April. 2010. "The [Sad] State of NJ School Libraries." *Librarygarden* (November 7). Accessed March 1, 2012. http://librarygarden.net/.

Callison, Daniel. 2007. "Data on the Instructional Role of the Library Media Specialist: Are Schools Getting Their Money's Worth?" *School Library Media Activities Monthly* 23(10): 55–58. Accessed March 1, 2012. http://www.schoollibrarymonthly.com/articles/Callison2007-v23n10p55.html.

Chapin Hall Center for Children at the University of Chicago. 2005. "Adolescence and the Transition to Adulthood: Rethinking Public Policy for a New Century." Philadelphia: The MacArthur Research Network on Transitions to Adulthood and Public Policy Accessed March 1, 2012. http://www.transad.pop.upenn.edu/downloads/Conference_Summary_Final.pdf.

Clark, Patty. 2011. "I Hate to Read! Part 3: The Elimination of Licensed School Librarians." Examiner.com. Accessed March 1, 2012. http://www.examiner.com/young-adult-literature-in-portland/i-hate-to-read-part-3-the-elimination-of-licensed-school-librarians.

Coburn, Cynthia E., Meredith I. Honig, and Mary Kay Stein. In press. "What's the Evidence on Districts' Use of Evidence?" In *Research and Practice: Towards a Reconciliation*, ed. J. Bransford, L. Gomez, D. Lam, and N. Vye. Cambridge, MA: Harvard Education Press. Accessed March 1, 2012. http://gse.berkeley.edu/faculty/CECoburn/coburnhonigsteinfinal.pdf.

Crowley, Bill. 2008a. "Lifecycle Librarianship." *Library Journal* 133(6): 46–48. Accessed March 1, 2012. http://www.libraryjournal.com/article/CA6542287.html.

Crowley, Bill. 2008b. *Renewing Professional Librarianship: A Fundamental Rethinking*. Westport, CT: Libraries Unlimited.

Crowley, Bill. 2010a. "Know Your ROEI." *Library Journal* 135(3): 34–35. Accessed March 1, 2012. http://www.libraryjournal.com/lj/ljinprint/currentissue/853644-403/know_your_roei.html.csp.

Crowley, Bill. 2010b. "Solving Problems and Building Coalitions: Survival Strategies for the Teacher-Librarian, School Library Media Specialist, and School Librarian." Paper presented at the 2010 Illinois School Library Media Association Conference, St. Charles, Illinois, October 9.

"Definitions." 29 U.S.C. Sec. 152.12. Office of the Law Revision Counsel, U.S. House of Representatives. Accessed March 1, 2012. http://uscode.house.gov/uscode-cgi/fastweb.exe?getdoc+uscview+t29t32+93+0++() AND ((29) ADJ USC)%3ACITE AND (USC w%2F10 (152))%3ACITE.

De Rosa, Cathy, and Jenny Johnsons. 2008. *From Awareness to Funding: A Study of Library Support in America. A Report to the OCLC Membership*. Dublin, OH: OCLC Accessed March 1, 2012. http://www.oclc.org/reports/funding/fullreport.pdf.

Dessoff, Alan. 2008. "8th Annual Salary Survey." *District Administration* (August). Accessed March 1, 2012. http://www.districtadministration.com/article/8th-annual-salary-survey.

Dewey, John. 1957. *Reconstruction in Philosophy: Enlarged Edition, With a New Introduction by the Author*. Boston: Beacon Press.

Diamond, Randy, and Martha Dragich. 2001. "Professionalism in Librarianship: Shifting the Focus from Malpractice to Good Practice." *Library Trends* 49(3): 395–414. Accessed March 1, 2012. http://www.ideals.illinois.edu/bitstream/handle/2142/8346/li brarytrendsv49i3c_opt.pdf?sequence=1.

Dougherty, Conor. 2010. "New Library Technologies Dispense With Librarians." *Wall Street Journal* (October 25). Accessed March 1, 2012. http://online.wsj.com/article/SB 10001424052702304354104575568592236241242.html?mod=googlenews_wsj.

Downing, Margaret. 2010. "Lamar High's Library Ousts Books, Re-Opens as Coffee Shop." *Houston Press* (November 23). Accessed March 1, 2012. http://blogs.hous tonpress.com/hairballs/2010/11/lamar_highs_library_ousts_book.php.

Haycock, Ken. 2011. "Advocacy Revisited: New Insights Based on Research and Evidence." Paper presented at the 2011 Graduate School of Library and Information Science Follett Lecture, Dominican University, February 9.

Heinauer, Lauren. 2011. "School Board OKs Plan That May Cost 485 Jobs." *Austin American-Statesman* (January 25), sec. Local News. March 1, 2012. http://www.statesman.com/news/local/school-board-oks-plan-that-may-cost-485-1207704.html?cxtype=rss_ece_frontpage.

House Bill 493, 82 Legislature, Regular Session (2011). Texas Legislature. Accessed March 1, 2012. http://www.capitol.state.tx.us/tlodocs/82R/billtext/pdf/HB00493I.pdf#navpanes=0.

Idaho Commission for Libraries. 2010. *The Idaho School Library Impact Study, 2009: How Idaho Librarians, Teachers. and Administrators Collaborate for Student Success.* Boise, ID: Idaho Commission for Libraries. Accessed March 1, 2012. http://libraries.idaho.gov/doc/idaho-school-library-impact-study-2009.

Kelley, Michael. 2011. "Proposed Budget in Texas Nearly Zeros Out Key State Library Funds." *LibraryJournal* (January 21). Accessed March 1, 2012. http://www.li braryjournal.com/lj/home/888925–264/proposed_budget_in_texas_nearly.html.csp.

Kenney, Brian. 2006. "Seeing Is Believing." *School Library Journal* (December 1). Accessed March 1, 2012. http://www.schoollibraryjournal.com/slj/printissue/cur rentissue/865212-427/seeing_is_believing.html.csp.

Kenney, Brian. 2007. "Getting It Together." *School Library Journal* 53(7): 9. Accessed March 1, 2012. http://www.schoollibraryjournal.com/slj/printissue/currentissue/863387-427/editorial_getting_it_together.html.csp.

Kenney, Edward L. 2010. "More Schools Losing Their Librarians." *Delawareonline* (November 9). March 1, 2012. http://www.delawareonline.com/article/20101109/NEWS/11090329/More-schools-losing-their-librarians?nclick_check=1.

Lance, Keith Curry, Marcia J. Rodney, and Bill Schwarz. 2010. "The Impact of School Libraries on Academic Achievement: A Research Study Based on Responses from Administrators in Idaho." *School Library Monthly* 26(9): 14–17. Accessed March 1, 2012. http://www.schoollibrarymonthly.com/articles/Lance2010-v26n9p14.html.

LaRue, James. 2010. "The Visibility and Invisibility of Librarians." *Library Journal* (November 15). Accessed March 1, 2012. http://www.libraryjournal.com/lj/reviews-reference/887361–283/the_visibility_and_invisibility_of.html.csp.

Lehmann, Chris. 2007. "High-Stakes Testing Threatens School Librarians." *School Library Journal* (July 1). Accessed March 1, 2012. http://www.schoollibraryjournal.com/article/CA6456393.html?industryid=47078.

Litwin, Rory. 2009. "Professionalism and Attitudes toward Change." *Library Juice* (August 10) Accessed March 1, 2012. http://libraryjuicepress.com/blog/?p=1591.

Massey, Pat. 2010. "Testimony by Pat Massey, NJASL President." New Jersey Legislature (March 25). Accessed March 1, 2012. http://www.njleg.state.nj.us/legislativepub/budget_2011/Other_Submitted_Testimony/P_Massey.pdf.

McGarry, Michelle. 2009. "The School Library Is the Link to Connecting with Parents." *School Library Monthly* 26(3): 45–47. Accessed March 1, 2012. http://www.the schoollibrarylink.com/storage/michellemcgarry_articleSLM.pdf.

Moran, Mark. 2010. "School Libraries Cut Databases; Effective Web Research Skills Will Become Paramount." *The FindingDulcinea Blog* (February 3). Accessed March 1, 2012. http://blog.findingdulcinea.com/2010/02/the-silver-lining-to-school-li brary-budget-and-database-cuts.html.

"No New Library Books for Boise Schools This Year." 2010. *KTVB News* (August 18). Accessed March 1, 2012. http://www.nwcn.com/news/idaho/No-new-library-books-for-Boise-schools-this-year-101042249.html.

Park, Loretta. 2011. "Advocates of School Libraries Push for State Funding." *Standard-Examiner* (January 30). Accessed March 1, 2012. http://www.standard.net/top ics/utah-legislature/2011/01/30/advocates-school-libraries-push-state-funding.

Shannon, Donna M. 2009. "Principals' Perceptions of School Librarians." *School Libraries Worldwide* 15(2): 1–22. Accessed March 1, 2012. http://www.iasl-online.org/pubs/slw/july09.htm.

Shockley-Zalabak, Pamela S. 2006. *Fundamentals of Organizational Communication: Knowledge, Sensitivity, Skills, Values.* Boston: Pearson.

Staino, Rocco. 2010. "Illustrators Join the Fight to Save California School Libraries." *School Library Journal* (April 28). Accessed March 1, 2012. http://www.schoollibraryjour nal.com/slj/articlesfunding/884777-347/illustrators_join_the_fightto_save.html. csp.

Staino, Rocco. 2011. "Maryland's Prince George's School District Could Fire 90 Librarians." *School Library Journal* (February 8). March 1, 2012. http://www.school libraryjournal.com/slj/newslettersnewsletterbucketextrahelping2/889146-477/marylands_prince_georges_school_.html.csp.

Tales, Dafney. 2010. "Teachers' Union Chief Pushes for Funding for School Libraries." *Philly.com* (November 24). Accessed March 1, 2012. http://articles.philly.com/2010-11-24/news/24955684_1_school-libraries-school-assessment-scores-high-schools.

"The State of America's Libraries: A Report from the American Library Association." 2011. *American Libraries,* special issue (April). Accessed March 1, 2012. http://american librariesmagazine.org/archives/issue/state-americas-libraries-2011.

Weinstein, Susan Parkou. 2010. "Teachers Union Grieves Lack of Librarians in Raynham and Bridgewater Schools." *Wicked Local* (October 12). Accessed March 1, 2012. http://www.wickedlocal.com/raynham/news/education/x123460234/Teachers-union-grieves-lack-of-librarians-in-Raynham-and-Bridgewater-schools#axzz1nvIcePiz.

Whelan, Debra Lau. 2008. "Three Spokane Moms Save Their School Libraries." *School Library Journal* (September 1). Accessed March 1, 2012. http://www.schoollibrary journal.com/article/CA6590045.html.

Whelan, Debra Lau. 2011. "California Hands Out Scores of Pink Slips to School Librarians." *School Library Journal* (March 15). Accessed March 1, 2012. http://www.school libraryjournal.com/slj/newslettersnewsletterbucketextrahelping2/889671-477/california_hands_out_scores_of.html.csp.

6

FUTURE-PROOFING
THE ACADEMIC LIBRARIAN

Lenora Berendt
Graduate School of Library and Information Science, Dominican University

Maria Otero-Boisvert
*San Jose State University/Queensland University of Technology
Gateway PhD Program.*

It's been said that the library is the heart of the university. Since the advent of the Internet and other recent technologies, librarianship has changed and evolved at a considerable pace, and nowhere has this been more apparent than in academic libraries. Thanks, in part, to Google and other Web search engines, information queries have diminished at reference desks, and the nature of today's questions has changed significantly. No longer do we produce answers for our patrons. Instead, we teach them how to locate, evaluate, and use information in all its forms for themselves. Users now request assistance in locating more specialized types of information and materials, a substantial number of which are found using subscription databases and other reliable deep Web resources. Perhaps most importantly, libraries are now both physical and virtual spaces for users. They are simultaneously at the center and reaching into the peripheries of their parent organizations. Rather than the heart, perhaps today academic libraries ought to aspire to be the central nervous system of the organization—constantly reacting to internal and external stimuli and coordinating responses as appropriate.

It is crucial that academic librarians take a more proactive role in order to be relevant to the future of higher education (Sennyey, Ross, and Mills 2009; Mays, Tenopir, and Kaufman 2010). Academic librarians must continue to meet the needs and expectations of their users while also striving to anticipate future needs. They must also appeal to external audiences and implement outcome-based approaches demonstrating the value of their services as library educators (Loesch 2010). Now, more than ever, it is critical for librarians to develop strong collaborative relationships with students, faculty, and university administrators based on their shared vision and institutional goals and within a climate of respect, understanding, and trust (Bjatti 2009). In the following pages, we discuss the various areas in which the college library has already begun the metamorphosis that will carry it into the future.

CURRENT ENVIRONMENT

Historically, academic libraries have faithfully and adeptly attended to the information and research needs of students and faculty. In return, they have generally been viewed as support services providers rather than partners in higher education. Ironically, while librarians have always embraced and adapted to new technologies, they have seldom taken the lead in the creation and innovation of instructional and revenue producing entities (ACRL Research Planning and Review Committee 2010). Perhaps the time has come for us to step into those leadership positions and outside of our comfort zone.

Most academic librarians have adapted their services to meet the needs of today's users who expect fast, convenient access to the information and materials they seek. In addition to traditional reference services, librarians now also interact with their patrons via email, IM, chat, Skype, and so forth, and greater amounts of information are available online than ever before. This has resulted in reduced gate counts and face-to-face interaction at the reference desk. Studies have shown that many academic library users are intimidated by the reference desk yet will readily seek and/or accept assistance from a librarian seen roving through the library or who approaches with an offer of help. To take proactive service one step further, librarians ought to be implementing the use of mobile devices to provide assistance to users whenever and wherever they may be (ACRL Research Planning and Review Committee 2010). For example, the use of iPads and/or iPhones by roving public service librarians would certainly result in increased reference interaction with students and faculty.

The traditional goals of academic librarians continue to be internally rather than externally focused, and most librarians do a poor job of promoting their services and resources to users and other university stakeholders (Jankowska and Marcum 2010). In order to be significant, relevant players in higher education, academic librarians need to take a more active leadership role both on and off campus and collaborate with other university entities to attract and retain students in their institutions (Shuler 2007; Bjatti 2009). For example, in addition to working collaboratively with faculty to participate in the teaching and learning process, reaching out to the staff of other university units, such as information technologies, tutoring and learning assistance centers, instructional design, and university recruitment and admissions, can cement the importance and relevance of the library on many levels.

The library instruction movement has long advocated teacher–librarian collaboration (Bjatti 2009; Loesch 2010). Its focus on communicating and partnering with faculty to encourage their participation in teaching students how to develop solid research skills has heightened the image of academic librarians and strengthened their relations with faculty in recent years (Association of College and Research Libraries 2011). However, several issues remain, including assumptions on the part of faculty that students know how to do research when they enter the university and the fact that faculty and student definitions of research skills often vary in terms of quality of information.

Faculty often understand research to involve scholarly, peer-reviewed content, while many students generally consider anything they find on the Internet to be research quality material. However, when in-depth ethnographic studies of student use of the Internet are conducted, the research demonstrates that university and college faculty, librarians, and students have overestimated student abilities to use this vital information resource (Kolowich 2011). It is therefore essential that librarians and faculty continue the research dialogue and partnership to ensure that current and future students know and understand how to locate, evaluate, and use information in all its formats.

Former User Education Coordinator and chapter co-author, Lenora Berendt, developed a successful partnership with School of Business Administration and MBA faculty at Loyola University Chicago's Lewis Library during the 1990s. As Berendt recalled,

> I started by building professional relationships with 2–3 faculty members who were regular library users, convincing them that their students' assignments would improve as they learned about the research process. By visiting the various departments and chatting casually with faculty in their offices on a weekly basis, word spread that research sessions taught by library faculty were effective and a good use of class time.

During the next few years, instruction statistics steadily increased as additional faculty got on board, resulting in a heavily used instruction program that continues today.

As academic library services and adaptation to new technologies continues to grow, the need for library instruction will increase, resulting in the demand for highly skilled and experienced librarians (Loesch 2010). Continuing education and staff development will become even more important to both current and future academic librarians. Given the funding cuts and flat budgets of the recent past, libraries and library schools may want to collaborate in order to provide access to the necessary training and skills development needed for current and future academic librarians (Mullins, Allen, and Hufford 2007).

OUTREACH AND ADVOCACY

In order to remain relevant in higher education, academic librarians must expand their outreach activities both within and outside the university community (Mays, Tenopir, and Kaufman 2010). Universities continue to move toward a business model, and librarians must learn what that means to their respective institutions and find ways to justify their relevance and existence. Julie Todaro, dean of Library Services at Austin Community College and a well-known columnist and writer on library leadership issues, stresses the importance of influence and persuasion as advocacy tools. She describes that crucial 15-minute opportunity that a librarian may have in which to deliver a well-crafted advocacy message to an administrator, legislator, or department chair, whether it is a scheduled opportunity or a chance encounter. Aside from these so-called elevator moments, there are also the more long-term opportunities, such as serving on college-wide committees and task forces in which librarians must also be prepared to employ all of their influence and persuasion principles (Todaro 2006). Reaching out to university administrators (president, provost, trustees) as well as academic and professional communities both on and off campus can provide academic librarians with the opportunity to become strong, effective players in higher education, as will continuing and growing teacher–librarian partnerships (Staley and Malenfant 2010).

Budget constraints have seriously impacted higher education on the local, state, and federal levels for a number of years (Loesch 2010). Given the current state of the U.S. economy, these challenges will not likely disappear any time soon. This means that academic librarians will have to add new skills to their toolkits:

sharpening their marketing abilities, becoming adept at writing successful grant proposals, developing effective fundraising skills, and reaching out to the surrounding community in order to remain key players in their institutions (Association of College and Research Libraries 2011). It is the responsibility of all academic librarians to continually promote the libraries' resources and services while attending to their everyday duties as information providers and educators.

Another important undertaking is strategic thinking and planning, which is key to the success of higher education entities (Jankowska and Marcum 2010; O'Connor and Au 2008). A thorough knowledge and understanding of the university's mission, vision, and strategic plan is critical, and contributing to that process is the responsibility of all librarians and staff (Howard 2010). The corporate sector has long understood the need for effective marketing strategies, yet many academic libraries do not possess a marketing plan. In order to remain relevant, academic librarians must learn to promote their services and resources more forcefully to their users, administrators, and faculty.

Successful marketing does not work in isolation; it needs to be part of every academic library's strategic plan, and librarians must know how to incorporate that into their daily interactions and work with users and faculty. A simple starting point might include a SWOT analysis to identify the library's strengths, weaknesses, opportunities, and threats. Incorporating that into the library's and university's strategic plan is one way of illustrating that academic librarians are key players and partners in higher education, not just service providers. Jean Zanoni and Scott Mandernack co-authored a chapter titled "Library Advocacy in the Campus Environment," which was published in a monograph by Welburn, Welburn, and McNeil (2010). In it they describe the strategic marketing process as being continuous, cyclical, and data-driven, with the data derived from market research of the target audience. They also stress the importance of librarians understanding the decentralized nature of the academic organization. By this they mean that every campus has several interest groups acting on their own behalf and those of their perceived allies. Decisions are often made in political contexts as opposed to rational ones. Policies and procedures that emerge can be seen as treaties among different sectors. In this scenario it is crucial that librarians have a seat at the table, a voice that is heard, and a clear message to relay (Welburn, Welburn, and McNeil 2010, 93–94).

ASSESSMENT

A principal tool in the struggle to demonstrate our value to the larger institution as well as our funding bodies is that of assessment. It is the battle cry of the economic recession in higher education and closely tied to the accountability movement. A quick look at recent job postings reveals that large academic librarians are hiring people to fill jobs such as Assessment Director, Assessment Projects Librarian, Assistant Director for Assessment, and Service Quality Librarian. It is no longer sufficient, as it was in the past, to prepare monthly and annual reports that indicate gate counts, circulation statistics, and instruction sessions. These may be useful bits of information for library managers planning services, but they do not begin to paint a compelling picture of institutional impact and value. Institutional decision makers are now demanding more clear cut evidence of return on investment (ROI), a business world concept that some would argue does not translate well into the academic paradigm. Nevertheless, it is a trend that cannot be ignored by academic libraries.

The Association of Research Libraries (ARL) holds an assessment forum twice a year before every American Library Association (ALA) Midwinter and Annual Conference. A group of librarians that participate in a very active blog called *The Library Assessment Blog* (libraryassessment.info) have chosen a definition of *assessment* that emphasizes the quantitative measurement of all library activities impacting teaching, learning, and research.

The profession's keen awareness of the need to verify the value of its services is no more evident than in the publication this year of a comprehensive study published by the Association of College and Research Libraries (ACRL). Dr. Megan Oakleaf of Syracuse University wrote *The Value of Academic Libraries: A Comprehensive Research Review and Report*, a 172-page behemoth of critical interest to the profession. Dr. Oakleaf's study offers a guide to the current situation as well as lessons learned along the way (Howard 2010, 1). She outlines 22 steps in her assessment primer, starting with "Defining outcomes" (Oakleaf 2010, 12) and ending with "Leveraging library professional associations" (Oakleaf 2010, 17).

In between the author advises librarians to link academic library outcomes to institutional outcomes, such as student enrollment, retention, graduation rates, student success and achievement, student learning, faculty research and teaching, and to develop systems for data collection where they don't already exist and track the library's impact on all of these outcomes. Although Oakleaf does go into some details on assessment tools currently available on the market, there do not appear to be many geared explicitly toward library services. It is a challenge for the library profession to create a data-tracking system that will closely follow a student's library use throughout her or his academic career and then tie that usage to specific outcomes. For example, a library can attempt to correlate student library interactions to their GPA or their GRE scores or their admittance to graduate schools, and so forth.

Perhaps one way to do this is by utilizing existing smart-card technology. Today's college students are well acquainted with the multiple uses of smart-cards. Their college ID cards function as card keys at their dormitories, admit them into the dining hall at dinner time, make purchases at the bookstore, and send them a text message when their load of laundry is done spinning. For them it would be an easy adjustment to learn to swipe their card for every interaction in the library. Our professional concerns about the possible awkwardness of these interactions and the clear need to safeguard individual privacy can be dealt with.

At Villanova University's Falvey Memorial Library, reference librarians use an online database in order to keep track of research support interactions. By creating a short entry for every interaction with a library patron, librarians create a record that can be mined for different kinds of information. For example, Jutta Siebert reports that the database is used to determine peak usage times and that staffing decisions are based on this information. The data is also used for annual reports and quality control. Because librarians often record how they have responded to a query, supervisory librarians can check those answers for accuracy. "I recently discovered that some of my colleagues recommended the wrong database to history students, and this prompted me to schedule a short tutorial on history resources for our next team meeting" (e-mail correspondence with the author, February 2, 2011). A great deal of information can be mined over the four years of a student's undergraduate work. We fail to do so at our peril.

It may well happen that these correlations do not show significant library impact. In those cases, libraries ought to take the opportunity to modify their services, facilities, and resources to better meet the needs of their clients. No doubt every library has numerous services, procedures, and even collections that have existed for time in memoriam that may no longer function adequately. Assessment data ought to lead to targeted improvements to align the library's outcomes with the institution's outcomes. Martha Kyrillidou, Senior Director, Statistics and Service Quality Programs for ARL, writes in a recent Research Libraries Issues (RLI) that "LibQUAL+® has now been used for a decade by upwards of 1,200 libraries around the world in 20 language versions. The results have helped librarians understand users' perceptions of library service quality" (Kyrillidou 2010). For more information on specific libraries' use of this quantitative instrument this entire issue of RLI is of special interest. Oakleaf calls on the library profession to rouse itself out of its previously passive role and take responsibility for its own continued success (Oakleaf 2010, 28–29).

Others, such as Carol Tenopir of the University of Tennessee, Knoxville, and Paula Kaufman of the University of Illinois at Urbana-Champaign, are currently working on a three-year study funded by the Institute of Museum and Library Services. Their study, originally conducted by the University of Illinois at Urbana-Champaign and titled "Value, Outcomes, and Return on Investment of Academic Libraries" (or Lib-Value for short), seeks to investigate the issue of ROI on grants, library collections, "and services to research, teaching and learning, and social and professional areas" (Mays, Tenopir, and Kaufman 2010, 36).

It should be mentioned that there may be an anti-assessment backlash in the works as evidenced by the published conference program for the 2011 ACRL Conference. In it is listed a program titled "Stop the Madness: The Insanity of ROI and the Need for New Qualitative Measures of Academic Library Success." The presenter for this alluring program is James Neal, Vice President for Information Services and University Librarian, Columbia University. Although the program has yet to be presented, as of this writing a glance at the description indicates that Neal will make the case for finding new qualitative measures of success. He calls the ROI movement both relentless and foolish (ACRL, 2011 Conference Program). One has to wonder if qualitative measures will ever carry the same weight as quantitative ones in a time of economic austerity.

Academic librarians must come to understand how they fit into the overall institutional mission and how they can best serve that mission. Furthermore, they must be able to quantify the outcomes of those efforts. They must become expert at writing organizational outcomes, creating assessment plans, using assessment tools and methods, preparing reports, disseminating results, and instituting changes (Oakleaf 2010, 38); and when they are done, they must do it all over again on a regular schedule. We prefer to think of this as job security.

STUDENT SERVICES

Library instruction, both general and specialized, is an integral part of the services provided by academic librarians in today's colleges and universities. Recent statistics suggest that the majority of incoming freshman students are not equipped with the skills necessary to do scholarly research and that they rely on Google and other search engines to do their research. This has prompted librarians to increase their efforts to provide tailored, course-related, and course-integrated instruction sessions and to promote these services to faculty and students (Bjatti 2009; Loesch 2010). In addition, they provide one-on-one assistance by appointment for those students needing individual assistance, yet many students go through college without ever having attended a library instruction session or met with a librarian for assistance with their information/research needs.

One option is to assign a research librarian liaison to every student and follow up with an email message periodically, briefly informing them of the research and information assistance available to them. At Yale University the library offers a Personal Librarian Program at both the undergraduate college and the medical school, which it defines as a "single point of contact for the library." The libraries' website describes the various services that students can expect, such as periodic email messages highlighting new services and resources, general information notices, basic reference service, research assistance, the ability to schedule in-person consultations, and so forth. The site is just as clear in what patrons may not expect: photocopying services, computer set-ups, and paper-writing. This is not a passive service in which librarians wait to be contacted, rather they are proactive in getting their message and services out to their assigned students (http://www.library.yale.edu/pl/).

The *Chronicle of Higher Education* recently featured an article about an embedded librarian at Baylor University who followed a class in real time via Twitter. As the class met, students were encouraged to turn on their laptops and open their Twitter accounts. Ellen Hampton Filgo would follow the postings of the class members and provide links to relevant resources as they came up in conversation. The librarian reported that all involved in this innovative new service model were very satisfied with the experience. The only caveat being the difficulty inherent in attempting to "upscale" the experiment to include many more classes (Young 2011).

Promotion and marketing of information literacy and assessment to students, faculty, and other university departments/units is critical to student success in the university (Bjatti 2009). Many academic librarians have created interactive Web tutorials aimed at instructing students in the research process using resources such as Qarbon, Camtasia, Captivate, and YouTube, which provides 24/7 access. These are excellent options for those who prefer this method of instruction, but for those who do not, one-on-one research appointments should always be available to students.

It bears repeating that as new technologies continue to drive changes in the provision of information to students in academic libraries, librarians must stay ahead of the curve and adapt their services in order to provide what their users want when and how they want it (Association of College and Research Libraries 2011). The increased use of mobile devices such as smart phones and tablet PCs are among the tools students will use to quickly and conveniently access the information and resources they need, and libraries must be ready to meet that challenge.

FACULTY SERVICES AND SCHOLARLY COMMUNICATION

Once considered the "handmaidens" to scholarship, today's librarians are more akin to personal coaches, brought in when needed by faculty who have learned to appreciate how they can assist in raising performance levels. They work hard at keeping them up to date with new developments, teaching them new ways of working, introducing new equipment, and setting higher goals. Faculty members who opt to go it alone may find themselves outperformed.

In his 2009 article for the *Journal of Academic Librarianship*, Pongracz Sennyey and his co-authors talk about the changing staffing patterns brought about by the increasing digitization of library collections and the expanded use of outsourcing library services. They make the point that maintaining the old print collections was a hands-on process that made experts of the library staff at all levels. Traditional in-house activities such as acquisitions, selection, cataloging, circulation, and inter-library loan services kept the library staff firmly in place as the "experts" standing between the faculty and the collections. Many of these processes and services are now outsourced or automated. Books arrive in shelf-ready condition—selected, acquired, cataloged, and processed remotely. Digital content is made available directly to library users with only minimal intervention of library staff. All of this, added to the plethora of digital resources such as blogs, alert services, and RSS feeds, allow Sennyey to conclude that researchers may now be just as expert at finding information as librarians once were (Sennyey, Ross, and Mills 2009, 255).

Our own observations, though, have shown that while faculty may be in a position to be as knowledgeable as the library staff, there is no guarantee that they actually are. Even the most dedicated and plugged-in faculty members have only so much time to constantly scan their digital environment for items relevant to their research. They may find themselves dependent on a few RSS feeds or blogs that result in too narrow a focus. Subject specialist librarians still have a role to provide any number of information services. We may no longer be the gatekeepers, but we are very expert coaches.

Pongracz Sennyey and his co-authors make the case that the new digital/out-sourced environment creates an opportunity to redirect staffing in more valuable ways. They call for more proactive services such as liaison programs, literacy programs, outreach activities, website development, digitization projects, institutional repositories, and publishing programs, as well as enhanced research commons facilities and services (Sennyey, Ross, and Mills 2009).

It was common in the past for subject specialists to keep office hours in the academic departments to which they were assigned. This practice made it possible to interact on a regular basis and in informal ways with the faculty, thus maintaining a higher profile and keeping track of faculty and graduate student needs. The new reality calls for even more aggressive practices. The term du jour is *embedding*. Librarians cannot sit passively at the reference desk or in their offices waiting for a request for information to come by. Those little "Ask a Librarian" pop-up menus look very sad and neglected on most library websites. Nor can librarians throw together a website or blog and hope someone will notice it.

After an anthropological study was done at the University of Rochester to fully understand how faculty and students do their work, many changes were implemented in the library's service model as well as its web presence. One example is the addition of pictures of assigned subject specialists to automated course management web pages along with contact information and links to recommended resources (Carlson 2007).

Push technology transforms passive service into proactive library service. Librarians must position themselves so as to anticipate faculty needs and design a suite of services around those needs. Then they must publicize and market those products and services. To a certain extent, librarians must even create the need. David Lewis writes about the need in the 21st century for librarians to insinuate their expertise into all aspects of teaching and learning (Lewis 2007, 425). Others take it even further. A recent ALA/ACRL publication on advocacy included a chapter titled "Using Interactive Technologies to Reassert Library Value." In it, the term *predatory reference* is introduced. It is attributed to Bill Pardue of Arlington Heights Memorial Library in Illinois (Welburn, Welburn, and McNeil 2010, 139). Pardue was the impetus behind the "Slam the Boards" movement of 2007 in which librarians across the country took it upon themselves, on a prearranged date, to answer as many questions as possible on popular answer boards such as Yahoo! Answers. The point to this exercise has been to include a tag line after each answer asserting that the question had been handled by a professional librarian, thus demonstrating the value of a professional.

Another example of predatory reference is the proactive participation in the writing and editing of Wikipedia articles by librarians. Aside from authoring articles, librarians have been enriching existing articles by providing ISBNs, citations to source materials, additional links, and so forth. Librarians have also been adding links to their own institution's catalogs, digital resources, and websites to encourage use (Welburn, Welburn, and McNeil 2010, 141).

What we see happening at the community college level is the linking of units such as "Centers for Teaching and Learning" to the library or learning resource center. At Moraine Valley Community College in Illinois, the Dean of Academic Development and Learning Resources position oversees a collaborative unit that "is committed to supporting faculty and staff and providing professional development opportunities to all Moraine Valley employees so that innovative learning-centered instruction and services can be provided to our students and community" (http://www.morainevalley.edu/CTL/). This is a natural combination of services and resources that benefits all parties and a trend that will only continue to expand in the future. In a recent interview, Leslie Warren, an Associate Professor and Information Literacy Librarian at Moraine Valley, described the work of this unit as supporting the mission of the college, facilitating communication, and placing librarians in leadership positions within the context of teaching and learning. The librarians work with instructional designers to develop workshops on copyright, instructional technology, and online learning (e-mail correspondence with the author, January 11, 2011).

The fact that this combined unit reports to an administrative position requiring an MLS degree is significant. It indicates that the college administration views the library as a leader within the organization, uniquely suited to managing this kind of service to the faculty and staff, a view that bodes well for the future.

This leads to a subject of tremendous concern within the library profession, that of scholarly communication (the production and dissemination of knowledge). Several circumstances that have been building for decades and have only been exacerbated by the rise of the digital scholarship include the on-going cancellation of journal and database subscriptions; the failure of small, nonprofit publishers as a result of flagging sales; the slow demise of scholarly societies as memberships drop; and the impact of slow sales on monographic publishing at even the larger imprints. All of these conditions are discussed in a 2009 study published by the ARL (Lowry 2009) and can be tied to the economic recession of the early

21st century. As universities feel the pinch, librarians must face budget reductions in all areas of operations. Collection budgets are reduced, impacting monograph, serials, and database collecting and access. The costs of these reductions are then passed on to publishing houses and scholarly societies that create knowledge. What we see happening is the movement away from print toward digital publishing, away from the proprietary toward open education resources. The ACRL study concludes that there will be a continued need in the future for libraries to reinvent themselves and their staff members. Diversity, new skills development, and an entrepreneurial spirit will allow librarians to take leadership roles in the future of academia (Lowry 2009, 8).

One excellent example of a research library providing this service to the greater academic community is that of the "Scholarly Communication" pages available at the University of Illinois' library website. They offer a comprehensive guide to the subject, covering issues such as author's rights, copyright awareness, support for new-model publishing initiatives, research alerts for current awareness, citation management support, and a scholarly communication blog. The University of Illinois also operates an online archive for scholarly works called IDEALS (Illinois Digital Environment for Access to Learning and Scholarship), "which collects, disseminate, and provides persistent and reliable access to the research and scholarship of the University of Illinois faculty, staff, and students" (www.library.illinois.edu/scholcomm/SCServices.html).

Librarians will continue to collaborate with faculty at ever greater levels as they enter into new areas such as publishing support and repository services. To do so, librarians are also entering into partnerships with other units on campus as well as other institutions (Lowry 2009, 9). It is this very process of reaching out into new areas of services, creating new resources, and seeking new opportunities for collaboration that will keep libraries at the heart of the organizations they serve. Activist librarians push their services, anticipate needs, and publicize their successes.

INFORMATION COMMONS

The concept of library as space, both physical and virtual, has become the subject of much discussion and debate (Gayton 2008; Webster 2010). Information commons are springing up in universities and colleges nationwide, providing both individual and collaborative opportunities for students and faculty. Is this really a new idea, or have academic libraries always been a gathering place for students and faculty engaged in research? Are they adopting the current bookstore model of comfy chairs and cafes, or is library space simply evolving into learning space? How will this affect future services, resource access, and facilities in academic libraries?

The days of the library as being a place where quiet and scholarly pursuits were fiercely enforced are disappearing. Many academic librarians realize the need for additional computers and study space for users, which has resulted in the growth of electronic collections, remote storage for seldom used materials, and the expansion of social areas available to students in the library. There are several schools of thought on this issue: the concept of social versus communal space in academic libraries. Gayton defines the social model as being "a library in which students and faculty collaborate and communicate with each other in the creation of new knowledge" (Gayton 2008). Do cafes and other social spaces, such as information commons facilities, undermine and detract from the communal spirit of the academic library? How is space related to students' research and learning activities?

A space study done at Queensland Library by Jordan and Ziebell concluded that, while students are heavy consumers of online resources, they still value the library as a learning space, and students spent most of their time in the library using computers and quiet study spaces (Webster 2010). Most chose to work in the library for reasons of convenience and availability of study space. Students were regular library visitors. All respondents put location, atmosphere, and study space above social reasons for visiting the library (Webster 2010; Moncrieff, Macauley, and Epps 2007). Another interesting result of the study was the prominence of the library in students' lives: "nearly 60%visit a library each day," with approximately half spending anywhere from 30–120 minutes and "almost a quarter spending more than two hours in the library" (Webster 2010).In an interesting conversation recently taking place in the blogosphere, Brian Mathews, assistant university librarian at the University of California at Santa Barbara, poses the following scenario: What will become of the Information Commons as we now understand them as mobile devices, such as the iPad, smart phones, and netbooks, become more and more prevalent? Will librarians still see a need to provide hundreds of desktop computers (which require frequent, expensive updating and maintenance), or will they begin to divest themselves of these bulky units? What then will the Information Commons become (Young 2010)?

Additional features students identified as important were group study rooms, wireless networks, and TV monitors and projectors; during exam periods they suggested access to "break-out areas with soft furnishings, couches, coffee and fresh air" (Webster 2010). It is evident that academic librarians must reconsider space use in their libraries and take into account the needs of their users by providing the right forum, ambience, and flexibility needed by students to be successful.

LIBRARY BUILDING AS UNIVERSITY CENTER

Academic librarians contribute to higher education in a variety of ways. They build collections that support faculty research activities; provide "library services and resources that support institutional engagement in service to their communities" (ACRL Research Planning and Review Committee 2010) by providing reliable, valid, and valuable information to community members; build special collections in their libraries, which can result in attracting prestigious faculty and research projects; and create strong, award-winning libraries that may impact the university/college's rank by bringing attention to the institution.

Library instruction continues to be one of the strongest links between academic librarians and faculty, primarily through instruction sessions, library guides, online tutorials, and guest lectures. Librarians select resources that are integrated into course materials and that support teaching and learning, and many contribute to their institutions by partnering with learning support centers and student affairs staff (ACRL Research Planning and Review Committee 2010); they support faculty research productivity in terms of scholarly needs related to tenure and promotion; and librarians assist faculty engaged in grant writing and other research funding activities by providing library resources for citations and other relevant materials.

As academic libraries continue to change and evolve with respect to services, technology, and collections, it is of paramount importance that librarians illustrate their worth to faculty and students by improving and honing their skills (Howard 2010). The role of academic librarians has changed substantially in recent years and will likely continue to do so as new technologies are introduced and patrons become more sophisticated users of information resources and tools. Given this scenario, it is obvious that continuing education opportunities for librarians and staff are crucial to the success of academic libraries; library administrators must support staff training and professional development initiatives despite recent economic challenges.

Universities and colleges have recently begun developing centers for teaching, learning, and technology, providing faculty development resources such as continuing education opportunities in the form of workshops, seminars, and conferences; professional networks for sharing best practices; instructional development grant opportunities; and leadership development (ACRL Research Planning and Review Committee 2010).

It is unfortunate that such centers are generally created without the participation and/or input of librarians, another signal that they must be more proactive, perhaps even forceful, in sharing their expertise and illustrating their worth in higher education. They must be part of the conversation early on in such initiatives and consider supporting teaching and learning efforts by creating space in their libraries for faculty and students to engage in the production of scholarship. If librarians are to truly participate as major stakeholders in their institutions, they must insert themselves into the professional lives of all those they serve and instruct and consistently provide them with exceptional services, resources, technologies, and support.

LOOKING DOWN THE ROAD

Just as our parent institutions prepare enrollment and budget projections, librarians have to position themselves to engage in strategic thinking. It is not enough to have a realistic grasp on our present realities and challenges. As a profession we must also do our best to gauge our future reality. The plans we make in the present will have an impact on the directions we take in the future. With this in mind, ACRL has published a new study titled *Futures Thinking for Academic Librarians: Higher Education in 2025* (Staley and Malenfant 2010). The 25 scenarios presented in this study use current academic trends as a springboard off of which to jump into the theoretical future. They range from the highly probable to the wildly improbable and too awful to contemplate. Some would have very high impact on our institutions, while other would have less of an impact. The ACRL study forecasts, for example, the rise of the nontraditional student, the continued growth of distance education programs, and the expansion of lifelong learning services—all phenomena that have become quite familiar in our present realities.

Several of ALA's divisions and sections have already established guidelines for services to many of these nontraditional user groups. One example is the recently revised guidelines issued by ALA's Reference and User Services Association, which has a committee looking at services for aging populations ("Guidelines" 2008).

The ACRL study goes on to predict a widening economic divide between haves and have-nots on campus, signifying that more undergraduate students will arrive at college needing remedial information instruction. The real challenge lies in persuading those students that they don't already know everything they need to know. Melissa Gross, in a 2005 article for *Reference and Users Services Quarterly*, warns us that inadequate information literacy skills impacts not only our users' outcomes but also how well they are able to assess the value of available library services and resources (Gross 2005, 155). One can take that step forward and say that the need for remedial information-seeking skills training goes beyond undergraduate students to include faculty and university administration. Any library advocacy effort aimed at college administrators must include a component of information literacy skills instruction. Students cannot be expected to assess or value what they do not comprehend or have never utilized. The dedicated library leader, therefore, seeks teachable moments at every committee meeting, board meeting, and lunch date.

Futures Thinking predicts the emerging use of "pop-up" campuses or temporary or removable educational facilities that are placed strategically for a period of time and then removed as needed and the pervasiveness of hand-held devices and the dominance of virtual services. Any one of these scenarios can be dealt with by engaging existing technology and only slightly modifying our service models. So far, so good, but how should we confront the growing privatization of college facilities ("this library brought to you by Groupon!") or the increased use of outsourcing (e.g., LSSI, Inc.) to salvage institutional budgets? Will we survive the disappearance of tenure, the collapse of the textbook monopoly, and the growth of Open Education Resources in which faculty, with the blessing of their institutions, create course materials and share them openly online?[1]

The answer, of course, is yes. We will not only survive but thrive, if only because librarianship as a profession is already beginning the evaluative and transformational process needed to do so. A glance at any recent conference program demonstrates the incredible depth and breadth of our intellectual inquiry as a profession.

One caveat to bear in mind is discussed by Susan Stickley in her recent ARL report (Stickley 2010) in which she explores the viability of higher education itself. For college and research libraries to survive, their librarians must come to the assistance of the institutions with which they are affiliated. All of the economic and technological tsunamis that impact our libraries first assault our parent organizations. As a profession, we must not look only to our own survival but that of our entire organization (Stickley 2010, 7). Among the participants in this ARL study, there was quite a lot of concern over the current "disinvestment in the humanities" and the move toward vocational education over the purely theoretical (Stickley 2010, 8). This shift can be seen quite clearly in our own struggle to brand our profession. The debate over library science vs. information science may never be decided to the satisfaction of all. (For a more in-depth discussion of this issue please refer to Bill Crowley's (2008) monograph, *Renewing Professional Librarianship: A Fundamental Rethinking*).

What is of most interest in the ACRL study is the assessment of each future scenario by members of the association. In many cases the librarians responding to the survey see opportunities for new service models and a strengthening of the role of libraries and library specialists embedded within each scenario. Demonstrating not so much a Pollyanna approach to the future as a courageous, "bring it on" attitude, librarians stand ready. As long as librarians continue to look forward and outward, as long as they become ever more engaged within their institutions and larger communities, and as long as they then come together as a profession to discuss possible options and create new service models, the future holds no threat.

NOTE

1. For more information on the OER movement here and abroad see Gutenplan (2010). Gutenplan's article describes the explosive growth of the OER movement among wealthy universities in this country (e.g., Harvard, Yale, Stanford, Michigan) and many Open Education institutions in Europe (e.g., Britain, Netherlands, and Catalonia).

REFERENCES

ACRL Research Planning and Review Committee. 2010. "2010 Top Trends in Academic Libraries: A Review of the Current Literature." *College and Research Library News* 71(6): 286–92.

Association of College and Research Libraries. 2011. Conference Program website. Accessed March 2, 2012. http://www.goeshow.com/acrl/national/2011/conference_sched ule.cfm.

Bjatti, Rubina. 2009. "Teacher-Librarian Collaboration in University Libraries: A Selective Review." *Pakistan Library and Information Science Journal* 40(2): 3–12.

Carlson, Scott. 2007. "An Anthropologist in the Library." *Chronicle of Higher Education* 53(50): A26. Accessed March 2, 2012. http://chronicle.com/article/An-Anthropologist-in-the/22071/.

Crowley, Bill. 2008. *Renewing Professional Librarianship: A Fundamental Rethinking.* Westport, CT: Libraries Unlimited.

Gayton, Jeffrey T. 2008. "Academic Libraries: 'Social' or 'communal?' The Nature and Future of Academic Libraries." *Journal of Academic Librarianship* 34(1): 60–66.

Gross, Melissa. 2005. "The Impact of Low-level Skills on Information-seeking Behavior: Implications of Competency Theory for Research and Practice." *Reference and User Services Quarterly* 45(2): 155–62.

"Guidelines for Library and Information Services to Older Adults." 2008. American Library Association. September 29. Accessed March 2, 2012. http://www.ala.org/rusa/resources/guidelines/libraryservices.

Gutenplan, D. D. 2010. "For Exposure, Universities Put Courses on the Web." *New York Times* (November 1). Accessed March 2, 2012. http://www.nytimes.com/2010/11/01/world/europe/01iht-educLede01.html?pagewanted=all.

Howard, Jennifer. 2010. "A Tool Kit to Help Academic Librarians Demonstrate Their Value." *The Chronicle of Higher Education* (September 14). Accessed March 2, 2012. http://chronicle.com/article/A-Tool-Kit-to-Help-Academic/124391/.

Jankowska, Maria Anna, and James W. Marcum. 2010. "Sustainability Challenge for Academic Libraries: Planning for the Future. *College and Research Libraries* 71(2): 160–70.

Kolowich, Steve. 2011. "What Students Don't Know." *Inside Higher Ed.* (August 22). Accessed March 2, 2012. http://www.insidehighered.com/news/2011/08/22/erial_study_of_student_research_habits_at_illinois_university_libraries_reveals_alar mingly_poor_information_literacy_and_skills.

Kyrillidou, Martha. 2010. "Library Value May Be Proven, if Not Self-Evident." *Research Library Issues: A Bimonthly Report from ARL, CNI, and SPARC* 271: 1–3. http://www.arl.org/resources/pubs/rli/archive/rli271.shtml.

Lewis, David W. 2007. "A Strategy for Academic Libraries in the First Quarter of the 21st Century." *College and Research Libraries* 68(5): 418–34. Accessed March 2, 2012. https://scholarworks.iupui.edu/bitstream/handle/1805/1592/Strategy%20 for%20Academic%20Libraries%20Article.pdf?sequence=1.

Loesch, Martha Fallahay. 2010. "Librarian as Professor: A Dynamic New Role Model." *Education Libraries* 33(1): 31–37.

Lowry, Charles B., Prudence Adler, Karla Hahn, and Crit Stuart. 2009. Transformational Times: An Environment Scan Prepared for the ARL Strategic Plan Review Task Force. Washington, DC: Association of Research Libraries. Accessed March 2, 2012. www.arl.org/bm~doc/transformational-times.pdf.

Mays, Regina, Carol Tenopir, and Paula Kaufman. 2010. "Lib-Value: Measuring Value and Return on Investment of Academic Libraries." *Research Libraries Issues* 271: 36–40. Accessed March 2, 2012. http://www.arl.org/bm~doc/rli271-libvalue.pdf.

Moncrieff, Joan, Peter Macauley, and Janine Epps. 2007. "My Universe Is Here: Implications for the Future of Academic Libraries from the Results of a Survey of Researchers." *Australian Academic and Research Libraries* 38(2): 71–83.

Mullins, James L., Frank R. Allen, and John R. Hufford. 2007. "Top Ten Assumptions for the Future of Academic Libraries and Librarians: A Report from the ACRL Research Committee." *College and Research Libraries* News 68(4): 1–2.

Oakleaf, Megan. 2010. *The Value of Academic Libraries: A Comprehensive Research Review and Report.* Chicago: ALA/ACRL.

O'Connor, Steve, and Lai-chong Au. 2008. "Steering a Future through Scenarios: Into the Academic Library of the Future." *Journal of Academic Librarianship* 35(1): 57–64.

Sennyey, Pongracz, Lyman Ross, and Caroline Mills. 2009. "Exploring the Future of Academic Libraries: A Definitional Approach." *Journal of Academic Librarianship* 35(3): 252–59.

Shuler, John A. 2007. "Information Policy: The Civic Value of Academic Libraries and the Open Source University." *Journal of Academic Librarianship* 33(2): 301–3.

Staley, David J., and Kara J Malenfant. 2010. *Futures Thinking for Academic Librarians: Higher Education in 2025.* Chicago: American Library Association, Association of College and Research Libraries.

Stickley, Susan. 2010. "Preparing for the Future Scenario Planning Process." Association of Research Libraries. Accessed March 2, 2012. http://www.arl.org/bm~doc/scenarios-data-gathering-summary-082010.pdf.

Todaro, Julie. 2006. "The Power of Persuasion: Grassroots Advocacy in the Academic Library." *College and Research Libraries News* 67(4): 228–29, 268.

Webster, Keith. 2010. "The Library Space as Learning Space." EDUCAUSE Review 45(6): 10–11.

Welburn, William C., Janice Welburn, and Beth McNeil, eds. 2010. *Advocacy, Outreach, and the Nation's Academic Libraries: A Call for Action.* Chicago: American Library Association, Association of College and Research Libraries.

Young, Jeff. 2010. "If Libraries Remove Computers, Will Anyone Come?" Wired Campus. *The Chronicle of Higher Education* (April 29). http://chronicle.com/blogs/wiredcampus/if-libraries-remove-computers-will-anyone-come/23600.

Young, Jeff. 2011. "'Embedded Librarian' on Twitter Served as Information Concierge for Class." Wired Campus. *The Chronicle of Higher Education* (February 25). http://chronicle.com/blogs/wiredcampus/embedded-librarian-on-twitter-served-as-information-concierge-for-class/30000.

7

UNDERSTANDING THE WORTH
OF THE PROFESSIONAL LIBRARIAN
IN THE RESEARCH UNIVERSITY
OR INSTITUTION

Cleo Pappas
University of Illinois at Chicago

INTRODUCTION: INCIDENT AT JOHNS HOPKINS

In June 2001 a healthy research volunteer, Ellen Roche, who had participated in a National Institutes of Health–funded asthma study at Johns Hopkins University, died due to progressive failure of her kidneys and lungs. The principal investigator of the study, Alkis Togias, MD, had performed a literature review on the investigational drug hexamethonium prior to approval of the study by Hopkins' Institutional Review Board (IRB). The search he performed, although labeled as a "good faith effort" by the subsequent investigation, failed to reveal the potential toxicity inherent in inhalation of the drug. In addition to the tragic consequence of Roche's death, the federal Office for Human Research Protections (OHRP) temporarily suspended federally funded research at Hopkins and its affiliates (Steinbrook 2002). The impact of the event had a profound effect on Johns Hopkins, its IRB, and IRBs in general, to say nothing of the financial losses incurred by the university. In addition, a total of 2,400 protocols were temporarily halted, putting the trial participants at risk of not receiving protocol medications (Keiger and De Pasquale 2002).

While the inadequacy of the IRB supervision was a specific criticism of the OHRP, one of the many lessons drawn from this event was to draw attention to the importance of a professionally trained researcher in the clinical investigation process. Investigators failed to uncover previously published research revealing an association between hexamethonium and lung toxicity (McLellan 2001). In addition, the danger of the notion that everything is available on the Internet and can be retrieved by anyone was refuted.

Following the event at Hopkins, the Medical Library Association's (MLA) discussion list Medlib-l asked association members whether they would have been able to make known the dangers inherent in hexamethonium prior to the clinical study's volunteers receiving it. Medical librarians around the country performed what was for them routine searches that quickly revealed relevant articles citing potential adverse effects of the drug, including inhalation dangers and lung toxicity

(Perkins 2001). Interestingly, they discovered this information using databases other than those Dr. Togias used. Togias had used, in addition to PubMed, the open Web, including Google, Yahoo!, LookSmart, and GoTo.com (Perkins 2001). The information that would have saved Roche's life appeared in the medical literature of the 1950s, literature that has only recently been added to PubMed, whose coverage at the time began with the mid-1960s. The medical librarians mined Toxline and Micromedex's Poison Index Toxicologic Management (Perkins 2001).

The purpose of this chapter is to define those areas in which research librarians' special skills and training come in to play, to defend the value of the training that a skilled and degreed librarian employs in the context of highly specialized content areas, and to discuss the impact of the theoretical training degreed librarians receive in accredited schools of library and information science in their real-world library practice within the intensity of a research environment. The rigors of a research environment demand standardized training and practice from its librarians. Trained librarians' skills are transferable across content areas. They move stepwise from selecting appropriate databases, developing search terms that include keywords as well as the concept terms unique to each database, and determining appropriate limits.

Because medical librarians work in an area in which, unless they hold clinical degrees, they are not content specialists, they rely on highly developed search skills to generate comprehensive topic coverage, skills taught in library science reference programs. One of the principles taught in library science reference programs is not to rely on a search restricted to one database, and it is born out in medical research. Lawrence's conclusion was that a single database search will fail to identify anywhere from 16.7–81.5 percent (median 43.4%) of the articles relevant to injury prevention and safety promotion (Lawrence 2008). By practicing this multiple database search, the medical librarians answering the call by Medlib-l not only uncovered but also verified that participants in Togias's research with known lung impairments should never have received hexamethonium via inhalation.

The Accreditation Manual of the American Library Association (ALA) reinforces the principles of quality and standardization of education that accredited library programs offer. It is the *Standards for Accreditation of Master's Programs in Library & Information Studies* (American Library Association, Office of Accreditation 2008) that the Committee on Accreditation (COA) uses to evaluate the degree-granting programs of Library and Information Science institutions. The manual lists six standards, each of which is divided into detailed subdivisions: Mission, Goals, and Objectives; Curriculum; Faculty; Students; Administration and Financial Support; and Physical Resources and Facilities. It is under the Objectives section of the first standard that is stated the main argument for the graduate degree in Library and Information Science. The program's objectives aim to train the students in organization of knowledge and its efficient retrieval (American Library Association, Office of Accreditation 2008, 6). Without such standardized training, an individual may function as a librarian without hewing to the theoretical constructs that explain why processes and procedures exist.

A helpful analogy to a non-MLS librarian may be that of a teacher who has a wealth of content knowledge but has never faced a classroom before the first day of school. The content is there, but the process of how best to retrieve and deliver the content is not.

One of the many important skills included in formalized training of librarians is a basic understanding of the structure of and differences among databases. Most proprietary databases may be searched either using keywords or concept terms. Keyword search retrieval includes those citations that quote the word exactly anywhere in the article. The word appears in the article, but the article is not necessarily *about* the word. A concept search or subject heading search, sometimes called a controlled vocabulary search, requires access to a thesaurus of predetermined vocabulary that has been developed specifically for that database. Every database that allows conceptual searching has such a thesaurus. Thesauri are not easy to find, however, and their contents are not identical. For example, the thesaurus in PubMed is called MeSH; in the Cumulative Index of Nursing and Allied Health Literature (CINAHL), the thesaurus is called CINAHL headings; and in the European counterpart of PubMed, EMBASE, the name is EMBASE Tree.

In addition, controlled vocabulary or terminology in each database may be different. A MeSH search of the keyword "computing" in PubMed leads to the MeSH terms "computing methodologies," "mathematical computing," "medical informatics computing," and "point of care systems." In CINAHL, the first term suggested is "Computers and computerization." In EMBASE, the major term is "computer." Although the research of Chang, Heskett, and Davidson suggests that the best way to search PubMed is to begin with MeSH and then move on to a related articles search, Jenuwine and Floyd's work suggests that the two search strategies should be used together for maximal retrieval (Chang, Heskett, and Davidson 2006; Jenuwine and Floyd 2004).

Skilled librarians also use the "pearl culturing" technique of uncovering additional relevant articles from the seed of one significant article. Pearl culturing may be achieved by related article availability in specific databases, bibliography searches, determining the concept search terms (subject headings) of the chosen article, author searches, and "forward" searching (cited by) searches in Web of Knowledge.

To perform a systematic and comprehensive search of more than one database, a librarian needs to be aware of concept searching, its idiosyncrasies, the value of combining concept searching with keyword searching, a related articles search, pearl culturing, and the effective applications of limits in the method that each database allows them to be put in operation. Such database searching skills are taught in library schools. This allows librarians with a library degree and a new job to land on their feet running rather than learning the idiosyncrasies of proprietary databases during on-the-job training. And, although redundant, it bears repeating that, had Hopkins employed degree-trained librarians in the course of Togias's research, a tragedy may have been averted.

DEFINITION OF A RESEARCH UNIVERSITY

Before proceeding to a discussion of the highly specialized work and environment in which research university librarians function, it may be helpful to establish the definition of a research university. The Carnegie Commission on Higher Education developed a classification system for post-secondary education in 1970. Organized by degree level and specialization, the Carnegie Classification became the tool researchers used to describe an institution's mission. The system has been updated several times and differentiates between Associate's Colleges, Doctorate-granting

Universities, Master's Colleges and Universities, Baccalaureate Colleges, and Special Focus Institutions. Further refinements within Doctorate-granting Universities are now based on research produced and funding awarded. Doctorate-granting universities are so designated because of the number of doctorates they award annually (Carnegie Foundation for the Advancement of Teaching 2012a).

A quick scan of the doctorate-granting universities available through the Carnegie Foundation for the Advancement of Teaching reveals the variety of fields in which doctorates are awarded and, therefore, research is performed. In 409 institutions with doctoral programs, 313 offer degrees in more than one field (Carnegie Foundation for the Advancement of Teaching 2012b). It is important to note that an expert in one of these fields would need to play a quick game of catch-up in the other fields to offer adequate information services and suitable collection development without the theoretical models that formalized librarian training offers. Although the very existence of these classifications within research universities implies a fundamental difference among institutions of higher learning, librarians serving within them confront the same issues.

In addition, librarians within research universities offer curriculum-based instruction within a variety of classroom settings. Such instruction involves grounding in the subject content and the library resources related to that content. Universities do not have enough librarians to have one for every field in which the university performs research and offers higher degrees according to classification. Yet, the processes involved in teaching information literacy are similar across the board. The ALA website uses word "abilities" when defining information literacy, suggesting that it involves a compendium of skills rather than content (American Library Association, Association of College and Research Libraries 2006). It is significant that this definition offers the generic term *information* that may be applied to multiple fields. Librarianship teaches information literacy as a skill that is transferable among multiple content areas.

MEDICAL LIBRARIANSHIP

Medical librarians work in medical centers, hospitals, medical associations, and academic medical colleges, supporting the work of clinicians, researchers, and health consumers. Identified as a distinct profession in 1939, Columbia University held the first course in medical librarianship in 1948. Schacher described the evolution of clinical librarianship, a highly specialized niche within medical librarianship (Schacher 2001). Clinical librarians participate in walking rounds with physicians, research questions that arise in patient care, and attend morning report. Research on Clinical Medical Librarian (CML) services finds them timely and efficient, assisting in clinical decision making, revealing information resources unfamiliar to clinical practitioners, enhancing the practice of evidence-based medicine, and economical (Vaughn 2009).

Besides being able to perform timely and efficient searches, clinical librarians are able to summarize the information retrieved from medical databases, point out conflicting or contradictory findings within the literature, and anticipate subsequent questions that will arise. The ability to anticipate problems before they arise is especially helpful in a research environment. It may include everything from being aware of the chronic diseases physicians are treating and creating alerts in various databases regarding newly developed therapies, drugs, and other modalities that may be on the research horizon to suggesting that clinicians (doctors or nurses) involved in hospital quality improvement (QI) initiatives research completely the IRB process just in case they want to take their results out of their institutional walls by publishing or presenting at conferences.

Medical librarians function as teachers, instructing attending physicians, residents, and medical students in search strategies and working as consultants with researchers. This author regularly experiences the irony of the teaching role of clinical librarianship. As end users, in this instance physicians and nurses, become more proficient in searching, the questions they bring to librarians tend to be the difficult questions involving highly complex or time-consuming searches. As the Johns Hopkins incident tragically demonstrates, what may seem to be a simple search may require the unique perspective and skill of a trained librarian rather than a content expert.

Furthermore, even within the relatively small niche of medical librarianship there lie distinct and unique areas. At the author's university, medical librarians serve the university medical center, the College of Medicine, the College of Nursing, the College of Dentistry, the College of Pharmacy, and the College of Applied Health Sciences. Each field requires knowledge of specialized databases, subscriptions to content-rich periodicals, and familiarity with a different set of professional associations. Health fields each maintain a unique perspective toward their specialty. It is common anecdotally to hear that physicians are data driven while nurses are more holistic in outlook; additionally, the field of Disability and Human Development rejects the medical model altogether, having adopted an advocacy model echoing the civil rights movement of the 1960s from which many of its leaders emanate (Bickenbach et al. 1999). Working successfully with such a variety of clientele requires specific training that library programs offer in reference classes that teach the reference interview process and in access services classes that emphasize public service.

EMBEDDED LIBRARIANS

The Special Libraries Association (SLA) funded an 18 month research grant in 2007 to explore the Embedded Librarian model, to define it, to uncover those innovations and characteristics that enhance services provided under the model, and to make recommendations regarding its successful implementation (Shumaker and Talley 2009). Methods included surveys, site visits, and a literature study. The sample for the study was the membership of SLA: 11,000 members from 75 countries.

The authors of the report discovered several layers of description for *embeddedness,* including academic librarians involved in curriculum-integrated instruction, librarians working in research-dedicated institutions, and clinical medical librarians. For the majority of the report, the authors examined librarianship performed by "those who provide specialized services within their organizations" (Shumaker and Talley 2009, 4). Their activities included "collaborating and contributing to their customers' work," meeting regularly to discuss information needs, providing training, reporting to and collaborating with senior administration of the customer area, devoting time to continuing education in the customer area of expertise or subject knowledge, and participating in the customers' electronic work spaces such as email, wikis, and blogs (Shumaker and Talley 2009, 5).

The results of the study most pertinent to this discussion are that 84 percent of the embedded librarians reported holding an ALA-accredited Master's in Library or Information Science. This number supports how important the degree is within the concept of embeddedness.

CONFIDENTIALITY/HIPAA

Long before the Health Insurance Portability and Accountability Action (HIPAA) of 1996 (P.L.104–191) was enacted, librarians have been trained to maintain confidentiality in all librarian–patron interactions. The ALA explicitly defends all patrons' right to privacy and "uninhibited access to information" and has done so since its 1939 Code of Ethics for Librarians (ALA 2007). The right to privacy extends to "closed-stack call slips, computer sign-up sheets, circulation records, web sites visited, reserve notices, or research notes." Every library is encouraged by ALA to develop a local privacy policy. "The Code of Fair Information Practices" developed by the U.S. Department of Health, Education, and Welfare Secretary's Advisory Committee (1973) evolved from five principles, including the avoidance of secret record keeping and the prohibition of not allowing individuals access to information within their own records.

Furthermore, the political climate post–9/11 resulted in the Patriot Act, which has grave implications for library policies (Jaeger et al. 2004). A thorough grounding in the theory behind confidentiality policy is a prerequisite for navigating the minefield the Patriot Act has created.

Library privacy laws are determined at the state level (Nicholson and Smith 2007). Yet, not all libraries have developed confidentiality policies, and federal laws supersede state laws (Magi 2007, 458). This is alarming when one study performed collaboratively by the Vermont Department of Libraries and the Vermont Library Association revealed that their librarians had received in one year approximately 1,228 requests for personally identifiable information about an individual's use of library resources (Magi 2007, 462). The same study found that libraries "at which the director holds the Master of Library Science (MLS) degree are more likely to have written policies than are libraries with smaller staffs and libraries at which the director does not hold the MLS degree" (Magi 2007, 464). The importance that directors who hold an MLS place on such a written policy underscores the notion that, because such confidentiality is counterintuitive to the otherwise transparent policies of libraries, a content specialist would need to be trained specifically in its provisions and reinforces the breadth of training that MLS programs offer.

COPYRIGHT

In the digital age instructors face the hurdle of teaching students who are used to copying and pasting from their e-mails, Facebook, and blogs without worrying about or comprehending the concept of intellectual property and plagiarism. Although instructors make efforts of varying stringency to curb plagiarism, it is falling to librarians to assist students to determine when to use quote marks, when to cite an original author, and under what circumstances they need do neither. In addition, libraries need to observe copyright law when utilizing or providing interlibrary loan services and when making electronic reserves available for distance learning. Copyright law affects librarians involved in curriculum-integrated instruction and in access services.

The No Electronic Theft Act (NET Act) (1997) allows criminal prosecution for violation of copyright breaches whether or not the act results in financial gain. Signed into law in 1997, the NET Act stiffened previous law, which did not punish individuals engaged in copyright violation if there was no profit. The NET Act includes provisions for a maximum of five years in prison and $250,000 in fines.

In 1998 President Clinton signed the Digital Millennium Copyright Act (DMCA). The law makes it illegal to create software that is able to control access to works under copyright. (For example, it is illegal to make a copy of a movie in DVD format.) The law also offers protection to online service providers whose subscribers violate copyright law. The DMCA protects the audio and video creations of the entertainment industry. "A Citizen's Legal Guide to the Digital Millennium Copyright Act" is available online to answer inquiries regarding media and to offer pro bono legal resources (New Media Rights 2007). In 2002, President George W. Bush signed the Technology, Education, and Copyright Harmonization Act (TEACH). The law deals specifically with the parameters instructors teaching a distance education class must comply when performing or displaying copyrighted works (Copyright Clearance Center 2012). Several universities have developed full-fledged courses about copyright aimed at librarians with the purpose of clarifying the issues of copyright for instructors' fair use of materials and for students' correct citation practice.

In March 2010 Harvard University's Berkman Center for Internet and Society (2010) announced the opening of its free program Copyright for Librarians. Developed in conjunction with Electronic Information for Libraries (eIFL.net), Copyright for Librarians seeks to clarify copyright law as it exists today and as it most affects libraries, as well as to expand future policies regarding copyright. The ALA has published *Complete Copyright: An Everyday Guide for Librarians* by Carrie Russell (2004) as a resource for libraries. The Purdue Online Writing Lab (OWL) includes a module on avoiding plagiarism (Purdue University 2012). Understanding and implementing the evolution of copyright requirements in the digital age requires awareness, training, and time devoted exclusively to its study. Librarians who observe copyright principles keep signs stating the laws next to copy and scanning machines as reminders to patrons and staff. Research libraries whose collections tend to be large often serve as resource libraries for local and state consortia, filling interlibrary loan requests on a frequent and regular basis. The librarian in charge of interlibrary loan and document delivery must be thoroughly grounded in copyright principles that determine how many copies from a specific journal may be loaned before copyright is violated.

SCHOLARLY COMMUNICATION

Scholarly communication includes the topics of open access initiatives and institutional repositories. Open access can be a thorny issue in research institutions where faculty who vie for tenure are required to publish in refereed journals. Although some major areas of expertise such as cancer, pediatrics, and physics have long recognized open access publishing, most academic journals of high impact factor are based on a subscriber model. The impact factor of journals is calculated by dividing the number of citations to articles published in a certain year by the number of articles published in that same year (Institute for Scientific Information 2005). It behooves faculty who are facing tenure juries to have their publications in journals with a high impact factor to demonstrate their influence on their field.

Several factors are surfacing that dictate a revisiting of this procedure. Impact factor is computed by Thomson Reuter's Journal Citation Reports (JCR). For a brief but interesting discussion of the criticisms of impact factor, see "Not-so-Deep Impact" (2005). The increasing prices of subscription journals are leading to fewer libraries being able to afford them. Research libraries, yet, are bound to maintain subscriptions to those journals in which their faculty publish. In addition to the expense involved in the acquisition of such journals, the creation and maintenance of institutional repositories is inhibited by publishers' keeping or embargoing copyright of articles. SHERPA, a consortium of research universities dedicated to "opening access to research" (http://www.sherpa.ac.uk/index.html) maintains RoMEO, a database that cites publishers' copyright and self-archiving policies. Furthermore, The Federal Research Public Access Act (FRPAA), H.R. 5037 and S. 1373 requires federal agencies with large research portfolios to allow public access to the results of that research. Such research would be available without charge within six months of its publication within a journal. The "National Institutes of Health Public Access Policy" already requires that scientists whose research is federally funded be published within the public archives of PubMed Central upon acceptance for publication (U.S. Department of Health and Human Services, National Institutes of Health 2012).

A master's program in library science that meets the standard of maintaining currency in relevant issues will prepare the librarian to deal with faculty resistance to the open access issue by providing a theoretical grounding in the reasons for it, as well as prepare the librarian to develop or participate in the process of an institutional repository.

EVIDENCE-BASED LIBRARY AND INFORMATION PRACTICE

In 2000 Jonathan Eldredge wrote a seminal article on evidence-based librarianship (Eldredge 2000). In the article, Eldredge demonstrates how the principles of evidence-based medicine (EBM) and evidence-based health care (EBHC) can be applied to health sciences librarianship. Previously, then MLA president J. Michael Homan had called for evidence-based librarianship (EBL) as a desirable goal (Homan 2000). Eldredge stated that the decision-making roles of librarians need to be based on the best researched evidence possible, the guiding principle of EBM. EBM is defined as "the conscientious, explicit and judicious use of current best evidence in making decisions about the care of the individual patient. It means integrating individual clinical expertise with the best available external clinical evidence from systematic research" (Sackett 1996). Eldredge contends that evidence-based librarianship offers a systematic strategy for making decisions regarding reference provision, collection development, and staff training.

Since 2006, the publication of *Evidence Based Library and Information Practice* (EBLIP), an open access, peer-reviewed journal published quarterly by the University of Alberta Learning Services (2012), has provided a forum for examining and publishing current research in the EBL process.

Although it is not impossible, it is unlikely that a content specialist would be inclined to perform and publish research in the librarianship area. But it is very likely that that the graduate of an MLS degree program would be interested in contributing to his/her profession by performing primary research in the field.

GREY LITERATURE

Knowing that grey literature exists, knowing where to find it, and understanding how to evaluate it are skills that require training, continuing education, collegial cooperation and collaboration, time, and effort. Grey literature refers to that literature that is not indexed by proprietary databases. It tends to be written in English and may consist of research in its earliest forms. The ALA says of Grey Literature that "It is commonly defined as any documentary material that is not commercially published and is typically composed of technical reports, working papers, business documents, and conference proceedings" (Mathews 2004). Research reveals that there is a tremendous amount of information presented at conferences that is never published (von Elm et al. 2003). Finding aids for grey literature are not always immediately apparent (Weintraub 2006). Grey literature demands that the searcher apply rigorous evaluation skills in its discovery and its appraisal (Weintraub 2006). Doctoral students, faculty presenting at national and international conferences, and clinicians researching orphan illnesses are some of the clientele for whom grey literature is crucial.

INFORMATION LITERACY, HEALTH INFORMATION LITERACY, HEALTH LITERACY

The ALA defines *information literacy* as "a set of abilities requiring individuals to recognize when information is needed and have the ability to locate, evaluate, and use effectively the needed information" (American Library Association 1989). The National Library of Medicine awarded the Medical Library Association funds to conduct a Health Information Literacy Project in 2006. The project was aimed at hospital libraries, and its goal was to determine the value administrators and health care providers put on consumer health information and the role that librarians can play in educating consumers (Shipman, Kurtz-Rossi, and Funk 2009). Part of the project involved the development of a curriculum project still in existence that trains librarians in the impact health information literacy has on patient/consumer health and safety (Medical Library Association 2012b). As a result of the project, participants became aware of consumer health resources that the National Library of Medicine provides and became more responsive to the importance of health information literacy. Furthermore, they recognized the unique role that hospital librarians play in patient health and safety (Shipman, Kurtz-Rossi, and Funk 2009, 1). What is relevant to our argument is that this was a librarian-driven research project that benefited health consumers.

INSTITUTIONAL REVIEW BOARDS (IRB)

The purpose of an IRB is to protect the human subjects who participate in research. IRBs are federally mandated and governed by the Office for Human Research Protections (OHRP) under the purview of the Department of Health and Human Services (http://www.hhs.gov/ohrp/). All researchers must register their research protocols with their institution's IRB prior to conducting their research. Research universities also require education in the history behind and implementation of IRBs by all faculty members. Such education must be updated on a regular basis to maintain currency in regulations. Research universities take IRBs very seriously as violation or noncompliance can and has shut down institutional research that is a major source of institutional revenue. Librarians who are on a tenure track and, thus, expected to perform original research and publication complete the IRB process for their own research, a skill that enables them to counsel their patrons as they pursue the process.

CONCLUSION

In conclusion, the argument for master's degree–trained librarians may be enhanced by comparing content expertise versus librarianship to several knowledge versus skill scenarios. Imagine the physician, scientist, or biologist who knows every aspect of the human body but who has never held a scalpel. He knows where everything is, and, if he has ever eaten a steak, he knows how to use a knife. Yet, I doubt anyone would want him operating.

Alternatively, envision the musicologist or music historian who cannot play an instrument. These persons may know the biography of all the important composers, the theory behind their work, and the historical era in which they composed. Nevertheless, although each may be an excellent performance critic, neither would be able to perform.

Finally, envision the teacher of whom we spoke earlier who had never faced a class before the first day of school. In each of these instances, there is information that the individual cannot utilize appropriately because of the lack of a specific skill set. The processes involved in information delivery, behavior management, and documentation are skills that cannot be learned on the fly, skills that years of practice and theoreticians have standardized into a core curriculum.

The skills that the MLS teaches include an understanding of various schemes for the organization of knowledge. Such organization provides the fundamental understanding for efficient retrieval; retrieval that may be sensitive, catching everything on a subject, or specific, revealing only the most relevant results, or both. Database classes offer the skills necessary to manipulate the wide variety of interfaces that proprietary databases use. Reference classes offer techniques for interacting with a wide variety of individuals who will eventually comprise future clientele and emphasize the mantra of customer service. Such classes guarantee to the consumer of library services a uniform standard of performance and excellence.

In the research environment particularly, librarianship is a skill valued by the researchers, authors, conference presenters, physicians, professors, graduate students, and medical students who rely on the librarian's ability to teach them the search skills they need, perform mediated searches when they are in a time crunch or have reached an impasse, and anticipate the challenges they face.

REFERENCES

American Library Association. 1989. *Presidential Committee on Information Literacy: Final Report*. Chicago: American Library Association. Accessed March 2, 2012. http:// www.ala.org/ala/mgrps/divs/acrl/publications/whitepapers/presidential.cfm.

American Library Association. 2007. Privacy Tool Kit. Accessed March 2, 2012. http://www.ala.org/ala/aboutala/offices/oif/iftoolkits/toolkitsprivacy/introduction/introduction.cfm.

American Library Association, Association of College and Research Libraries. 2006. Information Literacy Competency Standards for Higher Education. Accessed March 2, 2012. http://www.ala.org/ala/mgrps/divs/acrl/standards/information literacycompetency.cfm.

American Library Association, Office of Accreditation. 2008. Accreditation of Master's Programs in Library and Information Studies. Accessed March 2, 2012. http://www.ala.org/ala/educationcareers/education/accreditedprograms/standards/standards_2008.pdf.

Association of Research Libraries. 2012. "Mission Statement & Guiding Principles." Accessed March 3, 2012. http://www.arl.org/arl/governance/mission.shtml.

Bickenbach, J. E., et al. 1999. "Models of Disablement, Universalism and the International Classification of Impairments, Disabilities and Handicaps." Social Science and Medicine 48(9): 1173–87.

Carnegie Foundation for the Advancement of Teaching. 2012a. March 2, 2012 Classification Description. Accessed March 2. http://classifications.carnegiefoundation.org/descriptions/basic.php.

Carnegie Foundation for the Advancement of Teaching. 2012b. Graduate Instructional Program Part Two: Institutions with Doctoral Programs. Accessed March 2, 2012. http://classifications.carnegiefoundation.org/downloads/grad_prog_diagram.pdf.

Center for Measuring University Performance. 2012. "The Top American Research Universities." Accessed March 3, 2012. http://mup.asu.edu/research.html.

Chang, A. A., K. M. Heskett, and T. M. Davidson. 2006. "Searching the Literature Using Medical Subject Headings versus Text Word with PubMed." The Laryngoscope 116: 336–40.

Copyright Clearance Center. 2012. "The TEACH Act: New Roles, Rules and Responsibilities for Academic Institutions." Accessed March 3, 2012. http://www.copyright.com/media/pdfs/CR-Teach-Act.pdf.

Digital Millennium Copyright Act of 1998. U.S. Copyright Office Summary. December 1998. Accessed March 3, 2012. http://www.copyright.gov/legislation/dmca.pdf.

Eldredge, J. D. 2000. "Evidence-Based Librarianship: An Overview." Bulletin of the Medical Library Association 88(4): 289–302.

Federal Research Public Access Act (FRPAA), H.R. 5037 and S. 1373. SPARC Accessed March 3, 2012. http://www.arl.org/sparc/advocacy/frpaa/index.shtml.

Harvard University, Berkman Center for Internet and Society. 2010. Copyright for Librarians. Accessed March 3, 2012. http://cyber.law.harvard.edu/copyrightforlibrarians/Main_Page.

Homan, J. M. 2000. "2000/2001 Priorities." MLA News 325: 27.

Institute for Scientific Information. 2005. The Impact Factor. Accessed March 3, 2012. http://www.biotechmedia.com/y2005-Impact-Factor-Def.html.

Jaeger, Paul, T. Charles, R. McClure, John Carlo Bertot, and John T. Snead. 2004. "The USA PATRIOT Act, the Foreign Intelligence Surveillance Act, and Information Policy Research in Libraries: Issues, Impacts, and Questions for Libraries and Researchers." The Library Quarterly 74(2): 99–121.

Jenuwine, E. S., and J. A. Floyd. 2004. "Comparison of Medical Subject Headings and Text-word Searches in MEDLINE to Retrieve Studies on Sleep in Healthy Individuals." Journal of the Medical Library Association 92(3): 349–53.

Keiger, Dale, and Sue De Pasquale. 2002. "Trials and Tribulations." Illustrations by Naomi Shea. Johns Hopkins Magazine 54(1). http://www.jhu.edu/~jhumag/0202web/.

Lawrence, D. W. 2008. "What Is Lost When Searching Only One Literature Database for Articles Relevant to Injury Prevention and Safety Promotion?" Injury Prevention 14(6): 401–4.

Lombardi, John V. 2000. "Academic Libraries in a Digital Age." *D-Lib Magazine* 6(10). http://www.dlib.org/dlib/october00/lombardi/10lombardi.html.

Magi, Trina J. 2007. "The Gap between Theory and Practice: A Study of the Prevalence and Strength of Patron Confidentiality Policies in Public and Academic Libraries." *Library and Information Science Research* 29: 455–70.

Mathews, B. S. 2004. "Grey Literature: Resources for Locating Unpublished Research." *College and Research Libraries* 65: 125–28. http://chaptercouncil.mlanet.org/roundtables/2006/GreyLit.pdf.

McLellan, Faith. 2001. "1966 and All That—When Is a Literature Search Done?" *Lancet* 358(9282): 646.

Medical Library Association. 2012a. "About the Medical Library Association." Accessed March 3, 2012. http://mlanet.org/about/.

Medical Library Association. 2012b. "Resources." Accessed March 3, 2012. http://www.mlanet.org/resources/healthlit/define.htmlandhttp://www.mlanet.org/resources/healthlit/hil_project.html.

New Media Rights. 2007. "A Citizen's Legal Guide to the Digital Millennium Copyright Act." Accessed March 3, 2012. http://www.newmediarights.org/guide/legal/copyright/citizens_legal_guide_digital_millenium_copyright_act_dmca.

Nicholson, Scott, and Catherine Arnott Smith. 2007. "Using Lessons from Health Care to Protect the Privacy of Library Users: Guidelines for the De-identification of Library Data Based on HIPAA." *Journal of the American Society for Information Science and Technology* 58(8): 1198–1206.

No Electronic Theft (NET) Act. 1997. http://www.justice.gov/criminal/cybercrime/17–18red.htm.

"Not-so-Deep Impact." 2005. *Nature* 435: 1003–4. Accessed March 3, 2012. http://www.nature.com/nature/journal/v435/n7045/full/4351003b.html.

Perkins, Eva. 2001. "Johns Hopkins Tragedy: Could Librarians Have Prevented a Death?" *Information Today* 18(8): 51, 54. Accessed March 3, 2012. http://newsbreaks.infotoday.com/nbreader.asp?ArticleID=17534.

Purdue University 2012. Purdue Online Writing Lab (OWL). Accessed March 3. http://owl.english.purdue.edu/owl/resource/589/01/.

Russell, Carrie, ed. 2004. *Complete Copyright: An Everyday Guide for Librarians.* Chicago: American Library Association.

Sackett, D. 1996. "Evidence-based Medicine: What it Is and What it Isn't." *British Medical Journal* 312: 71–72. Accessed March 3, 2012. http://www.bmj.com/cgi/content/full/312/7023/71.

Sampson, Margaret, Jessie McGowan, Carol Lefebvre, David Moher, and Jeremy Grimshaw. 2008. *PRESS: Peer Review of Electronic Search Strategies.* Ottawa: Canadian Agency for Drugs and Technologies in Health. Accessed March 3, 2012. http://www.cadth.ca/media/pdf/477_PRESS-Peer-Review-Electronic-Search-Strategies_tr_e.pdf.

Schacher, L. F. 2001. "Clinical Librarianship: Its Value in Medical Care." *Annals of Internal Medicine* 134(8): 717–20.

Shipman, J. P., S. Kurtz-Rossi, and C. J. Funk. 2009. "The Health Information Literacy Research Project." *Journal of the Medical Library Association* 97(4): 293–301.

Shumaker, David, and Mary Talley. 2009. "Models of Embedded Librarianship: Final Report." Prepared under the Special Libraries Association Research Grant 2007. Accessed March 3, 2012. http://www.sla.org/pdfs/EmbeddedLibrarianshipFinalRptRev.pdf.

Steinbrook, Robert. 2002. "Protecting Research Subjects: The Crisis at Johns Hopkins." *The New England Journal of Medicine* 346(9): 716–20.

University of Alberta Learning Services. 2012. Evidence Based Library and Information Practice (EBLIP). Accessed March 3. http://ejournals.library.ualberta.ca/index.php/EBLIP.

U.S. Department of Health and Human Services, National Institutes of Health. 2012. "Public Access Policy." Accessed March 3. http://publicaccess.nih.gov/.

U.S. Department of Health, Education and Welfare, Secretary's Advisory Committee on Automated Personal Data Systems. 1973. *Records, Computers, and the Rights of Citizens: Report of the Secretary's Advisory Committee on Automated Personal Data Systems,* iiv. Washington, DC: U.S. Sup. of Docs. ("The Code of Fair Information Practices" is posted on the Electronic Privacy Information Center Web page, "The Code of Fair Information Practices." Accessed March 3, 2012. http://epic.org/privacy/consumer/code_fair_info.html.)

Vaughn, C. J. 2009. "Evaluation of a New Clinical Librarian Service." *Medical Reference Service Quarterly* 28(2): 143–53.

von Elm, E., et al. 2003. "More Insight into the Fate of Biomedical Meeting Abstracts: A Systematic Review." *BioMed Central Medical Research Methodologies* 10(3): 12.

Weintraub, Irwin. 2006. The Role of Grey Literature in the Sciences. http://chaptercouncil.mlanet.org/roundtables/2006/GreyLit.pdf.

APPENDIX

ORGANIZATIONS

Even though in some instances they accept membership of nonprofessionally trained staff, associations provide mentoring, continuing education, networking, and conferences that encourage members to pursue the advanced degree. Some universities provide librarians with money to maintain memberships in professional organizations and to attend professional conferences. These monies are, however, limited, and it is questionable whether a subject specialist would demonstrate a preference for a library organization over one that represents a chosen area of expertise.

American Library Association (ALA): Founded in Philadelphia, Pennsylvania, in 1876, ALA is the oldest and, with more than 62,000 members, the largest library organization in the world (http://www.ala.org and "Report to Council and Executive Board," by ALA Executive Director Keith Michael Fiels, EBD#12.36 2009–2010, 18 June 2010 [misdated as 18 June 2009]. "Overall ALA Membership as of May 2010 stands at 62,251"). The organization currently espouses seven key action areas: Diversity, Equitable Access to Information and Library Services, Education and Lifelong Learning, Intellectual Freedom, Advocacy for Libraries and the Profession, Literacy, and Organizational Excellence. Members have access to scholarship, professional development assistance, continuing education offerings, research and surveys topics concerning all types of libraries and librarian roles.

The Canadian Agency for Drugs and Technologies in Health (CADTH): CADTH recognized the importance of the search process in determining the evidence on which its Health Technology Assessment is based and developed PRESS: Peer Review of Electronic Search Strategies. PRESS employed several strategies : a systematic review of major databases, a web-based survey of expert searchers, and peer review forums. The final report, *PRESS: Peer Review of Electronic Search Strategies* (Sampson et al. 2008), includes those elements with sufficient data to support them as vital to electronic search strategies in addition to a list of the most common errors that occur in sub-standard searches such as a failure to re-translate the search strategy in more than one database, missing relevant subject headings and spelling variations, and inadequate or inappropriate use of keywords (32). Librarians who work in research venues concern themselves with a constant re-evaluation of their search methods and the best way to mine databases successfully.

Medical Library Association: The Medical Library Association (MLA) first developed a specialized program for medical librarians in 1947. To this day, MLA offers continuing education programs for medical librarians and a credentialing program—the Academy of Health Information Professionals (AHIP). MLA boasts close to 4,000 members and more than 1,000 institutions in 56 countries (Medical Library Association 2012a). Members receive professional assistance through conferences, continuing education, discussion lists, as well as the sections devoted to specific topics such as hospital librarianship, research, and Allied Health, which includes nursing.

Special Libraries Association (SLA): Founded in New York in 1909, SLA is now a nonprofit global organization with more than 11,000 members from 75 countries. SLA offers continuing education, certificate programs, discussion lists, scholarships, and a report titled Competencies for Information Professionals of the 21st Century. SLA funded and supported "The Models of Embedded Librarianship Report."

Association of Research Libraries (ARL): ARL is a nonprofit organization of 126 research libraries. Membership is at the institutional level and is designed to provide a forum for the exchange of ideas and collective action. One of its stated guiding principles is to "build relationships with other higher education societies and associations that share our common goals" (Association of Research Libraries 2012). ARL is especially influential in the arena of scholarly communication; the impetus to correct the imbalance of the dissemination of research especially in the sciences.

The Center for Measuring University Performance (MUP): MUP maintains a Top American Research Universities Report (Center for Measuring University Performance 2012) covering more than 600 institutions. Evaluation is based on nine characteristics: total research, federal research, endowment assets, annual giving, national academy members, faculty awards, doctorates granted, postdoctoral appointees, and SAT/ACT range. MUP is also developing a methodology to identify excellent graduate programs (The Center for Measuring University Performance is available at http://mup.asu.edu/gradPrgQual.html). What do these measures have to do with research librarians? John Lombardi, co-editor of MUP and president of the Louisiana State University System, discusses in one of his publications the "chaos" and lack of organization of the digital world confronting academia, and he recommends that librarians hone their skills in accessing content. "Helping clients find resources in a digitally chaotic world is the first priority" (Lombardi 2000). If universities are to be evaluated by their research, the research will be evaluated by its comprehensiveness. Trained librarians know the difference between a representative search and a comprehensive search. How will researchers know that they have, indeed, found everything available on a topic except with the assistance and guidance of a librarian trained in just how to perform that monumental task.

8

VALUING THE RETURN ON INVESTMENT OF THE INFORMATION PROFESSIONAL IN SPECIALIZED INSTITUTIONS (CORPORATIONS, GOVERNMENT AGENCIES, NGOS, ETC.)

Michael E.D. Koenig
Long Island University

Valuing the information specialist, in any context, is difficult. The most obvious reason is that the value of information and knowledge is such a slippery topic and so difficult to pin down. It is not for nothing that in the literature of knowledge management (KM), the technique most often mentioned and discussed for justifying KM is story telling.

While studies of the impact of information professionals are therefore few and far between, there has been substantial literature on the impact of libraries and information centers. Those functions of course would not have much of an impact without the work and input of information professionals. Therefore, in this chapter we conduct a review of the highlights of this literature, particularly as it relates to specialized institutions such as corporations, government agencies, nongovernmental organizations (NGOs), and other institutions. For a more thorough consideration of this topic, the reader is referred to the section on the productivity impact of libraries and information centers in the recently enlarged and expanded *Encyclopedia of Library and Information Sciences* (Koenig and Manzari 2010).

THE RELATIONSHIP OF LIBRARY AND INFORMATION SERVICES TO PRODUCTIVE ORGANIZATIONS

This area is particularly germane, but it is exceedingly difficult to measure. In addition to the squishiness of measuring information or knowledge, there are few good measures of organizational performance or productivity and a very complex array of potentially very relevant and confounding variables. The principal studies to date, both examining research and development (R&D) performance, are those by Orpen (1985) in the electronics and instrumentation field and by Koenig (1983, 1990a, 1992a, 1992b) in the pharmaceutical industry. Their results are similar and congruent.

Orpen found that in the more productive organizations (as defined by rates of growth and return on assets) the organizational culture was one in which the managers were perceived to be significantly more characterized by the following

three behaviors: (1) they routed literature and references to scientific and technical staff, (2) they directed their staff to use scientific and technical information
(STI) and to purchase STI services, and (3) they encouraged publication of results
and supported professional visits and continuing education. Furthermore, Orpen
found in his investigations that only those aspects of managerial behavior *that were
directly concerned with information* differentiated in any way between the "high-
performance" and "low-performance" companies.

Koenig (1990a) studied the relationship between research productivity and the
information environment in the pharmaceutical industry. The measure of productivity was the number of approved new drugs per research dollar expended,
but refined further by weighting in regard to (1) whether or not the FDA (U.S.
Food and Drug Administration) regards the drug as an important therapeutic
advance, (2) the drug's chemical novelty, and (3) the filing company's patent position with regard to the drug as an indication of where the bulk of the research
was done. The more productive companies were characterized in particular by
the following:

- Greater use of their libraries and information centers
- Greater openness to outside information
- Somewhat less concern with protecting proprietary information
- Greater attendance by employees at professional meetings
- Greater information systems development effort
- Greater end user use of information systems, more encouragement of browsing
  and serendipity, and more time spent browsing and keeping abreast
- Greater technical and subject sophistication of the information services staff
- Relative unobtrusiveness of managerial structure and status indicators in the
  R&D environment.

In a review of the corpus of work on R&D innovation, Goldhar, Bragaw, and
Schwartz (1976) concluded that there were six characteristics of environments
that are conducive to technological innovation and productivity. Of those six, four
are clearly related to the information environment, specifically (1) easy access to
information by individuals; (2) free flow of information both into and out of the
organizations; (3) rewards for sharing, seeking, and using "new" externally developed information sources; and (4) encouragement of mobility and interpersonal
contacts. The other two characteristics are (5) rewards for taking risks, and (6)
rewards for accepting and adapting to change.

After reviewing a number of studies on innovation, principally from the management literature, Utterback (1971, 1974) concluded,

> In general, it appears that the greater the degree of communications between
> the firm and its environment at each stage of the process of innovation, other
> factors being equal, the more effective the firm will be in generating, devel-
> oping, and implementing new technology. (Utterback 1974)

Wolek and Griffith (1974) reviewed the sociologically oriented literature on this
topic and came to the same conclusion. McConnell (1980, 1982), writing on how

to improve productivity, reviewed the literature in less formal fashion and summarized his conclusions as,

> Information flow, through both formal and informal networks, should be full and free—up, down, and across the organization. This requires continuous effort and attention . . . The more open and free communication is in the organization, the greater will be productivity. (McConnell 1982)

Abell and Winterman (1995) published an extensive review of these findings titled "Information Culture and Business Performance" in a study prepared for the British library. The very uniform conclusion of these and similar studies is that successful R&D operations are characterized by a *rich, deep,* and *open information environment.*

More recently, Strouse (2003) obtained questionnaire feedback from a very large number of corporate library users. He reports that 40 percent of users reported that using the corporate library saved them time; 21 percent reported that library use generated revenue, with an average figure of $777 of revenue generated per library use; and 22 percent reported an immediate cost savings averaging $42 per library use.

The literature about productive and innovative organizations is remarkably clear and consistent in emphasizing a consistent theme of the need for greater openness toward and greater access to information, both internal and external, in order to facilitate creativity and innovation. What is also consistent is that information access–related factors emerge in positions of very high priority in comparison to other factors under management control. It is of course the information professional who facilitates that information flow and those rich, deep, and open communications and who provides the "continuous effort and attention."

An intriguing phenomenon, but also a very distressing phenomenon, is that the comparatively high importance of information and information access is often unremarked upon by the researchers documenting it, particularly, it seems, if they come from a management or engineering background rather than from an information services background. In Orpen's (1985) study, information-related behavior successfully discriminated between high-performance and low-performance companies (enhancing access to or encouraging use of information was positive) while non–information-related behavior did not, but Orpen made no remark on this distinction. Similarly, the win, place, and show, as well as number 6, of Goldhar, Bragaw, and Schwartz's (1976) six factors are all information related, but the authors make nothing of it./

In the medical context there is clear evidence that better access to information produces positive results. A study by Marshall (1992) examined Medline searching in 15 hospitals in Rochester, NY, and concluded that Medline searching by a clinician was associated with a number of positive clinical outcomes, such as reduced hospital stay in 19 percent of the cases and avoidance of tests or procedures in 49 percent of the cases. A study by Klein et al. (1994), based on several Detroit hospitals, concluded that the initiation of early Medline searches by clinicians resulted in shorter hospital stays and reduced cost. While these studies are based on clinician use of information systems rather than information professional mediated use, it is certainly reasonable to project that use supported by an information professional would only magnify the effect.

In the legal context there are two recent articles substantiating the contribution made by KM to law firms (Forstenlechner et al. 2007; Forstenlechner, Lettice, and Bourne 2009). The salient contributions were in quality of counsel and legal opinions and in improved ease of use of information systems.

A recent study substantiating the importance of the skills of information professionals was contained in the Business Information Survey 2009 (Foster 2009). The most critical conclusion was that information discovery skills, the core expertise of information professionals, are increasingly being recognized as a key priority by senior information managers looking at their skill mix.

THE RELATIONSHIP OF LIBRARY AND INFORMATION SERVICES TO PRODUCTIVE INDIVIDUALS

Voluminous literature exists on the information use styles of scientists, engineers, businesspersons, and the like. The reader is referred to the *Annual Review of Information Science and Technology,* which contains numerous chapters on this topic; indeed the cumulative index for the first 35 volumes of the *Annual Review of Information Science and Technology* (Shaw 2001) lists 13 chapters on "Information Needs and Uses" in which this literature is reviewed. The recent article in the *Encyclopedia of Library and Information Sciences* on "Productivity Impacts of Libraries and Information Services" (Koenig and Manzari 2010) is also useful. The literature is much too extensive to review in detail in this chapter. That extensiveness, however, provides the virtue that the consistency of its findings is compelling. What these studies have in common, and what they overwhelmingly conclude, is that the more use the researcher makes of information services, the more productive that researcher is. By obvious extension, those information services depend on information professionals, and therefore, the more use the researcher makes of information professionals, the more productive that researcher is.

Work by Strouse (Griffin 2007) solicited library end-user feedback from users in corporate, government, and the health and education sectors and found that, on average, information end users reported that they saved nine hours of their time for each session with an information professional and more than $2,000 in costs ($3,107 in the corporate sector).

CALCULATIONS OF THE VALUE OF INFORMATION SERVICES

Another way to implicitly look at the relationship of information services and the information professionals behind them with organizational effectiveness is to attempt to derive a value for those information services.

Again, the literature is extensive, but a few highlights are reported here. The seminal study was that done by Ben Weil (1980) at Exxon in the 1960s, which reported a benefit-to-cost ratio of 11 to 1, and this number was based only on those results with quantifiable benefits, while nonquantifiable benefits were ignored.

A more extensive study using similar techniques was conducted in the late 1970s on NASA's information services (Mogavero 1979). The benefit versus cost ratio was determined to be 7.6:1.

Table 8.1   Summary of Reported Findings of King Research Methodology in Various Organizations on Benefit to Cost Ratios of Using Information Professionals

SAVINGS IN TERMS OF	PSE&G	AT&T BELL LABS	KODAK	AIR PRODUCTS	DEPARTMENT OF ENERGY
Willingness to pay measured in terms of professional's time	19: 1	4.4: 1	4.3: 1	2.5: 1	26: 1
Cost to use alternative services	8: 1	3.6: 1	2.7: 1	2.6: 1	Not calculated
Research cost avoidance	17: 1	14: 1	16: 1	4.8: 1	25: 1

Source: Taken from Koenig (1990b), chapter 2, 55–86, p. 68. Summary of reported findings of King research methodology in various organizations on benefit to cost ratio of using information professionals.

The most extensive work in this area is that compiled by King and Griffiths in their studies of various organizations (Griffiths and King 1985; Griffiths 1982, 1988, 1990, 1993; King and Griffiths 1988; King and Roderer 1978; Roderer, King, and Brouard 1983; King et al. 1982, 1984). This work is valuable particularly because it has been applied to numerous organizations, and it reveals clear and consistent patterns. Table 8.1 is a summarization of the findings from their major studies regarding benefit to cost.

King Research also examined the value of the energy database (EDB) of the U.S. Department of Energy (King et al. 1982, 1984), looking not only at use by government employees, but by contractors as well. Their conclusion was that the return on investment was approximately 2.2 to 1.

The Federal Highway Administration (U.S. Department of Transportation and the Federal Highway Administration 1999) summarized interviews with state DOTs on the value of information services. The most thorough study, that done by the state of Minnesota, found a benefit cost ratio of between 9 and 10 to 1 when searching was done by information professionals rather than having end users finding information on their own.

Revisiting these classic studies, Tenopir and King (2000) determined that newer studies with different methodologies have not challenged earlier results. If there were no library it would cost scientists 2.9 times the library cost. They determined that employing librarians and information professionals *saves* the equivalent of nearly five scientists' time for every library or information professional staff member working for an organization.

For further reading, there are five review articles on this subject or in close proximity to it. Two, by Koenig (1990b, 1992a), are similar to this chapter but contain further references. Another two, by Bearman, Guynup, and Milevski (1985) and by Cronin and Gudim (1986), discuss the topic and contain further references but little data. Finally, a review by Bawden (1986) on the related topics of information and creativity pulls together a very disparate literature on a cognate topic.

THE IMPORTANCE OF THE
INFORMATION PROFESSIONAL

In addition to the documented importance of the information center and, conse-quently, information support to effective organizational function, there is strong evidence as to the importance of the information professional as well. Note par-ticularly Tenopir and King's conclusion mentioned previously, based on a review of many studies, that the ratio of the information professional's time worked to researchers' time saved was nearly one to five.

In Koenig's (1990b) study of the correlates of successful pharmaceutical R&D, one of the significant correlations was that the researchers in the more productive companies used their company library/information center more and also rated the expertise and technical competence of their library/information center staff as above average.

Matarazzo and Gauthier (1990) and Matarazzo and Prusak (1995) conducted a study in which they asked senior management about the library's impact. Their study included 164 corporations in the United States. While most corporations had no procedures for measuring the value of the library, the librarians, that is, the *information professionals,* were highly rated for their contribution to the success of the organization.

KNOWLEDGE MANAGEMENT: TAXONOMIZATION
AND THE INFORMATION PROFESSIONAL

Another clear indicator of the importance of access to information and of the contribution of the information professional is to be seen in the development of KM. KM has *evolved* with three clearly delineated stages (Koenig and Neveroski 2008).

Stage One

The initial stage of KM was driven primarily by information technology. The first stage is well described with an equestrian metaphor as "by the internet out of intel-lectual capital." The large international consulting organizations understood quite well that their stock in trade was information and knowledge; if they could share that knowledge, they could operate more effectively. When the Internet emerged, KM emerged, and initially it was all about how to deploy that new technology to accomplish those goals.

Stage Two

The second stage of KM added recognition of the human and cultural dimen-sions. It was soon recognized that "If you build it they will come" is a recipe that can easily lead to quick and embarrassing failure if human factors are not sufficiently taken into account. The second stage might be described as the "If you build it they will come is a fallacy" stage. The second stage focused on human relation (HR) issues and human computer interaction (HCI) and emphasized communities of practice (COPs) and the capturing of implicit knowledge in ex-plicit form.

Stage Three

The third stage came with the realization of the importance of content and, in particular, an awareness of the importance of the retrievability and, therefore, of the importance of the arrangement, description, and structure of that content, the domain of the information professional. Continuing the metaphor stated previously, perhaps the best description for the etiology of the third stage is the "it's no good if they can't find it" stage, or perhaps "it's no good if they try to use it but can't find it."

If one peruses the content of the 1999, 2000, and 2001 KMWorld conferences, one can see the emergence of Stage III clearly. At KMWorld 2000 a track on Content Management appeared for the first time, and at KMWorld 2001 in October/November Content Management was the dominant track, constituting the largest cluster of topics in the conference. In 2006 a "Taxonomy Boot Camp" was added to the KMWorld Conference and has become an increasingly important component of the conference. This third stage that emerged is well described as the *taxonomy/content* stage.

Another bellwether of the third, taxonomy, stage is that TFPL, a major UK consulting group, in a report of their October 2001 Chief Knowledge Officer (CKO) Summit, reported that for the first time taxonomies emerged as a topic, and it emerged full blown as the major topic (TFPL 2001). Stage three is the salient development in KM from the perspective of this chapter.

The point of course is that in the rapidly expanding world of KM, the importance of information and knowledge organization, and therefore the importance of the role of the information professional, is increasingly being recognized as central. Furthermore, this realization was arrived at on the part of KM efforts that were for the most part unpopulated by information professionals as they are considered in this book.

It should be mentioned in passing at this point that there is substantial bibliometric and informetric evidence for the importance and continued growth of the business community's interest in KM (Koenig 2008). Resting a case on the importance of KM is building on solid ground.

THE INFORMATION PROFESSIONAL: SYSTEM IMPLEMENTATION AND USER TRAINING

The developments in KM also attest to the importance of the information professional in another way. KM implementation efforts have been characterized by a very high failure rate. One can posit with some confidence that a very major component of this high failure rate has been a result of what one might call the tendency for well meaning "amateurs" to jump on the KM bandwagon without the involvement of information professionals in any central role.

The largest study on KM implementation to date is that undertaken by KPMG Consulting (2000). The study included more than 400 firms, and it provides fascinating and compelling evidence concerning the reasons for failure. KPMG reported that of the 288 firms that had KM in systems in place or were setting up such a system, there were 137 cases, that is nearly half, where the benefits failed to meet expectations, a very high failure rate indeed. The reasons for failure, as reported by the company, were as shown in Table 8.2.

Table 8.2   KPMG Findings for KM Implementation Failure

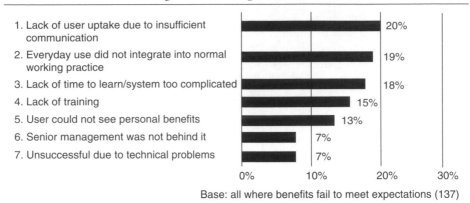

Base: all where benefits fail to meet expectations (137)

Note: These percentages add to 99 percent due to rounding error; there is no overlap.

What is striking however, and striking on two levels, is the importance of user training and education. What are presented as three reasons—(1) lack of user uptake due to insufficient communication, (2) lack of time to learn/ system too complicated, and (3) lack of training—are all fundamentally the same reason: inadequate training and user education. With that recognized, the table can be recast in a much more informative fashion; see Table 8.3.

Table 8.3   Restated KPMG Reasons for KM Implementation Failure

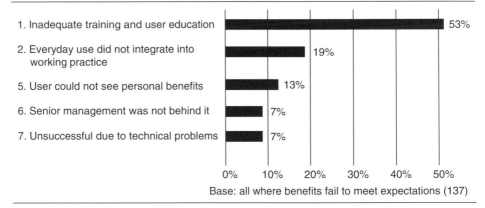

Base: all where benefits fail to meet expectations (137)

It is also quite likely that some component of reason 5, "User could not see personal benefits," is also reflective of inadequate training and user education.

When reanalyzed, it is clear that inadequate training and user education is by far the most prominent reason for why benefits failed to meet expectations, accounting for the majority of failures. In fact, inadequate training and inadequate user education exceeded all other reasons combined.

The relevance here is that the failure to recognize the importance of user training and education on such a large scale would have been very unlikely if information professionals had been centrally involved. The importance of user training and education is something that information professionals take for granted. The business community, however, does not take it for granted or adequately recognize its importance. The KPMG study is a wonderful example in terms of making the point that the importance of user training and education was staring the study team in the face, and it failed to see the most salient fact that emerged from the study. The KM failure rate, though a back-handed compliment, is a persuasive argument for the importance of the involvement of the information professional.

THE PENALTY OF WRONG OR USELESS INFORMATION

A consistent theme in the study of business use of information is how much of the information used by businesspeople is wrong or useless. Accenture (2007) reports that managers confirm that the majority of information obtained for their work is useless. A Dow Jones and Special Libraries Association (SLA) (2010) study similarly reported that the prevalence of incorrect information on the web is a major cause of concern for businesses. Clearly, this problem is a reason for the involvement of information professionals in providing and analyzing information and for coaching information users as to how to avoid falling into the wrong or useless information trap.

IN SUMMARY, HOW IS THE VALUE, THE RETURN ON INVESTMENT, OF THE INFORMATION PROFESSIONAL DEMONSTRATED?

- The value of information services in specialized institutions is very clearly demonstrated; without information professionals, those services would be dysfunctional.

- Studies like those of Koenig (1990a, 1990b); Matarazzo and Gauthier (1990); Matarazzo and Prusak (1995); and Tenopir and King (2000) attest directly to the value of the information professional.

- Productive individuals make more use of information services and information professionals.

- The burgeoning KM has evolved in a fashion that clearly shows its dependence on taxonomization and, therefore, its dependence upon the information professional.

- Analyses of KM failures point directly to inadequate user education and training and by default and logical extension to the point that the involvement of information professionals is a key ingredient for success.

FURTHER READING

The following works are recommended for those seeking a further understanding of the value of information professionals in specialized institutions.

Bryant, S. L., and Anne Gray. "Demonstrating the Positive Impact of Information Support on Patient Care in Primary Care: A Rapid Literature Review." *Health Information and Libraries Journal* 23, no. 2 (2006): 118–25.
    Recounts much discussion and finds six articles that to at least some degree do document a demonstrable impact.
Chartered Institute of Library and Information Professionals. "Demonstrating the Value and Impact of Special Library and Information Services: Complete List." Accessed September 2010. http://www.cilip.org.uk/get-involved/advocacy/special-library-information-services/Pages/special-library-resources-list.aspx.
    This is a good well annotated list of articles and other documents on the subject, interpreted broadly, of special library impact. It contains references to and descriptions

of a number of studies in gray literature domain that is not well covered in conventional bibliographic databases. First compiled for the CILIP (Chartered Institute of Library and Information Professionals) Information and Advice Team in collaboration with Peter Griffiths and the Special Library and Information Services Panel. It is being updated and maintained.

Kadell, M. *The New Face of Value: Best Practices for Government Libraries 2010.* Albany, NY: Lexis/Nexis, 2010. http://www.lexisnexis.com/tsq/gov/Best_Practices_2010.pdf. A compendium of some seventy plus articles relating to the value of library and information service in the context of U.S. government operations. Most items however are more inspirational rather than fact filled.

Oakleaf, M. "Value of Academic Libraries: A Comprehensive Research Review and Report." American Library Association. http://www.ala.org/ala/mgrps/divs/acrl/issues/value/val_report.pdf.

This report focuses obviously on academic libraries and of course some of that is relevant to specialized institutions, but it also has a section on Special Library Value Studies (pp. 84–93).

Weightman, A.L., and J. Williamson. "The Value and Impact of Information Provided through Library Service for Patient Care: A Systematic Review." *Library and Knowledge Development Network Quality and Statistics Group* 22, no. 1 (2005): 4–25. http://nnlm.gov/mar/about/valuebibliography.html.

A periodically updated bibliography, including detailed abstracts, compiled by searching PubMed, Web of Science, CINAHL, Lisa, and library Literature. (NNLN is the National Network of Libraries of Medicine)

REFERENCES

Abell, Angela, and Vivienne Winterman. 1995. "Information Culture and Business Performance." In *Information Culture and Business Performance,* prepared for the British Library by Hertis Information and Research. Hatfield: University of Hertfordshire.

Accenture. 2007. "Managers Say the Majority of Information Obtained for Their Work Is Useless. Accenture Survey Finds." Accessed January 4. http://newsroom.accenture.com/article_display.cfm?article_id=4484.

Bawden, David. 1986. "Information Systems and the Stimulation of Creativity." *Journal of Information Science* 12(5): 203–16.

Bearman, Toni C., Polly Guynup, and Sandra N. Milevski. 1985. "Information and Productivity." *Journal of the American Society for Information Science* 36(6): 369–75.

Cronin, Blaise, and Mairi Gudim. 1986. "Information and Productivity: A Review of Research." *International Journal of Information Management* 6(2): 85–101.

Dow Jones and Special Libraries Association (SLA). 2010. *"Bad Info" Survey Results: The Impact of "Bad Info" on Business Decisions.* New York: Dow Jones.

Forstenlechner, Ingo, Fiona Lettice, Mike Bourne, and Carol Webb. 2007. "Turning Knowledge into Value in Professional Service Firms." *Performance Measurement and Metrics* 8(3): 146–56.

Forstenlechner, Ingo, Fiona Lettice, and Mike Bourne. 2009. "Knowledge Pays: Evidence from a Law Firm." *Journal of Knowledge Management* 13(1): 56–68.

Foster, Allen. 2009. "Battening down the Hatches: The Business Information Survey 2009." *Business Information Review* 26(1): 10–27.

Goldhar, Joel D., Louis K. Bragaw, and Jules J. Schwartz. 1976. "Information Flows, Management Styles and Technological Innovation." *IEEE Transactions on Engineering Management* 23(1): 51–61.

Griffin, Daniel. 2007. "New Report from Outsell Confirms What Librarians Knew All Along." *Information World Review* (August 30). http://www.iwr.co.uk/

professional-and-library/3008209/Organisations-with-access-to-an-enterprise-library-enjoy-significant-RoI.

Griffiths, Jose-Marie. 1982. *The Value of Information and Related Systems, Products and Services.* Vol. 17 of *Annual Review of Information Science and Technology,* ed. M. E. Williams, 269–84. White Plains, NY: Knowledge Industry Publications for the American Society for Information Science.

Griffiths, Jose-Marie. 1988. *An Information Audit of Public Service Electric and Gas Company Libraries and Information Resources: Executive Summary and Conclusions.* Rockville, MD: King Research.

Griffiths, Jose-Marie. 1990. *A Manual on the Evaluation of Information Centers and Services.* Paris: AGARD.

Griffiths, Jose-Marie. 1993. *Special Libraries: Increasing the Information Edge.* Washington, DC: Special Libraries Association.

Griffiths, Jose-Marie, and Donald W. King. 1985. *The Contribution Libraries Make to Organizational Productivity.* Rockville, MD: King Research.

King, Donald W., and Jose-Marie Griffiths. 1988. "Evaluating the Effectiveness of Information Use." In *Evaluating the Effectiveness of Information Centres and Services: Material to Support a Lecture Series Presented under the Sponsorship of the North Atlantic Treaty Organization, Advisory Group for Aerospace Research and Development (AGARD), Technical Information Panel and the Consultant and Exchange Programme,* 1:1–1:5. Neuilly-sur-Seine, France: AGARD.

King, Donald W., and Nancy K. Roderer. 1979. "Information Transfer Cost/Benefit Analysis." In *Information and Industry: Proceedings of the North Atlantic Treaty Organization, Advisory Group for Aerospace Research and Development (AGARD), Technical Information Panel Specialists' Meeting Held in Paris, France 18–19 October 1978,* 8:1–8:10. Neuilly-sur-Seine, France: AGARD.

King, Donald W., José-Marie Griffiths, Nancy K. Roderer, and Robert R.V. Wiederkehr. 1982. *Value of the Energy Data Base.* Rockville, MD: King Research.

King, Donald W., José-Marie Griffiths, Ellen A. Sweet, and Robert R. V. Wiederkehr. 1984. *A Study of the Value of Information and the Effect on Value of Intermediary Organizations, Timeliness of Services and Products, and Comprehensiveness of the EDB.* Rockville, MD: King Research.

Klein, M. S., F. V. Ross, D. L. Adams, and C. M. Gilbert. 1994. "Effect of Online Literature Searching on Length of Stay and Patient Care Costs." *Academic Medicine* 69(6): 489–95.

Koenig, Michael E. D. 1983. "Bibliometric Indicators versus Expert Opinion in Assessing Research Performance." *Journal of the American Society for Information Science* 34(2): 136–45.

Koenig, Michael E. D. 1990a. "Information Services and Downstream Productivity." In *Annual Review of Information Science and Technology,* vol. 25, ed. M. E. Williams, 55–86. New York: Elsevier Science Publishers for the American Society for Information Science.

Koenig, Michael E. D. 1990b. "The Information and Library Environment and the Productivity of Research." *Inspel* 24(4): 157–67.

Koenig, Michael E. D. 1992a. "The Importance of Information Services for Productivity: Under-recognized and Under-invested." *Special Libraries* 83(4): 191–210.

Koenig, Michael E. D. 1992b. "The Information Environment and the Productivity of Research." In *Recent Advances in Chemical Information,* ed. H. Collier, 133–43. London: Royal Society of Chemistry.

Koenig, Michael E. D. 2008. "KM Is Here to Stay." In *Knowledge Management in Practice: Connections and Context,* ed. Kanti Srikantaiah and Michael E. D. Koenig, 5–8. Medford, NJ: Information Today for the American Society for Information Science and Technology.

Koenig, M. E., and L. Manzari. 2010. "Productivity Impacts of Libraries and Information Services." In *Encyclopedia of Library and Information Sciences,* 3rd ed., ed. M. Bates and M. N. Maack, 4305–14. Boca Raton, FL: CRC Press.

Koenig, Michael E. D., and Kenneth Neveroski. 2008. "The Origins and Development of Knowledge Management." *Journal of Information and Knowledge Management* 7(4): 243–54.

KPMG Consulting. 2000. *Knowledge Management Research Report 2000.* New York: KPMG Consulting.

Marshall, Joanne Gard. 1992. "The Impact of the Hospital Library on Clinical Decision Making: The Rochester Study." *Bulletin of the Medical Library Association* 80(2): 169–78.

Matarazzo, James M., and M. R. Gauthier. 1990. *Valuing Special Libraries: A Survey of Senior Managers.* Washington, DC: Special Libraries Association in cooperation with Temple, Barker & Sloane.

Matarazzo, James M., and Laurence Prusak. 1995. *The Value of Corporate Libraries: Findings from a 1995 Survey of Senior Management.* Washington, DC: Special Libraries Association.

McConnell, J. Douglas. 1980. "Productivity Improvements in Research and Development and Engineering in the United States." *Society of Research Administration Journal* 12(2): 5–14.

McConnell, J. Douglas. 1982. "R&D Productivity Factors." *Resource. Management* 4(4): 32–37.

Mogavero, Louis N. 1979. "Transferring Technology to Industry through Information." In *Information and Industry: Proceedings of the North Atlantic Treaty Organization, Advisory Group for Aerospace Research and Development (AGARD), Technical Information Panel Specialists' Meeting Held in Paris, France 18–19 October 1978,* 14:1–14:6. Neuilly-sur-Seine, France: AGARD.

Orpen, Christopher. 1985. "The Effect of Managerial Distribution of Scientific and Technical Information on Company Performance." *R&D Management* 15(4): 305–8.

Roderer, Nancy K., Donald W. King, and Sandra E. Brouard. 1983. *The Use and Value of Defense Technical Information Center Products and Services.* Rockville, MD: King Research.

Shaw, Debra. 2001. "Cumulative Keyword and Author Index of ARIST Titles: Volumes 1–35." *Annual Review of Information Science and Technology,* vol. 35, ed. M. E. Williams, 531–80. Medford, NJ: Information Today for the American Society for Information Science.

Strouse, Roger. 2003. "Demonstrating Value and Return on Investment: The Ongoing Imperative." *Information Outlook* 7(3): 14–20.

Tenopir, Carol, and Donald W. King. 2000. *Toward Electronic Journals.* Washington, DC: SLA Publishing.

TFPL. 2001. *Knowledge Strategies—Corporate Strategies.* Presented at TFLP's Fourth International CKO Summit (October), London.

U.S. Department of Transportation and the Federal Highway Administration. 1999. *Value of Information and Information Services.* Publication No. FHWA-SA-99–038. Washington, DC: U.S. Department of Transportation.

Utterback, James M. 1971. "The Process of Technological Innovation within the Firm." *Academic Management Journal* 14: 75–88.

Utterback, James M. 1974. "Innovation in Industry and the Diffusion of Technology." *Science* 183(4125): 620–26.

Weil, Ben H. 1980. "Benefits from Research Use of the Published Literature at the Exxon Research Center." In *Special Librarianship: A New Reader,* ed. E. R. Jackson, 586–94. Metuchen, NJ: Scarecrow Press.

Wolek, Francis W., and Belver C. Griffith. 1974. "Policy and Informal Communications in Applied Science and Technology." *Science Studies* 4(4): 411–20.

9

DEFENDING THE
PROFESSIONAL ARCHIVIST

Cecilia Lizama Salvatore
Dominican University

"A tin of cocoa that was with the Scott of the Antarctic when he died," "a rare collection of hundreds of 1920s chocolate moulds," and "a collection of more than 300 Nestle films that were recently uncovered in a wall cavity at the company's base in Croydon." These are among the items of what can be found in the state-of-the-art archival facility that Nestle UK opened at the company's factory complex in York in summer 2011. Executives of the Nestle UK company stressed that the facility "demonstrated how serious Nestle UK was about preserving and promoting its history in the UK" (Laycock 2011).

The value of archives to historians, who look to primary resources while conducting their research, is common knowledge. Even at the National Park Service where researchers and historians work with structures, objects, and "other traces of human activity," the value of archives to historians is recognized. "Unlike an archeological site, which once excavated no longer exists for future archeologists seeking new information with more sophisticated techniques, a properly maintained archival collection can be researched repeatedly by historians asking new questions about the topics it covers" (Mackintosh 1998). In the Nestle UK state-of-the-art archive described here, we see that corporations join agencies, institutions, and communities in recognizing the need to preserve their history and cultural heritage and the need for staff expertise, skills, tools, and resources to properly maintain historical and cultural heritage resources.

The value of archives and archivists has been particularly articulated and illustrated by various Catholic orders of sisters. One Catholic sister recently described to the author the urgency in preserving the heritage of the order she belonged to through their records and archives. She referred to the fact that her community continues to decline in membership. Furthermore, she underscored the significance of preserving the sisters' history, particularly to "secular historians" who are increasingly interested in researching the history of orders that have contributed to society through the founding of hospitals, schools, and social institutions. The Sisters of Mercy is a Catholic order of sisters that has recently successfully launched a state-of-the art archives facility and has employed a professionally trained and certified archivist to manage it. The order has recently expanded a building in the former Sacred Heart College in Belmont, North Carolina (called the Mercy Heritage Center), that would be the central location of all archival records and materials of all the Sisters of Mercy communities in the continental United States (DeMars 2011).

THE TRANSFORMATION OF THE ARCHIVAL PROFESSION

Within North America there has been a large increase in the number of students seeking archival education in Graduate Schools of Library and Information Science accredited by the American Library Association (ALA). This is a far cry from years past when students sought archival education in public history programs (Cox and Larsen 2008). This points to a convergence—or perhaps, reconvergence, as Given and McTavish (2010) point out—of library science, museum studies, and archival education. With this convergence, we can surmise that an issue that affects one of the professions more than likely affects the other professions. As evident elsewhere in this volume, deprofessionalism is an issue that troubles librarians, library administrators, and library and information. It is likely that it has been increasingly confronted by the archival community.

Defending professionalism in the archival profession brings to my mind the time when I announced my intention to pursue a doctoral education with a focus on archives to my former librarian colleagues on Guam. One of the colleagues quickly remarked, "But why 'archives'"? I cannot remember all that ensued after this, but I do remember a further remark by this same colleague—a remark to the effect of, "Well, archivists work in basements or some secluded workspace, and I didn't think you would like that." I had served as Guam Territorial Librarian/Archivist but was recognized primarily as a librarian, so I can forgive my colleague because she was perhaps more surprised that I was considering a doctoral education that focused on archives and archival work (I should note that, in the end, my dissertation focused on information-seeking behavior and discourse in a library or special collection).

I bring up this story to illustrate a perception, common at the time, that archivists worked in seclusion with old, historical records that were disorganized, worn, and even deteriorating. Those who had this perception likely believed that the archivist's work with these records of paper, photographs, film, and ephemera consisted of conducting an inventory of them, creating a list of them, assessing their condition, and rehousing and preserving them. They perhaps also saw that the archivist's work was focused primarily on the record and material and significantly less on the user of that record and material.

The perception of the archivist has improved and, notwithstanding my former colleague's observation regarding secluded spaces, the basement is never the rational place to put an archival collection. Nevertheless, there are still those who believe that the archivist is only concerned with old and historical records. An accurate perception of archivists is that they appraise and acquire a collection, arrange and describe records and materials of enduring value, and develop and carry out strategies to preserve them. It should be pointed out that archivists describe one of the work functions as arrangement and description, instead of cataloging and classification. Furthermore, they seek to gain legal, intellectual, and physical control of the collection, including control and preservation of the authenticity and context of the records in that collection (Pearce-Moses 2005).

Archival work has always required professional skills and competencies. Archivists should be versed in specific professional domains, and in fact, as of 1989, they are graded on for certification through the Academy of Certified Archivists. This is an independent nonprofit certifying organization, founded in 1989, that, incidentally, is not at all an arm of the Society of American Archivists. Specifically, and primarily, archivists should be versed in the domains of selection, appraisal, and acquisition; arrangement and description; reference services and access; preservation; outreach, advocacy, and promotion; management; and professional, ethical, and legal responsibilities.

In the modern, competitive information environment, so much is changing in the way information is created, organized, used, and preserved that the archival profession, similar to other professions, is rethinking and restating these skills and competencies. This chapter describes the way the complex nature in which information is created, organized, used, and preserved is affecting the archival profession and why it is imperative, now more than ever, that archivists are educated and academically and professionally trained. Archivists must have specialized skills and knowledge to carry out the increasingly complex tasks and functions of their job. To be sure, they must have a professional education that instills the necessary, deep conceptual knowledge of records and other forms of documentary evidence and associated legal requirements, awareness and sensitivity to diverse communities and sociohistorical contexts, robust professional ethics and values, and applied research skills. In this chapter, the specific focus is on the need for professional archivists in archives and related cultural heritage institutions in order to (1) deal with the complex format and nature of records, (2) identify and apply modern information technology, (3) deal with the needs of diverse communities, and (4) provide the foundation for justifying archival professionalism and professional education.

BRIEF HISTORY AND BACKGROUND OF THE PROFESSION

The archival profession has come a long way, and much credit is due it for willing to evolve to get to the point of successfully addressing the challenges of new information environments. While the archival profession is relatively a young profession in the United States, its roots can be traced back almost 5,000 years to Mesopotamia. A defining moment in the development of the archival profession came during the French Revolution when the French "established the principle that records were critical because they protected the rights of the people" and "the corollary principle that the public at large had the right to inspect and examine the records produced and kept by its government" (O'Toole 1990, 29). In the United States, private and subsequently state historical societies that primarily focused on publishing and sometimes collecting historical documents were first established on the east coast, beginning with the Massachusetts Historical Society in 1791. In 1901 the first public archives were established with the founding of the Alabama State Archives; in 1934, the National Archives was established for the preservation of the public records of the Federal Government (O'Toole 1990).

At the beginning of the archival profession in the United States, it was not difficult for fundamental archival principles and practices to be sustained and maintained. Generally, archivists played a passive, back-end role. They took care of the volumes of records and artifacts that were being created by their institutions or were being entrusted to their state historical societies. In government archives, papers and records arrived at the archives, and the archivist appraised, accessioned, and arranged and described them most likely without disturbing the order in which they arrived and while reinforcing the context in which they were created. Archivists in government archives could determine in which record group and in which series they would put the papers and records as these arrived in the archives. The archivist at a state or local historical society would carry out similar activities, although chances are the papers and records (more likely to include photographs, film, and ephemera) did not belong to a prescribed record group or series. It was common during that time for an archivist to have gained knowledge about archival principles and best practices through an introductory course and an extensive and broad internship and apprenticeship (Fleckner 1991; Hensen 2002).

This is an important point because as those in the profession now know, the profession is facing many issues that require that an archivist completes more than a rudimentary course in archival practices and management. It should also be added that while archivists were doing their job well at the time, because of limited staff and resources and the large volume of materials in the archives and historical institutions, the existence of a large backlog of materials that needed to be processed was commonplace. It was also commonplace for archivists to work very closely with users, going through materials in files, folders, boxes, and cabinets.

The Archivist, Technology, and the Authentic Archival Record

If students in other graduate archival programs are like the students in my beginning archives classes, they enrolled in their programs with some awareness of some of the challenges confronting the archival profession because of technological advances. These students have formulated their diverse career goals based on these challenges. This is good news; it points out that the old image of the archivist is gone. When students in my recent class were asked about their career aspirations, I learned that several wanted to build digital archives, several wanted to be audio archivists, still others wanted to preserve rare books and manuscripts. A few wanted to document and preserve, using technological tools, a diaspora, and so on. It would be easy to simply teach these students the practical use of the technological tools that would allow them to carry out particular archival tasks and functions, but there is more to archival work than the use of technological tools. Archival work includes the application of theories and complex principles, standards, and methodology, learned through formal professional education.

To be sure, new and changing information technology has been the major impetus in the rethinking of theory, methods, and practices in the archival profession, just as it has been in other professions. The use of technology in the creation, organization, use, and preservation of records and materials has presented challenges to archivists as they work within the domains of their profession. For instance, archivists are used to looking at a print record, a photograph, a film, or an artifact and appraising its value for selection and acquisition, based on institutional mission, scope of collections, and their resource capacity. But more is involved in the appraisal, selection, and acquisition of born digital materials and archivists.

One concern that archivists have is the authenticity of the electronic record or material that ends up in their care. Beyond appraising a record for preservation, description, or reference purposes, the archivist generally leaves it up to the end user of the record to determine its utilization and trustworthiness (Gilliland-Swetland 2002). In the case of fluid electronic records and born digital materials, however, archivists have to be concerned that they are authentic and genuine and not tampered with. For example, the existence of cloud computing and open source and interactive systems greatly increase the potential for electronic and born digital records to be tampered with. In a nutshell, in the proliferation of records and information, they have to answer the basic question, "what is a record?" To answer this question is not an easy task.

Duranti and Thibodeau, Gilliland, MacNeil, McKemmish, and other scholars and researchers representing several major countries have been investigating the authenticity, as well as the permanence, of records in electronic systems in a series of phases through The International Research on Permanent Authentic Records in Electronic Systems (InterPARES) Project (Gilliland-Swetland 2002; Duranti and Thibodeau 2006; InterPARES Project 2011; MacNeil 2005; McKemmish et al. 1999). During each phase of the project, the investigators focused on specific goals and tasks. For example, in InterPARES1, they focused on developing theory and methods for determining authenticity and preserving records created and maintained in databases and records management systems. During InterPARES2, along with the authenticity, they also looked for the accuracy and reliability of records throughout the lifecycle of these records from creation to permanent retention. They also focused on records in interactive, experiential, and dynamic environments. In InterPARES3 they have been working with small and medium-sized archives and units putting the theory learned in InterPARES1 and InterPARES2 into practice, as well as developing training programs and curricula. The overarching goal of the InterPARES Project is to develop theoretical knowledge that addresses issues arising in the real world and assists archivists and other professionals, such as records managers, lawyers, and so forth, in creating standards, policies, and strategies in ensuring the authenticity and longevity of electronic records.

Expanding the description of InterPARES here is done for good reason. The extensive, long-term efforts of scholars and researchers in InterPARES (of course, as well as the ongoing debate about the place of electronic records or born digital records in the modern archives) illustrate the critical need for archivists to be actively involved in the lifecycle of the record, beginning with the creation and ending with the retention or destruction of that record. In other words, archivists cannot just sit back and wait for the records to come to them before they begin planning to care for and provide access to them. The involvement of international scholars and researchers in InterPARES, as well, point to the reality that electronic records cross national boundaries and points out the need for in-depth conceptual knowledge about electronic records on a grand, global scale. In selecting and appraising records, archivists should ask such questions as: How were the records created? What national boundaries have the records crossed? What was the purpose behind the creation of the record? Who had access to the records over time? What national information policy has shaped the record's lifecycle? To be sure, the efforts and debate, more importantly, illustrate the need for archivists with professional and academic training.

ARRANGEMENT AND DESCRIPTION AND ACCESS OF ARCHIVES IN THE MODERN INFORMATION ENVIRONMENT

Archivists, just like librarians, are implementing advanced technology in diverse functions, activities, and services. For example, there is much excitement about using social networking and participatory technology in engaging users and the community in archives. One does not have to look far on the Internet to find examples of this; however, the use of technology in archival work goes deeper than embracing, say Web 2.0. Consider the information created through social networking tools. Users of such tools may be quick to share their digital records with others or with the general, global commons. For the professional archivist, on the other hand, critical questions emerge in this scenario: (1) What should happen to the information or record created through social networking, and does it have enduring and archival value? (2) Can the record be "arranged" and "described" using traditional, long-standing archival principles and practices? (3) What are the rules and standards that should guide the storage and preservation of this type of information? In a very real sense, while the modern information environment offers new opportunities and approaches for creating archives (such as through Web 2.0), it also brings what Pymm suggests are "limitations that have to be acknowledged and where possible, worked around" (2010, 24).

Arrangement and description is another core component of archival work. In arrangement and description, archivists have been guided by the fundamental archival principles of *respect des fonds* and *original order*. To the nonarchivist, it should be pointed out that during *arrangement* the archivist organizes and sequences materials in a collection in order to maintain physical and intellectual control over them, while during *description* the archivist creates a *finding aid* or a similar access tool to facilitate browsing and access, as well as to improve security and preserve and protect the materials in the collection. Arrangement and description comprise the *processing* of archival materials, which also includes assessing the condition of the materials and rehousing and applying preservation strategies to them as necessary, seeking to understand the context in which they were created, and seeking to understand and appreciate their creator. The *finding aid* in archival processing normally includes general information about the creator and the scope of the collection and a list of access points to the collection, as well as brief descriptions of components of the collection.

Duchein explains that to apply *respect des fonds* is "to group, without mixing them with others, the archives (documents of every kind) created by or coming from an administration, establishment, person, or corporate body. This grouping is called the *fonds* of the archives of that administration, establishment or person" (Duchein 1983, 64). The International Council on Archives (2000) defines *fonds* as "the whole of the records, regardless of form or medium, organically created and/or accumulated and used by a particular person, family, or corporate body in the course of that creator's activities and functions" (10). In the United States, the *fonds* is analogous to the "collection" or "records group." In applying *respect des fonds*, the archivist respects the creator of the *fonds*. In applying *original order*, the archivist respects the order in which the creator maintained his *fonds*. An important goal of maintaining original order is to preserve the relationships among the records, but we cannot expect that all records come to the archives with clear original order. When this happens, the archivist can impose order on these records.

If the principles of *respect des fonds* and *original order* emerged out of a paper-based tradition, as explained previously, what is their place in the modern digital or electronic information environment? Furthermore, what is the place of the archival finding aid in the modern information environment? And why are professionally educated archivists needed to ensure that the information environment is "friendly" to those accustomed to first-rate archival services?

Professional archivists have taken a leading role in employing modern information technology to advance access to the collections by the user. They, and archival researchers and scholars, long recognized that this technology could transform the effectiveness and efficiency of traditional aids and access tools to archival records. Through database and markup technologies, archivists are able to put archival finding aids online where they would be accessed by users all over.

As was described, the traditional archival finding aid allows respect for the creator of a *fonds,* or a group, by making explicit the clear relationship between the record group and its creator. With the use of modern information technology and the capability to use markup language and code to annotate text that will be put online, additional relationships between the record group and other creators, as well as other record groups, can be created. As records are used more widely (again thanks to modern information technology) additional meanings about them are constructed. Relationships among records, among creators, and among functions are constructed, and in turn, relationships among these relationships themselves are formed. Pitti (2005) explains that "it is now possible to not only envision but also to begin developing and realizing an archival descriptive system with dedicated apparatus for the description and interrelating of the principle components of archival description: description of creators, description of functions, and description of records" (17).

Professional archivists have studied extensively the different types of technologies and their practical tools in order to identify which would be useful to and efficient for the archival profession. They have had the professional education and training necessary to understand which technology will be most effective and efficient in an archival setting, for example, which dedicated semantics (in computer science terms, semantics refers to the meaning of data structures and languages) should be used, and how would they encode existing finding aids. For example, after years of investigation, technology researchers at the University of California, Berkeley, with Daniel Pitti as the principal investigator, developed EAD (Encoded Archival Description) as a standard tool to encode finding aids and deliver them to the Internet, releasing a version of it in the fall of 1998. Since then, the Library of Congress has maintained the EAD homepage. More and more institutions are using EAD to encode their finding aids.

The implementation of EAD is complex and costly. With funding and staff shortages, professional archivists have intelligently pursued cost-effective ways to deliver their materials to the Internet. For example, they have investigated and utilized open source systems, such as Omeka, to show virtual exhibits of their collections.

Information technology also continues to change, and professional archivists also know the theory behind the development and the application of technology. They know how to respond when the technology changes.

We might ask ourselves now if it has come to the point where technology has debunked the standard archival principles of *respect des fonds* and *original order*, the standard archival approaches grounded in understanding the contexts and inter-relationships of documents within a collection or record group. If it has, then a question posed earlier, "Can the record [created through social networking] be 'arranged' and 'described' using traditional, long-standing archival principles and practices?" is irrelevant. In fact, however, implementing the traditional principles helps to ensure that the technology used is effective and efficient. By paying par-ticular attention to *respect des fonds* and *original order* in creating the archival find-ing aid, the archivist, as MacNeil (2005) describes, has a part in helping to ensure the authenticity of the records in a collection through ensuring that the records are linked to their descriptions and that the descriptions are at the forefront when the records are accessed by the user. Furthermore, the archivist can help to preserve the sociohistorical contexts in which the collection as a whole was created.

MacNeil and undoubtedly others as well recognize that finding aids are not simply neutral tools; they are "cultural texts, historically situated in time and place. They are shaped by particular ideologies and intentionalities which in turn shape what they include and exclude, what they emphasize and what they ignore" (Mac-Neil 2005, 274). To be sure, there is a "social construction of finding aids," as MacNeil (2005, 274) points out, that deserves investigation. Referring to the likely consequence that the finding aid will still change when it is converted to a record on the Web, MacNeil asks, "To what extent does their mode of dissemination af-fect their content and structure?" (274).

In a very real sense, what all this illustrates is that archival records are complex to begin with, so much so some sort of organization is necessary before they are trans-ferred to the fluidity of the Web. In the dynamic, interactive, global information environment, archivists have to be professionally trained and educated in modern information technology, and the theories and concepts that provide meaning to it, so that they can use this technology to carry out their tasks and functions while maintaining their jurisdictional and professional edge (e.g., ensuring intellectual control of records) and, at the same time, increasing the capability of the user to access archival collections.

ARCHIVISTS IN THE DIVERSE SOCIETY

Some time ago, I was called on by a community's indigenous members to help as-sess the status of its records and collections. I was cognizant of the political tension in the geographical area that was affecting the relationships among its different components, including the indigenous group. As one of the upper level indigenous community leaders pointed out, there is a feeling among the indigenous com-munity that its members are being pushed to the margins by other groups in the community. By the same token, newcomers to the community are feeling that they are no longer welcome to the community. Nevertheless, I agreed to assess the "entire" community's records and collections, as I was asked to do. The indig-enous members of the area had made it clear to me that the records and collections that had enduring value and represented the community's cultural memory would be preserved, but as a "user-centered" archivist who wanted to gain insight into which records and collections these might be, these records and collections were discussed with all members of the community. Inevitably, it became problematic to identify which records and collections should be preserved as the community's political tensions continued to manifest themselves. In the end, it was necessary to assist all members of the community in a negotiation process for identifying for each group what constituted its cultural records and collections. It was necessary for me to assist all members of the community in recognizing their cultures in terms of past population movements and cultural dispersions. Throughout this process I relied on both my professional training and experience to work through what could have been major stumbling blocks to preserving the multiple memories of this community.

This experience points to the dilemma of an archives that is user-centered. One borrows the notion of user-centered versus system-centered from Dervin and Nilan (1986), who, after reviewing use and user studies in Library and Information Science, wrote that research in the field had moved from a system-centered to a user-centered approach. The volume of use and user studies in the archival literature is not proportionally as large; nevertheless, the work of several significant researchers, including Yakel and Torres's (2007) study of the community of genealogists, Duff and Johnson's (2003) study of the information-seeking behavior of genealogists, and Prom's (2004) study of user interactions with electronic finding aids, have set new standards for quality.

Just as the library, information, and knowledge professions have become externally focused, user-centered professions, so too has the archival profession, particularly with the use of modern information technology. In our increasingly multicultural world, archivists who work closely with users and potential users equal archivists who work closely with a diversity of users. In order for archivists to fulfill the archival needs of all their users, they have to make changes in the way they select and appraise records, arrange and describe records, and so forth. As Jimerson (2007) explains, "responding effectively to the challenges of using the power of archives for the public good will require a broad commitment by the archival profession to reflect on underlying assumptions and biases, and to over come these through a renewed commitment to democratic values" (281). In the example of my own experience discussed previously, it was necessary to insert my conceptual knowledge of the record—that is, the record as cultural memory, as collective memory, as authentic and possibly less-biased history, and so forth, into an inclusive community-wide negotiation process.

It was the historian Howard Zinn who first made a stand calling for archivists to play an activist role. He labeled the archivist's "supposed neutrality" as "a fake." He argued that "the existence, preservation, and availability of archives, documents, records in our society are very much determined by the distribution of wealth and power," and archival collections were "biased towards the important and powerful people of the society, tending to ignore the impotent and obscure" (Zinn 1977, 20–21).

Since Zinn's address, others, such as Tom Nesmith (2002), Randall C. Jimerson (2007), and Mark Greene (2009), have called for the archival profession to be more inclusive in its functions, tasks, and services, at times referring to it as a postmodernist approach. The climate today is for archivists to work toward social justice and accountability in performing their archival tasks. Admittedly, definitions of *social justice* and *accountability* vary over the time and place. Nevertheless, as archivists are charged with the care and maintenance of archival records and collections, they will be held accountable by future generations who will use these records and materials expecting that their existence is a result of well-formulated, professional decisions in which the relationships between history, memory, and accountability are taken into consideration (Dirks 2004). Dirks points out that the availability of archives is essential to serve "a society's need for the prevalence of justice, and the preservation of rights, and values" (38). To be sure, the world needs archivists who are professionally and academically trained.

A NECESSARY PROFESSIONAL EDUCATION

Throughout this chapter, the need for archivists to obtain professional education and training was stressed, but what does this professional education and training consist of? It was noted that in earlier days it was common for an archivist to have gained knowledge about archival principles and best practices through an introductory course and an extensive and broad internship and apprenticeship. It is now known that that is not sufficient. What the modern-day professional archivist needs are the conceptual and theoretical knowledge of how a record is created, authenticated, and preserved; knowledge of technical skills, along with the ability to implement technology for the purpose of carrying out his or her tasks most effectively and efficiently; and knowledge of the diversity of users and uses of archives, records, and collections. All this requires an extensive graduate archival education. Gilliland-Swetland (2000) points out three primary functions of a graduate education in archival science: (1) inculcating the knowledge base, skills, ethos, and societal roles of the archival profession; (2) grounding these in the history and theory of the underlying disciplines; and (3) advancing all of the aforementioned through critical inquiry. To these three fundamentals there might be added another educational component: (4) communicating effectively in order to understand and meet the needs of present and potential users. Gilliland-Swetland further points out that archival education should include the conduct of research and the acquisition of research skills, such as narrative analysis, grounded theory development, bibliometrics, and sociometrics or social network analysis.

Wosh (2000) agrees that archivists should have acquired research skills, especially as their job responsibilities now require them to be active information experts rather than mere passive curators. He calls for graduate archival education to prepare students to have a "highly nuanced understanding of the research process" (Wosh 2000, 271), including the ability to develop research questions, the ability to make the right methodological choice to carry out the research that will help answer the research questions, and the ability to effectively analyze data. All this makes explicit and validates what Duranti states as the recognition of "the high degree of complexity reached by archival work, the consequent need of conducting critical inquiry into the conceptual and theoretical aspects of the archival discipline, the impossibility for practicing archivists to undertake it within their own institution, and the requirement for those who conduct it in academia of having been trained in archival research and have experienced diverse methodologies and research design" (Duranti 2000, 242).

Two projects point out the way in which the diversity of the profession is addressed. The first is the "first broadscale survey of individual archivists in the United States in nearly thirty years," conducted in 2004, which identified specific issues that the profession needed to address in an expedient manner in order to proceed effectively in the information age. The survey, which was published as a full Fall/Winter 2006 issue of the SAA's publication, *The American Archivist*, was supported by the Institute of Museum and Library Services (IMLS) and was conducted by a Working Group, working under the auspices of the Society of American Archivists (SAA), and involved the diverse demographic, geographic, and professional membership of the archival profession. Among the critical issues identified in the survey were the need to strengthen "the profession's collective technical skills by rethinking and retooling . . . recruitment and training efforts," the need to "attract archivists who reflect the diversity of society at large," and the need to identify "effective methods for transferring the knowledge and values acquired through decades of education" (Walch et al. 2006, 295, 312).

The second was the "Pluralizing the Archival Paradigm through Education" collaborative project among the University of California at Los Angeles, Monash University in Melbourne, Australia, and Renmin University in Beijing, China, which started out in 2005, in its first phase. The project reviewed the state of archival education across the Pacific Rim region and sought to identify a methodology that would pay particular attention to the different communities and their needs "as they increasingly interact with economic, political, and technological global forces" (Gilliland et al. 2008, 96). At the conclusion of Phase One, the project called for the need to pluralize the archival paradigm to take into consideration, for example, the vast linguistic, cultural, and religious diversities in the many individual nations in the Pacific Rim (all with diverse political, economic, and historical circumstances). The project determined that the existing core curriculum and work of current archivists were not fully addressing the needs of people in the Pacific Rim.

Issues of diversity are important. Issues of diversity must be taken into consideration in archival education in order for future archivists to truly gain the conceptual and theoretical knowledge of how a record is created, authenticated, and preserved. Issues of diversity must be taken into consideration in archival education in order for future archivists to have broad knowledge of technical skills, along with the ability to implement technology for the purpose of carrying out his or her tasks most effectively and efficiently. In this effort, whether monolingual or polylingual, whether their personal lives have been lived within one culture or among several, all archivists must receive a professional education that is permeated with the values of effective intercultural communication between and among often diverse language, ethnic, national, and other communities.

In his extensive discussion about the system of professions, the sociologist Andrew Abbott proposed that while a profession has several exclusive properties, its most important possession is its jurisdiction. He contends that a profession must occupy a professional jurisdiction that has been vacant or that it had come across. After occupying a jurisdiction, a profession can expand it (Abbott 1988). I contend that in the information environment, the archival profession still has its jurisdictional edge in that professional archivists are still the ones who hold true the tradition of making sure that an institution's or a community's history, memory, and/or heritage is protected and preserved and the tradition of sustaining and acknowledging national, community, or personal identity in society. Professional archivists and archives are key instruments of accountability and empowerment in ensuring that rights and responsibilities are documented and organizational actions are transparent. The pre-eminent role of archives is to serve as trusted repositories of legal, historical, cultural, social, and bureaucratic evidence; the distinctive professional activities and ethics of archivists flow from the need to serve as trusted and competent stewards of that evidence. In a world of powerful bureaucracies and competing political and cultural narratives, archivists have to maintain a constant awareness of their inevitable role in shaping historical and cultural legacies and privileging or excluding certain voices and experiences, and of the diverse demands on and expectations of their archives. Their work, involving experience built on a solid professional education, in the appropriate techniques, is an ongoing negotiation between the identification, preservation, and representation of the evidence of a complex past in the present and the contemplation of the relevance and usability of that evidence in an unknown and unforeseeable future.

REFERENCES

Abbott, Andrew. 1988. *The System of Professions: An Essay on the Division of Expert Labor.* Chicago: The University of Chicago Press.

Cox, Richard J., and Ronald L. Larsen. 2008. "iSchools and Archival Studies." *Archival Science* 8(4): 307–26.

DeMars, Sr. Jacqueline. 2011. "NyPPaW Prepares to Move Archives to Belmont, N.C." *In Harmony* (spring). Accessed August 9, 2011. http://www.mercynyppaw.org/storage/documents/in_harmony/spring%202011%20in%20harmony.pdf.

Dervin, Brenda, and Michael Nilan. 1986. "Information Needs and Uses." In *Annual Review of Information Science and Technology* (ARIST), vol. 21, ed. Martha E. Williams, 3–33. White Plains, NY: Knowledge Industry Publications.

Dirks, John M. 2004. "Accountability, History, and Archives: Conflicting Priorities or Synthesized Strands?" *Archivaria* 57(spring): 35, 49.

Duchein, Michel. 1983. "Theoretical Principles and Practical Problems of Respect des fonds in Archival Science." *Archivaria* 16: 64.

Duff, Wendy M., and Catherine A. Johnson. 2003. "Where Is the List with All the Names? Information-seeking Behavior of Genealogists." *American Archivist* 66(1): 79–95. Accessed August 9, 2011. http://archivists.metapress.com/content/l375uj047224737n/fulltext.pdf.

Duranti, Luciana. 2000. "The Society of American Archivists and Graduate Archival Education: A Sneak Preview of Future Directions." *American Archivist* 63(2): 237–42. Accessed August 9, 2011. http://archivists.metapress.com/content/l417x9l3840qn07l/fulltext.pdf.

Duranti, Luciana, and Kenneth Thibodeau. 2006. "The Concept of Record in Interactive, Experiential and Dynamic Environments: The View of InterPARES." *Archival Science* 6(1): 13–68.

Fleckner, John A. 1991. "'Dear Mary Jane': Some Reflections on Being an Archivist." *American Archivist* 54(1): 8–13. Accessed August 9, 2011. http://archivists.metapress.com/content/3607610316t66j42/fulltext.pdf.

Gilliland, Anne, Sue McKemmish, Kelvin White, Yang Lu, and Andrew Lau. 2008. "Pluralizing the Archival Paradigm: Can Archival Education in the Pacific Rim Communities Address the Challenge?" *American Archivist* 71(1): 87–117.

Gilliland-Swetland, Anne J. 2000. "Archival Research: A 'New' Issue for Graduate Education." *American Archivist* 63(2): 258–70. Accessed August 9, 2011. http://archivists.metapress.com/content/6226636045t48543/fulltext.pdf.

Gilliland-Swetland, Anne J. 2002. "Testing Our Truths: Delineating the Parameters of the Authentic Archival Electronic Record." *American Archivist* 65(2): 196–215. Accessed August 9, 2011. http://archivists.metapress.com/content/f036wp74710g1483/fulltext.pdf.

Given, Lisa M., and Lianne McTavish. 2010. "What's Old Is New Again: The Reconvergence of Libraries, Archives, and Museums in the Digital Age." *Library Quarterly* 80(1): 3–32.

Greene, Mark. 2009. "The Power of Archives: Archivists' Values and Value in the Post-modern Age." *American Archivist* 72(1): 17–41. Accessed August 9, 2011. http://archivists.metapress.com/content/k0322x0p38v44l53/fulltext.pdf.

Hensen, Steven L. 2002. "Revisiting Mary Jane, or Dear Cat: Being Archival in the 21st Century." *American Archivist* 65(2): 168–75. Accessed August 9, 2011. http://archivists.metapress.com/content/104w103270121021/fulltext.pdf.

International Council on Archives, ISAD(G). 2000. *International Standard for Archival Description (General)*. Ottawa, CA: ICA.

InterPARES Project. 2011. Accessed August 9. http://www.interpares.org/.

Jimerson, Randall C. 2007. "Archives for All: Professional Responsibility and Social Justice." *American Archivist* 70(2): 252–81. Accessed August 9, 2011. http://archivists.metapress.com/content/5n20760751v643m7/fulltext.pdf.

Laycock, Mike. 2011. "Nestle Opens Archives Facility in York." *The York Press*. Accessed August 9. http://www.yorkpress.co.uk/news/9118686.Nestl__opens_archives_facility_in_York/?action=complain&cid=9485223.

Mackintosh, Barry. 1998. "The Value of Archives to National Park Historians." *History E-Library*. Accessed August 9, 2011. http://www.nps.gov/history/history/his-nps/npsarchives/arch.htm.

MacNeil, Heather. 2005. "Picking Our Text: Archival Description, Authenticity, and the Archivist as Editor." *American Archivist* 68(2): 264–78. Accessed August 9, 2011. http://archivists.metapress.com/content/01u65t6435700337/fulltext.pdf.

McKemmish, Sue, Glenda Acland, Nigel Ward, and Barbara Reed. 1999. "Describing Records in Context in the Continuum: The Australian Recordkeeping Metadata Scheme." *Archivaria* 48: 3–44.

Nesmith, Tom. 2002. "Seeing Archives: Postmodernism and the Changing Intellectual Place of Archives." *American Archivist* 65(1): 24–41. Accessed August 9, 2011. http://archivists.metapress.com/content/rr48450509r0712u/fulltext.pdf.

O'Toole, James M. 1990. *Understanding Archives and Manuscripts*. Chicago: Society of American Archivists.

Pearce-Moses, Richard. 2005. *A Glossary of Archival and Records Terminology*. Chicago: Society of American Archivists.

Pitti, Daniel V. 2005. "Technology and the Transformation of Archival Description." *Journal of Archival Organization* 23: 17.

Prom, Christopher J. 2004. "User Interactions with Electronic Finding Aids in a Controlled Setting." *American Archivist* 67(2): 234–68. Accessed August 9, 2011. http://archivists.metapress.com/content/7317671548328620/fulltext.pdf.

Pymm, Bob. 2010. "Archives and Web 2.0: The Example of the September 11 Digital Archive." *Archives and Manuscripts* 38: 13–26.

Walch, Victoria Irons, Nancy P. Beaumont, Elizabeth Yakel, Jeannette Bastian, Nancy Zimmelman, Susan Davis, and Anne Diffendal. 2006. "A*Census (Archival Census and Education Survey Needs in the United States)." *American Archivist* 69(2): 291–419. Accessed August 9, 2011 http://archivists.metapress.com/content/d474374017506522/fulltext.pdf.

Wosh, Peter J. 2000. "Research and Reality Checks: Change and Continuity in NYU's Archival Management Program." *The American Archivist* 63(2): 271–83.

Yakel, Elizabeth, and Deborah A. Torres. 2007. "Genealogists as a 'Community of Records.'" *The American Archivist* 70(1): 93–113.

Zinn, Howard. 1977. "Secrecy, Archives, and the Public Interest." *Midwestern Archivist* 2(2): 20–21.

10

A CULTURALLY PRAGMATIC AND FEMINIST-INFLUENCED APPROACH TO DEFENDING PROFESSIONALISM

Bill Crowley
Dominican University

DEFINING THE PROBLEM

The aim of this chapter is to counter the deprofessionalization of librarians, information specialists, knowledge managers, and archivists through providing a defense of their professional educations, cultures, and values from the perspectives of cultural pragmatism and feminism. In doing so the author (1) provides a theoretical underpinning for the defense of the professionalism of appropriately educated practitioners; (2) explores the operation of Return on Emotional Investment (ROEI) in solidifying support for library, information, knowledge, and archival professionalism; (3) considers what role the female dominated nature of librarianship plays in complicating or solving the deprofessionalization problem; and (4) presents the reader with pragmatic and feminist reasons for supporting a spectrum of professionalism that effectively solves problems of personal significance of community, school, academic, or organizational importance.

TWO STORIES OF LIBRARIAN PROFESSIONALISM

Some time ago the author held an appointment with the Alabama Public Library Service and served with another consultant who had spent many years working in the American Southwest. On several occasions this consultant talked of the difficulty of convincing local officials of the value of hiring professional librarians, even describing how a community in one southwestern state had "solved the problem" of a formerly middle class but recently impoverished local resident by appointing her as the municipality's public librarian. Although the woman lacked professional training and was clearly unqualified for her position, she did have well-established community connections. In what was undoubtedly an emotional response to this woman's financial problems, the local decision makers on library matters determined that helping a respected community member avoid the embarrassment of receiving welfare was worth the negative impact her appointment might have on the quality of library service provided to local residents.

Several years later the author was sitting in the office of a senior public library administrator in a Midwestern city—which will be discussed under the pseudonym of "Franklin"—when a library assistant rushed into the room to inform the administrator that she, a staff member strongly connected to her community, was being threatened with the loss of her job. This announcement shocked the senior manager. Although the woman was a patronage appointee sent over by city hall, her work was satisfactory and the administrator had never considered recommending her discharge to his own supervisor, the library director. When he so informed the assistant, she reminded the administrator that it was an election year in Franklin. Her party, which had presided over the city and county government for decades, was unexpectedly facing the loss of a critical elected position, one that controlled many well-paid jobs and lucrative government contracts.

According to the library assistant, such an electoral defeat would strongly affect the public library, something she had just learned in a phone call from her city hall contact. That day, the county chair had announced to a meeting of party leaders that if the position controlling so much patronage was lost, many city and county government employees holding their jobs through political connections, regardless of who appointed them, would be fired after the election. A number of library employees, those who had been sent over by city hall for open positions, would be gone, regardless of how well they might be doing their jobs. The only way they could save their positions was to work night and day to turn out the vote for their party.

Within the Franklin Public Library the only personnel explicitly declared to be safe in their jobs were the professional librarians, people who had been hired on the basis of their educational qualifications and experience, not their political contacts. The librarians would not have to violate their professional ethics and state law by being forced to carry out partisan activities, including outside work on paid library time. Nonetheless, exemption from compulsory politicking did not leave the professional librarians untouched. As the campaign ramped up in intensity, they had to deal with service complications resulting from periodic absences of the support staff. The librarians also felt the need to bolster the morale of their politically connected coworkers, even as such staff routinely left their normal daytime assignments behind for what were euphemistically termed *external library activities.*

Ultimately, the critical elected position that controlled so many human and financial resources was retained by the party in power. With electioneering temporarily over, the library staff members involved were able to return to their normal duties. At this time the author had the opportunity to discuss the situation with a local official who liked libraries and librarians but who had spent his adult life thriving in Franklin's culture of patronage. In this conversation the author learned more about why the librarians had been exempted from forced political work. Franklin was a predominantly working-class community where college was not the norm and graduation from high school was an achievement. It was a city where local role models outside of the worlds of politics, sports, and criminal activities were rare. In this atmosphere, their dedicated work for the community had made the public librarians respected for their commitment and their professional education. Forcing them to participate in partisan politics as a condition of keeping their jobs would have been seen as appalling by many, including some who made their living on the basis of their political connections.

"Unlike a lot of city and county employees the librarians actually work to their job descriptions," the politician pointed out. "Anybody who uses the library knows their agenda is the good of the community. And their professional qualifications also mean that the party has less leverage with them. The librarians can go elsewhere if the county chair forces them to get out the vote by threatening their jobs."

The official smiled. "Obviously, the county chair and I wouldn't want that kind of situation. It would cause unnecessary problems, even for some of our precinct captains. Their kids love the librarians. Besides, if we had pressed the matter the media might have found out that we were treating professional librarians like patronage appointees. It's a mom, motherhood, and apple pie sort of thing. The negative publicity alone would have cost us votes."

DISCUSSION

In this author's years of service as a professional librarian and senior library administrator in New York, Alabama, Indiana, and Ohio, as well as his work as a library and information science faculty member in Illinois, he learned early and repeatedly that variants of the preceding stories occur with some regularity in the United States of America. Assuming certain similarities in human nature, it is likely that similar activities are going on, perhaps more discretely, in certain Canadian and British environments. It might well be something close to a multinational truism that, sometimes, people in authority are going to advance their political or social agendas by using the public library for purposes not enshrined in the relevant library law.

It is equally correct to observe that accounts of such illegalities and improprieties are seldom made public. All involved have reasons for keeping these offenses undetected. Community leaders, including elected or appointed library board members, fear the consequences resulting from awareness of their misuse of public funds, including criminal prosecution, civil litigation, or, at the very least, public embarrassment and loss of reputation. Employees appointed for political reasons want to keep their jobs. Library managers dread the possibility of negative social media postings and embarrassing articles in the professional media. The notoriety of being caught on a video recording while violating state, provincial, or national laws and then having the evidence posted online might have a fatal impact on a director's career.

Although there are strong reasons for stories like this to be concealed, sharing accounts of illegal or unethical employment practices over drinks at state or national conferences sometimes does occur. Such stories can also be related, albeit discretely, during one-on-one mentoring sessions of new professionals by supervisors or colleagues who believe that newcomers need to know that libraries, information and knowledge centers, and archives are not always exempt from the less positive ways in which the world sometimes works.

These two stories were selected for this chapter in order to provide dramatic examples of how the presence or absence of respect and support for their education and expertise, what the author has termed ROEI, can strongly impact the future prospects of library, information, knowledge, and archival professionals. The extended result is also a positive or negative effect on their employing institutions and the clientele they are charged with assisting. ROEI has been defined "as a continuing emotional connection between users and the libraries and professional librarians who provide the library services and programs that people deem vital to their lives" (Crowley 2010, 34), and the story of the Midwest library represents a textbook example of its operation. Yet the concept is not limited to public libraries alone. The emotionally driven support generated by ROEI is also present, or absent, when professionally educated practitioners operate, or fail to operate, well-run, market-focused, and customer-oriented information centers, knowledge centers, and archives.

In the case of the southwestern community, ROEI as support for librarian professionalism did not exist within the ranks of the local culture's leadership. The library itself was seen as a tool for other purposes, including saving a neighbor from public embarrassment over her new financial distress. In the southwest example, generating positive library-focused ROEI would likely have required more than an individual grateful for having avoided public assistance. It would have demanded the interaction with her or his community of a dedicated practitioner, intellectually equipped with both a professional education and a customer-driven commitment to service.

Paradoxically, the exceedingly partisan environment of the City of Franklin appears to demonstrate a high degree of ROEI in its support for librarian professionalism. The culture of the community made it acceptable, even preferable, for support staff positions in the library to be used as political rewards. However, professional librarians, whose job descriptions required a master's degree from an American Library Association (ALA)-accredited program, were valued for their nonpartisan contributions to the community's well-being. At a fundamental level the librarians had an undeniable emotional connection with the community and through their work helped shape its more positive cultural values. Even at a time when political appointees throughout Franklin and its surrounding county feared for their jobs, professional librarians, because of their graduate education and the quality of their services to local residents, were respected and appreciated, not terrified and exploited.

A (VERY) FEW WORDS ON THEORY

It is to be recalled that this chapter is written from the standpoints of cultural pragmatism and feminism, research philosophies that the author addressed in *Spanning the Theory-Practice Divide in Library and Information Science* (Crowley 2005) and *Renewing Professional Librarianship: A Fundamental Rethinking* (Crowley 2008). For the benefit of those who find theory useful, the author's comprehensive definition of cultural pragmatism and his definition of feminism, both of which first appeared in 2005, are provided in the appendix to this chapter.

The role of feminist theory in sustaining professionalism is addressed later. While this author's extended work on cultural pragmatism forms the other intellectual support on which this chapter is constructed, he has found that practitioners prefer a shorter, more memorable version of how pragmatism works. To this end I have borrowed a concise description of the process through which pragmatists solve problems from a 2001 issue of the *Hedgehog Review*. In their introduction to this special issue on the revival of pragmatism the editors of the Hedgehog Review stressed:

> For the most part, pragmatists offer us a simple means of thinking, talking, and deliberating about the things that matter most to us. They tell us to resist

abstraction, stay close to experience, allow for mistakes and uncertainty, and look to the consequences of what we propose to believe and do. Pragmatism can be seen as a way of approaching life, disagreements, hurdles, and decisions. "Test one hypothesis, answer, or solution against another," the pragmatist suggests. "Rather than strive to attain absolutes or certainty, try to come up with something that works and makes sense of your experiences." ("Introduction: Pragmatism" 2001, 5)

Each academic, school, organizational, or political culture has its own particular set of values, and the understanding of their impact is critical for those who would develop or sustain any sort of LIS professionalism. Nevertheless, even with such cultural diversity, it is possible to secure a general knowledge of the barriers to developing professional status from the library, information, knowledge, archival, and other professional literatures.

WHAT IS A PROFESSION?

Daniel Condon is a Dominican University professor and colleague of the author who teaches in the university's Brennan School of Business. He has also been a relatively frequent presenter during the university's Faculty Seminar Series, a weekly event where, over a university-provided lunch, professors can communicate their research to an audience of other faculty. In the question and answer session following one such presentation, Dan, a respected economist, pointed out that all professionalism is "restraint of trade." He then emphasized that the more formal the profession, the more elevated its requirements, and the stronger its legal support, the fewer people it allows to practice.

This point being made, Dan went on to observe that if the United States, Canada, or any other nation had a totally free market anyone could be a surgeon, with or without formal education, internships, and residencies. In such a totally unregulated market the primary criteria for a surgeon would be low cost and success on the operating table. Those who charged the least while killing the fewest were likely to be seen as the best surgeons, with or without formal training. It should be noted that Dan's example, drawn from the world of economics, intentionally ignores such nonprofessional yet often-present factors as "old boy" and "old girl" ties, family associations, political connections, and personal networks.

Professionalism supports values based on relevant education and experience as an alternative to the values of unrestricted free markets, family links, close friendships, or political contacts. Such an emphasis in a community or organizational culture presumably results in the delivery of higher quality services to citizens, customers, or consumers in return for the culture's support for requiring some level of professional education and training. Educational requirements undoubtedly limit the number of people who may serve in a profession. However, without professional standards as a basis for civil service rules, job descriptions, and other indications of minimum competency, how else can one avoid the very human tendency to discriminate among job applicants by inappropriately prioritizing often nonrelevant relationships and connections over relevant education, training, skill, and experience?

Studying the Library, Information, Knowledge, and Archival Professions

Examinations of the characteristics required of a profession have formed a virtual cottage industry within the library and information literature. The extent of this effort is well-documented in the third edition of Richard E. Rubin's (2010) *Foundations of Library and Information Science* (102–5). According to Rubin, approaches such as the analysis of traits (service oriented, altruistic, possessing a body of theory, etc.), control (power over work by professionals, clients, or shared by both), and values (dedication to improving lives of individuals and society, support for democracy, etc.) have been crucial to a number of attempts to construct an acceptable model for library and information professionalism.

Such analyses may reflect the interest of scholars in generalizing for analytical purposes. On a practical basis, specified criteria can also have an impact with bureaucratically oriented human resource departments in developing a city or university library's professional job descriptions. However, the reality is that professionalism of any type is usually not a status dependent on objective and universal criteria. It is a condition nearly always supported or undermined in particular contexts and subjectively judged by how well a given profession supports the values of an individual community, organization, or nation.

No foolproof checklist exists on which points are added or subtracted for a range of factors, which, when totaled, "objectively" determine professionalism in library, information, knowledge, or archival work. A profession is established, maintained, or lost within a given community, organization, or nation on internal cultural perceptions that the profession's professional values and their impact on service delivery are or are not advancing the values that are deemed important by the dominant culture.

Several years ago, the author and Deborah Ginsberg described how professionalism comes to be recognized and supported in an article published in the practitioner-oriented magazine *American Libraries*. With only a slight bit of editing to promote inclusiveness, this analysis captures the realities affecting the perceived professionalism of librarians, information scientists, knowledge managers, and archivists alike.

> 21st century librarianship [as well as information science, knowledge management, and archival professionalism] in the United States [Canada and the United Kingdom] may well live or die on its ability to harness expertise in support of a spectrum of values prized by significant subcultures within the broader national culture. To retain our professional status, librarians [and other LIS professionals] will need to trade on "intracultural reciprocity:" the changing, context-specific perceptions of mutual worth by participants in geographical, organizational, social, cultural, and other arenas. Librarians [and other LIS professionals] will enjoy intracultural reciprocity as long as they are components of a group that accepts and supports their professionalism. By design a dynamic and changing reality, intracultural reciprocity can be extended—or withdrawn—in response to alternations in societal, cultural, or market contexts. (Crowley and Ginsberg 2005, 53)

Admittedly, the term *intracultural reciprocity* is an ugly phrase for the process of mutually awarding and sustaining professional status. Even though there is no consensus on the criteria for professional recognition that is applicable within all community or organizational cultures, certain recurring factors do seem to be present in the process. With some exceptions, professional status in the United States, Canada, and Britain

- Requires some sort of advanced education;
- Tends to be awarded to the group when the professional education, experience, and commitment of group members are viewed as important resources for addressing what a given community or organizational culture determines to be its critical problems and priority needs;
- Is maintained through emotional support for the profession and its members, a natural response when members of a community or organizational culture see themselves as strongly benefiting from the profession's work on their behalf; and
- Is diminished or lost when undermined by the actions of practitioners and educators, as well nonprofessional decision makers.

BARRIERS TO RECOGNITION AS A PROFESSION

The broad range of barriers to securing and maintaining a particular culture's recognition and support for library, information, knowledge, or archival professionals was discussed in depth in chapter 1, "Why Are We Trashing the Professionalism of Librarians, Information Specialists, Knowledge Managers, and Archivists?" At this point a more limited consideration can begin with the reminder that, in the public library sphere, antiprofessionalism factors include

- fear for their jobs by "librarians" who gained their positions without the ALA-accredited master's degree;
- concern by elected officials, trustees, and customers in smaller communities over losing local library service—or at least control of such service—if required to pay the salaries of local professional librarians or accept supervision of a community's library services by a larger library system;
- willingness of certain library "leaders" to jettison librarian professionalism rather than carrying out the extended work of maintaining a climate of effective, responsive service that in itself makes the case for the retention of professional status;
- fear by professional associations that stressing the value of professional education will alienate librarians and others without the appropriate professional training, trouble public library trustees who have failed in their duty to acquire the financial support necessary to hire professional librarians, and weaken these associations by alienating dues-paying individuals and organizations who might discontinue their memberships if the issue of professionalism was emphasized; and
- absence of a critical mass of professional librarians whose values, transmitted through their professional education, provide the framework for meeting the personal or professional needs of customers, patrons, and users.

In any given occurrence, one or more of these factors can negatively influence the hiring of professional librarians and thereby lessen the levels of positive

ROEI for librarian professionalism. Variations of these factors can and do have their counterparts in virtually all library, information, knowledge, and archival sectors.

As discussed in Chapter 1, it is too-often the case that professional leaders will proclaim their allegiance to the concept that community or organizational support for service excellence is developed and maintained through a process of effective marketing. However, they fall short of turning this conceptual truth into an implemented reality. Such lack of follow-through generally means library, information, knowledge, and archival leaders and managers have not identified priority needs and/or aligned always limited resources to effectively address them. As a result, when a crisis occurs and funding is threatened, the value of library or information professionalism has not been established with external decision makers and must be defended, if at all, in a makeshift manner.

This predictable tendency of certain library and information leaders to undervalue, and undermine the value of the professionals may actually be welcomed by library governing boards, academic administrators, and corporate and other organizational managers who are dealing with imposed limits on available resources. Professionalism costs money. If LIS managers and leaders do not make the case for professional excellence in meeting priority community or organizational needs, who else is going to do so? One cannot expect the case for employing qualified library, information, knowledge, and archival professionals, including the trade-off of more money for better service, is going to be made by one's competitors in the competition for limited public or organizational funds.

Community perception of the long-standing, even systematic, failure of public libraries to market effectively became a significant factor in the interviews with local civic leaders conducted for *Long Overdue: A Fresh Look at Public Attitudes about Libraries in the 21st Century*, a valuable report prepared by Public Agenda. In addition to describing the concern for public libraries expressed by civic leaders, *Long Overdue* stressed that "public libraries' lack of marketing, impassive advocacy and isolation from the community were . . . cited as shortcomings in library performance" (Public Agenda Foundation 2006, 13).

From the perspective of cultural pragmatism, an effective marketing effort to align library, information, knowledge, and archival services with priority community or organizational needs is best undertaken with an understanding of what has been termed a culture's deep structure.

CULTURE AND ITS DEEP STRUCTURE

Every culture possesses a deep structure that defines a preferred model for existence, that prescribes for communities and organizations alike how to live and what makes life worth living. The three most enduring and most powerful components of culturally deep structures, the ones that library, information, knowledge, and archival professionals need to understand as forming the context within which to demonstrate their professionalism, are

1. Family
2. State (community)
3. Religion (worldview) (Samovar, Porter, and McDaniel 2010, 49)

While public libraries have long supported family friendly programs and, of late, have become enamored of the concept that libraries build community, it is likely that most libraries, information centers, knowledge management centers and archives have never adequately identified the components of their community or organizational culture's deep structure. In consequence, it is doubtful that they have mapped out their services to determine if programs advance or hinder achievement of the priorities of their employing culture. Identifying their place in advancing a community or organization's cultural priorities is key to developing a robust emotional response. A strong ROEI requires going beyond stressing the value of the institution. People relate to other people, not buildings or social networking sites. Both concrete and electronic "structures" are clearly necessary, but emotional connections are best developed by focusing on how the work of LIS professionals not only meets the identified needs of their service communities but assists such communities in obtaining a fuller understanding of how library, information, knowledge, and archival professionals help solve less visible, if equally important, cultural problems. Effective approaches to meeting identified and less understood, if equally critical, cultural needs, including how professionals can support the fundamental cultural structures of family, state/community, and religion worldview while strengthening their own professionalism and living up to its values, will be explored more in chapter 12 "The Political Case for Supporting the Value of Professionalism."

Effectively addressing the emotional component of community values is at the heart of the 2008 OCLC report *From Awareness to Funding: A Study of Library Support in America*, a compilation of research that helps validate the pragmatic concept of ROEI. As readers may recall, ROEI is defined "as a continuing emotional connection between users and the libraries and professional librarians who provide the library services and programs that people deem vital to their lives" (Crowley 2010, 34). The author cannot help but use the concept of ROEI when addressing what OCLC found were the perceptions of the librarian that were highly related to funding support. In what some might consider to be a counterintuitive finding, OCLC determined that such factors as how often one visits the library or how knowledgeable one is about library programs are not central to determining an individual's level of commitment to financial support of the public library (De Rosa and Johnson 2008, 4–8).

It is not a contradiction to observe that some of the most "anti-tax" people in a community can become heavy library users when they cannot purchase their own materials or services. Particularly in times of high unemployment, people who see themselves as lacking the money to pay additional taxes may desperately need and borrow multitudes of "free" library children's books, enjoy numerous "no charge" library programs, or use "no cost" library access to the internet to research job sites and submit electronic job applications.

Alternatively, according to OCLC,

> While frequency of library visitation and awareness of the full range of library services are not key determinants of library funding support, respondents' perceptions of the public librarian have a strong influence on funding support. Survey respondents rated the librarians at their local public libraries across a number of attributes. Analysis of the responses shows that a strong positive rating for the librarian across five of these attributes has a strong

influence on library funding support. These five attributes can be combined to describe the "passionate librarian":

- *True advocate for lifelong learning*
- *Passionate about making the library relevant again*
- *Knowledgeable about every aspect of the library*
- *Well-educated*
- *Knowledgeable about the community. (De Rosa and Johnson 2008, 4–8)*

Given OCLC's findings that these attributes of a "passionate librarian" can and do result in support for additional funding, the results of the entire study may be seen as forming a benchmark example of the reciprocal benefits of ROEI for public librarians, the institutions they represent, and the public they serve. It is often the case that individuals and communities make significant decisions on the basis of "feelings" and not "facts." Consequently, it is a poorly educated librarian, information specialist, knowledge manager, or archivist who neglects the importance of the emotional component of professionalism.

THE ROLE OF FEMINIST THEORY IN DEFENDING LIBRARY, INFORMATION, KNOWLEDGE, AND ARCHIVAL PROFESSIONALISM

"Doing Well by Doing Good"

Several years after capping an extensive library career by earning a PhD and accepting an appointment with Dominican University's Graduate School of Library and Information Science (GSLIS), I was participating in a meeting of the university's Planning Committee. It was a long session with the discussion focused on how to encourage students to become more engaged in social outreach and thereby advance the university's mission of helping to create a more just and humane world.

By this time I had become familiar with the altruistic motivations of many of the overwhelmingly female students in the GSLIS master's degree program. With that background, I also found myself thinking that in the area of self-sacrifice the university faculty and administrators had nothing to teach these students. When a break came in the discussion, I turned to share this observation with another committee member, who happened to be a Sinsinawa Dominican and a member of the order of nuns who had founded Dominican University a century before.

"My students don't need to be any more self-sacrificing," I told Sister Janet Welsh, O.P. "They already do too much of that. A lot of our students go into substantial debt while earning their MLIS degree. What they really need to do is get a good-paying job and become more skilled at looking after their own interests. They need to adopt that well-recognized southern Protestant approach of learning "How to do well by doing good." Sister Janet's understanding response was to laugh and remind me that I was still included in her prayers.

Feminism has many definitions, and this author even proposed one in *Spanning the Theory-Practice Divide in Library and Information Science*, a definition that is included in the appendix to this chapter (Crowley 2005, 203). However, for the

purpose of defending professionalism from a feminist perspective, that definition
is far from adequate. In this chapter I prefer to draw on that folksy southern truth
and offer the newer definition that feminism for librarianship, information science,
knowledge management, and archives is a philosophical approach designed to enhance the status of women by encouraging them to "do well" for themselves, their
gender, and their profession through adopting approaches that enable them to "do
good" for their communities and organizations.

The value, indeed necessity, of relying on feminist insights when addressing the
defense of professionalism in library, information, knowledge, and archival contexts
is difficult to dispute. Approximately 80 percent of the "professional master's degrees from program accredited by the American Library Association (ALA) . . . *are
earned by women*" (Crowley 2005, 77, emphasis added). This lopsided gender
division in higher education LIS programs has remained remarkably consistent as
reported in the annual "Earned Degrees, Conferred" (2010, 31) section "Almanac
Issue" of the *Chronicle of Higher Education*.

In this short examination of the role feminism can play in defending library,
information, knowledge, and archival professionalism, the most salient question
to be addressed is, Does supporting professionalism, particularly the requirement
for a master's degree from an ALA program, or equivalent recognition in the British context, advance or retard achieving equal status for women in contemporary
American, Canadian, and British workplaces?

Ironically, consideration of the value of the master's degree from an ALA-accredited program is complicated by the finding of Robert Flatley and Andrea Wyman
(2009, 33) that in public libraries serving less than 2,500 people only 14 percent
of the "librarians" possessed the ALA-endorsed degree. Moreover, those employed
as "librarian" without the MLIS degree may lack commitment to the professional
aims of librarianship, having secured their library position as a result of the simple
need for a job, preferably one with the possibility of "upward mobility" (Flatley
and Wyman 2009, 27). Although extensive discussion of the implications of gender was lacking in the Flatley-Wyman study, it was reported that the "majority of
respondents were women between the ages of 40–59" (Flatley and Wyman 2009,
36). From his extensive work experience in such states as Alabama, Indiana, Ohio,
and Illinois, and presentations and discussions in the Canadian provinces of British
Columbia and Ontario, the author believes that the percentage of women librarians of all ages in public libraries in Canada and the United States is likely to at least
mirror the 2009 figure of 83 percent female, which was asserted for contemporary
American librarianship as a whole in "Librarians in the U.S. from 1880–2009"
(Beveridge, Weber, and Beveridge 2011). Given the reality of so many "librarians"
without a professional education, the question naturally arises—What has feminism to say regarding the encouragement of the hiring of master's degree–holding
library professionals in Canadian and American rural communities?

Of late, urban and suburban libraries have seemingly embraced "downgrading professional work" under the guise of a "wise deployment of staff" (Oder
2009). Given the reality that many of the professional positions being diminished
to assistant or even clerical levels were previously held by master's degree–holding
women, another questions seems obvious—What has feminism to say regarding
the deprofessionalization of librarian positions, even if those later hired for the
downgraded positions are women?

Feminist Questions and Answers

Providing answers to the previous questions can help sharpen an awareness of the value of feminist thought in the protection of professionalism in library, information, knowledge, and archival contexts.

1. Does supporting professionalism, particularly the requirement for a master's degree from an ALA program, or equivalent recognition in the British context, advance or retard achieving equal status for women in contemporary American, Canadian, and British workplaces?

The development of librarianship, later library and information studies, into a series of professions has taken place in the midst of otherwise advanced societies nonetheless still afflicted with "sexist attitudes" (Garrison 1979, 241). As one of the professions with a majority of female professionals, librarianship may deprofessionalize more from a lack of internal support than from external pressures.

In my years of public service, research, and theory building, I have concluded that the actions of the directors and other administrators who make or recommend decisions that uphold or undermine feminist values in library, information, knowledge, and archival contexts, whether they be female or male, are immensely more important than their feminist or nonfeminist rhetoric.

It might be a surprise to some to learn that those who do not self-identify as feminists may yet advance feminist goals by supporting the professionalism of appropriately educated women. Directors or administrators, male or female, who adopt a dynamic marketing approach to identifying and meeting critical academic, public, school, or corporate/organizational needs and thereby secure the resources to employ credentialed professionals, the majority of whom are likely to be female, can be identified as supporters of feminist professionalism on the basis of their actions, regardless of their verbal expressions. Alternatively, managers who neglect a marketing approach, who do not identify and meet critical community or organizational needs for library, information, knowledge, or archival services, and, in consequence, are denied the resources to support professional services, are, for all practical purposes, nonfeminists.

The short feminist answer to this question is the argument that professionally educated women, using their advanced library, information, knowledge, or archival education to help solve priority community and organizational problems form the critical human examples that advance the goal of gender equality in American, British, and Canadian environments. Such examples and their valuable services should be found in all possible library, information, knowledge, and archival contexts, rural, suburban, urban, and online.

2. What has feminism to say regarding the encouragement of the hiring of master's degree–holding library professionals in Canadian and American rural communities?

Contemporary feminism would see the residents of rural communities as no less deserving of quality library, information, knowledge, and archival services than their urban and suburban counterparts.

Over the decades feminist theorists with a practical bent have joined their prag-matic counterparts advocating for the reforms necessary for women and men to have equal opportunities for lifelong success. This more-than-occasional common-ality of interests is the reason why this writer, steeped in cultural pragmatism, sees both feminism and pragmatism as essential components of any successful effort to expand and protect library, information, knowledge, and archival professionalism.

PROFESSIONALS AS VALUES KEEPERS IN COMMUNITY AND ORGANIZATIONAL CULTURES

Defining Library, Information, Knowledge, and Archival Values

The extended spectrum of library, information, knowledge, and archival environ-ments enormously complicates any discussion of how professionals educated for each and in such context carry out their vital if too-often underappreciated roles as important keepers of community and organizational values. Throughout the chap-ters of this volume, the reader will find specific and implied values statements, in-cluding those addressing a spectrum of fundamental beliefs that include the worth of providing library and information services as "public goods," freely distributed to users, and the equally acceptable concept of delivering information services for gain or implementing them in support of the profit-making operations of the larger organization. Nonetheless, from the perspective of the author's cultural pragma-tism it appears difficult to make a case for the application of the same library, infor-mation, knowledge, and archival values to all professional contexts. Even setting aside the matter of "free versus fee," finding fundamental values applicable to both corporate knowledge management centers and public libraries might require lin-guistic gymnastics in describing the work of the professionals involved.

Nonetheless, Richard E. Rubin (2010), in the third edition of his *Foundations of Library and Information Science*, found the ALA's compilation of "core val-ues"—access, confidentiality/privacy, democracy, diversity, education and lifelong learning, intellectual freedom, the public good, preservation, professionalism, and social responsibility—to be "a sensible and helpful framework" for "how LIS pro-fessionals should conduct themselves" (Rubin 2010, 414–15). The application of these ALA-endorsed core values to the work of library, information, knowledge, and archival professionals in for-profit, nonprofit, and governmental environments is also addressed in chapter 12.

VALUES IN CONFLICT OR VALUES IN COOPERATION

The library commentator Will Manley boasts online of 30 years service as a librar-ian and 7 years work as a city manager (Manley 2010). Drawing on this experience in his June/July 2010 *American Libraries*' column "Will's World," Manley warned against a public library defending its budget on the grounds of increased use by people in reduced financial circumstances. According to Manley, "it makes the library seem like a charitable institution for poor people, and like it or not, poor people carry zero political clout" (2010, 96).

Without a relevant professional education, how likely is it that "librarians" will understand the service imperatives derived from their history and service philoso-phy? Unlike the contemporary western politicians of Manley's acquaintance, the mid-19th-century political leaders of East Coast Boston adopted a report asserting that their public library would come into existence, in part, with an ideal of providing taxpayer-funded resources (books) to "poor families" and lending them "wherever they will be most likely to affect life and raise personal character and condition" (Boston Public Library 1852, 9 of 11).

The fundamental worth of service that underscores the ideal of the modern public library may be listed as one of the ALA's core values, but it is not something whose significance is proven scientifically. Rather, it is accepted as a belief held by the community of professionally educated librarians. Similar foundational beliefs can be found in other library, information, knowledge, and archival associations. Such a belief rests "on the authority of communities that have accepted a tradition of valuing equality and also on the intuitions of people who have been shaped by those communities" (Marsden 1996, 309). Although there are clearly individual exceptions, it is far more likely that librarians and other LIS practitioners who were shaped by professional values through their education in ALA-accredited graduate programs will accept and support the service imperatives of such values. Professionally endorsed values are not laws or city ordinances, but they provide a base from which to negotiate with vote-counting city councils or county commissions to advance public library service, including service to the new and old poor.

How such service is delivered is a practical matter and usually determined on a local or organizational basis. In localities with a commitment to social betterment, service to the disadvantaged may be an openly proclaimed priority program. In other communities, perhaps towns, cities, and counties more concerned with limiting taxes and preferring to fund services that directly benefit middle- and upper-class taxpayers, the library and information needs of the new and old poor may be met without drawing special attention to the process. This approach, however, does not foreclose the reporting of "success stories," with the permission of those involved, when library customers, patrons, and users take advantage of available library resources to better their life situations. Naturally, the politicians involved should be provided the credit for having allocated the necessary funding. Many library users vote and can support those who support the library at election time. Cultural pragmatism and feminism are both likely to support either the open or the more nuanced approaches to delivering service, provided that they are implemented without undermining values fundamental to each philosophy.

Variations of the process for securing resources for serving the new and old poor through public libraries are practiced by appropriately educated professionals over a variety of matters that arise in the wide spectrum of libraries, information centers, knowledge management centers, and archives. Academic administrators, corporate managers, research coordinators, and others who control financial and human resources have multiple demands for their allocation. However, practitioner standards rooted in professional educations and values can be effective in securing funding, particularly when they are combined with the demonstration of the benefits that accrue to those who make available the necessary resources.

CONCLUSION

By its very nature a chapter titled "A Culturally Pragmatic and Feminist-Influenced Approach to Defending Professionalism" must balance detail with theory. In doing so it provides the reader with the grounding necessary to evaluate the encouraging mix of solutions offered by practitioners and practitioners turned scholars throughout this work. In the definition of cultural pragmatism" contained in the appendix to this chapter, it is noted, "since cultural pragmatists deem the future 'workability' of a theory to be more important than its historical source, they are open to seeing philosophical competitors such as critical theory, feminism, and even revealed religion, as both potential collaborators and valuable repositories of human experience" (Crowley 2005, 202).

In the equally important area of how feminism supports relevant professionalism, this author believes it is best to conclude by elaborating on the working definition provided for this chapter—feminism for librarianship, information science, knowledge management, and archives is a philosophical approach designed to enhance the status of women by encouraging them to "do well" for themselves, their gender, and their profession through adopting approaches that enable them to "do good" for their communities and organizations. This approach, combining excellence in service ("doing good") with the enlightened self-interest of promoting the employment of female professionals "doing well"), is both appropriate and necessary for those raised in an American, British, or Canadian culture whose gendered expectations still support self-sacrificing behavior within strict limits rather than demonstrating the value of providing the resources necessary to achieve laudable service aims.

Inherent in the preceding is the contention that there is no single culturally pragmatic or feminist solution for solving the problem of defending library, information, knowledge, and archival professionalism. Professionalism is a complex human reality that is supported or undermined in multiple contexts by everything from fundamental cultural values affecting the career aspirations of women and the achievement of necessary laws and regulations to the claims of professional associations and the subjective decisions of policymakers. From the pragmatic point of view, while far from ideal, it is just how the world works. From the feminist standpoint, it is something that must be worked with until it can be changed.

With no available best solution capable of solving the professionalism problem in all library, information, knowledge, and archival contexts, those who would defend the value of appropriately educated practitioners are left with John Henry Newman's "practical best." Newman, the 19th-century author of the breakthrough *The Idea of a University*, memorably summarized such a situation when he sagely observed, "in a particular instance, it might easily happen, that what is only second best is best practically, because what is actually best is out of the question (Newman 1996/1873, 20).

Throughout, readers of this work have and will encounter quite a number of "practical best" solutions, approaches that may well prove to be exactly what is needed to defend professionalism in their own community or organizational cultures.

REFERENCES

Beveridge, Sydney, Susan Weber, and Andrew A. Beveridge. 2011. "Librarians in the U.S. from 1880–2009." *OUPblog* (blog). Accessed June 29, 2011. http://blog.oup.com/2011/06/librarian-census/.

Boston Public Library. 1852. *Upon the Objects to Be Attained by the Establishment of a Public Library: Report of the Trustees of the Public Library of the City of Boston.*

City Document Number 37. Boston: Boston Public Library. Accessed January 16, 2011. http://www.mcmillanlibrary.org/history/report_of_trustees.html.

Crowley, Bill. 2005. *Spanning the Theory-Practice Divide in Library and Information Science*. Lanham, MD: Scarecrow Press.

Crowley, Bill. 2008. *Renewing Professional Librarianship: A Fundamental Rethinking*. A Beta Phi Mu Monograph. Westport, CT: Libraries Unlimited.

Crowley, Bill. 2010. "Know Your ROEI: Emotional Investment in Service Delivery Can Return Lifelong Benefits." *Library Journal* (February 15): 34–35. Accessed June 29, 2011. http://www.libraryjournal.com/lj/communitymanaginglibraries/853644-273/know_your_roei.html.csp.

Crowley, Bill, and Deborah Ginsberg. 2005. "Professional Values: Priceless." *American Libraries* (January): 52–55.

De Rosa, Cathy, and Jenny Johnson. 2008. *From Awareness to Funding: A Study of Library Support in America: A Report to the OCLC Membership*. Dublin, OH: OCLC. Accessed June 29, 2011. http://www.oclc.org/reports/funding/default.htm.

"Earned Degrees, Conferred, 2007–8." 2010. *Chronicle of Higher Education* 57(1): 31.

Flatley, Robert, and Andrea Wyman. 2009. "Changes in Rural Libraries and Librarianship: A Comparative Survey." *Public Library Quarterly* 28(1): 24–39.

Garrison, Dee. 1979. *Apostles of Culture: The Public Librarian and American Society, 1876–1920*. New York: Free Press.

"Introduction: Pragmatism—What's the Use?" 2001. *Hedgehog Review* 3(3): 5–8. Accessed December 29, 2010. http://www.iasc-culture.org/HHR_Archives/Pragmatism/3.3BIntro.pdf.

Manley, Will. 2010. "Will's World: Winning the Budget Wars." *American Libraries* (June/July): 96. Accessed June 29, 2011. http://americanlibrariesmagazine.org/columns/wills-world/winning-budget-wars.

Marsden, George M. 1996. "Theology and the University: Newman's Idea and Current Realities." In *The Idea of a University*, John Henry Newman, ed. Frank M. Turner, 302–317. New Haven, CT: Yale University Press.

Newman, John Henry. 1996/1873. *The Idea of a University*. Edited by Frank M. Turner. New Haven, CT: Yale University Press.

Oder, Norman. 2009. "MLS: Hire Ground?" *Library Journal* (June 1): 44–46. Accessed June 29, 2011. http://www.libraryjournal.com/lj/ljinprintcurrentissue/855028-403/mls_hire_ground.html.csp.

Public Agenda Foundation. 2006. *Long Overdue: A Fresh Look at Public Attitudes about Libraries in the 21st Century*. New York: Public Agenda. Accessed June 30, 2011. http://www.publicagenda.org/files/pdf/Long_Overdue.pdf.

Rubin, Richard E. 2010. *Foundations of Library and Information Science*. 3rd ed. New York: Neal-Schuman.

Samovar, Larry A., Richard E. Porter, and Edwin R. McDaniel. 2010. *Communication between Cultures*. Wadsworth series in speech communication. Belmont, CA: Wadsworth/Cengage Learning.

APPENDIX

DEFINITIONS

Cultural pragmatism: A philosophy that builds upon classical pragmatism and holds, as does its intellectual progenitor, that "truth" is subject to construction in ongoing processes within cultural and other human communities. Cultural pragmatists hold that the true test of any theory resides in analyzed experience. It understands that everyday truths tend to be culture specific, but it is open to the possibility of constructing larger truths that transcend cultural and geographical boundaries. Cultural pragmatists value past experience but hold that "truths" are always more or less provisional and must be continually tested in a variety of contexts. Since cultural pragmatists deem the future *workability* of a theory to be more important than its historical source, they are open to seeing philosophical competitors—such as critical theory, feminism, and even revealed religion—as both potential collaborators and valuable repositories of human experience. As such, philosophical competitors are all capable of producing theories for testing in a variety of contexts (Crowley 2005, 202).

Feminism: A philosophy that puts issues related to gender and gender discrimination at the heart of its analysis. In part, feminism arose in reaction to cultural and intellectual traditions that identified "human" with "male" and neglected women's contributions and issues (Crowley 2005, 203).

11

THE LIS PROFESSIONAL COMMONS AND THE ONLINE NETWORKED PRACTITIONER

Kyle M. L. Jones
University of Wisconsin–Madison

Michael Stephens
San Jose State University

The interconnected and social state of the Internet has led to innumerable developments for professionals across fields, interests, and nationalities to collaboratively develop projects and share ideas. Not that long ago the Internet was a static environment, but it has evolved into a social platform enabled by a variety of Internet-bound information and communication technologies. As a mode for communication and information sharing, the Internet has no rival. "We now have communications tools that are flexible enough to match our social capabilities," writes Shirky (2008, 20), "these communication tools have been given many names, all variations on a theme: 'social software,' 'social media,' 'social computing,' and so on." No matter the term applied to this evolution of the Internet, it has changed the way society uses it, engages with it, and creates for it.

Like its influence on greater society, the Internet also shapes professionals in the way they approach their daily tasks, go about their projects, and develop throughout their careers. As a field forced to evolve by the information creation and exchange on the web, library and information studies (LIS) professionals must be aware of the role the social Internet has on the organization and dissemination of information, for this is a tectonic shift in the field. While it can be conservatively stated that, as a whole, LIS has taken note of the effects of the social Internet, with less confidence it can be said that professionals within the field truly understand the role the social Internet can have in shaping their own professional development from the start of their education while in graduate school, through the fledgling stages of their careers, and into their prime years as professionals solidified in their positions.

As LIS professionals consistently and actively engaged in the social Internet for a combined 12 years, writers of professionally focused blogs, and educators in LIS at a variety of levels (as technology trainers, consultants, and as a tenure-track professor at a degree granting institution), we can attest to the professional value gleaned from being active participants in the online social realm. It is through these observations and experiences that we have developed a model called the LIS Professional Commons (LISPC).

The LISPC is a stratified, interconnected environment, a part of the social Internet that, through continued engagement, library professionals should be members of as part of their professional development experiences. By doing so, library professionals will come to value and understand that online social engagement in the commons provides learning experiences, professional opportunities, and a heightened awareness of the issues at hand, opportunities ahead, and trends forthcoming that affect librarianship. The LISPC acts on part eight of the American Library Association (ALA) (2008) Code of Ethics, which states that "[w]e strive for excellence in the profession by maintaining and enhancing our own knowledge and skills, by encouraging the professional development of co-workers, and by fostering the aspirations of potential members of the profession." While the LISPC is an open online environment for anyone in librarianship, for example, circulation staff, student workers, and others, its potential to further the field rests in how professionals take part in the conversations that will surely shape the future of librarianship. We posit throughout this text that the LISPC cannot be denied as a formidable part of any library professional's development.

The LISPC is technology agnostic. It is not built on any specific online social network or networks. It is not reliant on a singular device. It is not dependent on applications, web-based or otherwise. It is, however, a dispersed network of individuals who, through the affordances of a broad set of technologies, are able to connect, engage, and educate each other about their profession. Through these affordances the professional commons for library professionals has organically grown and continues to thrive. The authors of this chapter have four aims:

- To clearly define the LISPC;
- To illustrate that the affordances of technologies, and not the specific technologies themselves, enable the LISPC;
- To map how a practitioner can engage with the LISPC and create a socially networked professional development action plan; and
- To provide an overview of the benefits of hiring a library professional who is entrenched in and adept at utilizing the LISPC.

DEFINING THE LIS PROFESSIONAL COMMONS

The Concept of the Commons

As it can be generally conceived, a commons is a shared place or space, physical or virtual in existence, that, in essence, is ungoverned and unstructured, but through shared aims and collaborative exchanges works toward the betterment of knowledge creation and acquisition. There is no singular blueprint for what a commons looks like, nor should there be as all commons are unique to their needs and communities. Furthermore, blueprints suggest a sense of rigidity for commons that, while at times may be beneficial, are hurtful for communities that need flexibility to evolve as they see fit.

As it is with all things in existence, the commons has a beginning; a moment of creation either from an idea, a collaborative exchange, or otherwise. Whoever initially creates a commons, however, does not own, govern, nor rule a commons. As a shared participatory experience, a commons is ruled only by the interchange of ideas. For example, participants sharing experiences and thoughts will tend to find themselves temporarily bound by the subjects of which they communicate, though never permanently. This inherent flow of loosely bound ideas and knowledge creation is what enables a commons to ever evolve.

Parallels exist between commons and Etienne Wenger's (1999) seminal publication Communities of Practice. Of greatest focus in Wenger's work is social learning, which is an "encompassing process of being active participants in the practices of social communities and constructing identities in relation to these communities" (Wenger 1999, 4). A commons, as described previously, is unarguably a social community filled with active participants, and, as we discuss later on, does relate to identity creation. Moreover, a commons includes Wenger's three dimensions that define community: Mutual engagement, joint enterprise(s), and shared repertoire(s) (Wenger 1999, 73). A commons is a community. And while communities are defined broadly (e.g., Chicago's "Little Italy" neighborhood, nunneries, writers groups, etc.), a commons—again, much like Wenger's "communities of practice"— is a uniquely defined type of community because of its purpose and process.

Many clear examples of thriving commons in action are available. Of easiest recognition are the discipline-specific commons who gather, communicate, and collaborate on research interests and practice within their fields. From chemistry to psychology, human resources to accounting, conferences and online communities exist as part of a general commons experience, or in some cases, peripheral commons emerge out of larger commons due to distinctly shared interests. Professionally focused commons are conventional and thriving due to Wenger's three dimensions of community, specifically the elements of shared repertoires and enterprises. In fact, we recognize that the online elements of professional commons have become so successful and replicable that they have evolved into an identifiable model for study.

The Professional Commons Framework

The framework of the professional commons is defined by its networked strata across the social Internet. Each individual stratum exists as a layer adding to the collaborative nature and knowledge building of the commons as a whole. What, exactly, a stratum's intended purpose, population makeup, and knowledge output is is unique; however, the married strata exist as one whole professional commons. This can be thought of as different sub-communities within an all-encompassing community. Without the sub-communities (the stratum), the entire community (the professional commons) is weaker in breadth and depth, if not completely eliminated.

The location of each individual stratum is uniquely placed, and their knowledge building actions are unable to be compared to other strata. To be concrete, let us compare two types of online strata: the professionally focused LinkedIn and the conversation centric Twitter.

Both are situated differently; they do not share the same space. Virtually, LinkedIn is accessible at http://linkedin.com and Twitter at http://twitter.com. As inhabitants of different spaces, each has its own set of members, and each member has a unique account. Accounts provide access to each site's features and tools. While LinkedIn and Twitter share a similar feature—the ability to update one's status—the purpose is inherently different. LinkedIn's professional aim affects how members post information about themselves or otherwise; Twitter's conversational tone has the same affect in a contrasting way. This simple example is just one of many, and it enables the general statement that each has its own affordances that allow for collaboration and knowledge building in separate ways. Removing (or ignoring) a stratum from the whole removes a layer that simply cannot be entirely replicated somewhere else.

Thoroughly understanding the role each stratum has in the professional commons is not necessary, but appreciating the complexity of the commons and what it has to offer on a variety of levels is of utmost importance. As each stratum is investigated, one will find that opportunities exist to connect with other professionals, to collaborate on projects, to gain knowledge, and to share what one knows with the greater community in a variety of ways.

The Value of the Professional Commons for LIS

To many, the professional commons sounds familiar; to some it may be an interesting concept, while others simply will not care. We firmly believe that the professional commons is something that all should recognize as a virtual professional development space stocked with potential for networking and knowledge building, for innovation and the fostering of ideas, and for critical reflection. The dialogue in the professional commons represents the current state of a profession or discipline. Being a part of the conversations enriches your professional development and keeps you attuned to ongoing developments and opportunities.

Our participation in the professional commons for LIS has a proven track record. We have grown into reflective practitioners who actively assess our past experiences, adjust our current practices, and plan for new projects based on our maturation as professionals. The professional commons has enabled this by collaborating with us on projects and ideas, by providing constant feedback. Only through this dynamic dialogue have we been able to mold what we do to better our field and, in turn, better serve our users and the students we teach. This could be enough of a benefit of being a participant in the professional commons, but we have also been given opportunities far and beyond what we ever thought could be reaped from our online conversations in the commons.

By refining our professional thoughts, ideas, and actions through collaborative participation in the commons, we have put ourselves out there for criticism and praise; for the most part, the criticism has been constructive. As individuals and organizations have learned more about us and our work in the commons, they have approached us for consulting and speaking arrangements, even job offers. These opportunities lead us out of the virtual commons but always connect us with new individuals who we continue to stay in touch with online, thus building our commons connections further.

Our stories are not unique. We can point to a sample of LIS professionals who, to some degree, have had similar experiences in the commons. Each individual could then point to different parts of the commons, demonstrating that the disparate features of individual stratum, not one specific online space, are how the professional commons is framed.

AFFORDANCES OF TECHNOLOGIES IN THE LIS PROFESSIONAL COMMONS

Building Blocks of the Professional Commons

As demonstrated previously, each type of network or social space on the Internet has its individual characteristics that lead to unique additions to the professional commons. And while the technologies employed by these sites or applications are unique, we believe that there are thematic elements that can be identified as crucial parts. Gene Smith (2007), an experienced information architect and chief officer for a Canadian user experience consulting firm, offers a list of "social software building blocks" as a way to model the affordances of these technologies. These aspects are available in disparate online networks to varying degree across the many networks. One network may have two or three of the blocks, while others may have different ones. Defining the building blocks within the context of the LIS professional, however, offers a concise way to define the similar aspects of the professional commons:

Identity

LIS professionals identify themselves within the various networks of the professional commons and craft user profiles that detail personal traits, interests, accomplishments, and more. Many will share a photo, known as an avatar. This allows recognition, especially if the avatar is used across various networks. This is a standard for almost all social networks.

Presence

The network includes mechanisms that report when a particular person is online and may include status reporting such as "Away" or "Busy." Facebook includes an example of this. ALA Connect, a social network community created by the ALA, displays a sidebar of "Who's Online." Other sites, such as Twitter, do not display online status.

Relationships

The system allows users the means to connect with each other as "friends" or some other similar language. ALA Connect, for example, allows users to define relationships as friends, colleagues, and contacts. Sites such as LinkedIn allow LIS professionals to define positions within the context of their libraries, professional associations, and consultancies.

Conversations

Conversations are the essence of any kind of commons. The ability to communicate with participants is a necessary element. In social networks conversations usually begin with a status update (see the following section, "Reputation") or a group forum posting. As LIS members of the commons read the initial posting, they add to it with responses and a conversation begins. How far they take the conversation and what it leads to is up to the community.

Groups

Parts of the professional commons naturally become segmented into groups based on interests, connections, and purpose. While not all networks explicitly have a groups function like LinkedIn, Facebook, and FriendFeed, others provide the opportunity to create ad hoc organized connections, like Twitter lists for archivists, technology librarians, or libraries that are on Twitter.

Reputation

Social sites include explicit ratings or reputation indicators that show how active a member is in terms of amount of user content published, peer ratings, or by other measurements. If these indicators are implicit, they can usually be uncovered by manual means. The true purpose of reputation is not about statistics, it is about quality and commitment to the community. As Smith (2007, para. 3) writes, "[Are] they good citizens? [Can they] be trusted?" (para. 3). A good judge of one's reputation is to ask questions. Who in the LIS commons answers? Who helps? Build your own reputation by helping others and being active.

Sharing

An important element of the LIS professional commons is sharing your skills, knowledge, and experiences. The most meaningful conversations occur in the commons when members assist other members. Additionally, publish your projects and presentations. Explore some specific strata like Slideshare and Vimeo to share your presentation slides, screencasts, and general videos; point other LIS commons members to your work, and gain valuable feedback for your growth.

MAPPING A PATH THROUGH
THE LIS PROFESSIONAL COMMONS

In this section we provide a map for LIS professionals to find their own useful and engaging passage into the professional commons. Participation may be different for each person depending on career paths and time in the profession. One given: for all, it is never too late to join and interact.

For the LIS Student

The professional commons should be part of your LIS education. It should be part of your curriculum to experience and engage with other students, your teachers, and practitioners around the world. If it is not part of your school's curriculum and you have not heard about it in your classes, use this chapter and other resources to create your own experiential immersion in the commons. Quick starts include commenting on librarian-authored blogs, following noted LIS professionals on twitter, and aligning with like-minded folks as well as those who offer opinions contrary to your own on social sites for balanced, fair conversation, debate, and exchange. As you build your connections within the LISPC, add notations to your resume. Just as a new graduate lists technology and other skills acquired in school, detailing your professional presence in the social networks and related experience enhances your curriculum vita further.

For the New Librarian

Now is the time. If you did not have exposure to the professional commons in your library education, follow the steps here to explore and interact. Utilize the LISPC as a means to stay in the know about issues and trends in LIS as you are starting your first professional position. Fine tune your focus—networks, people to follow, other strata—to your new position. Leverage your learning in meetings, on committees, and working with your colleagues and users to further the organization's mission.

For the Current Professional

We would urge you always to be engaged, always learning. The professional commons is one means to do this that requires little more than time and a connection to the online world. No time, you say? Then understand this: If you are not participating, you are not as valuable as you could be to your institution and to your most important stakeholders, your users.

You owe it to your users to be a competent, engaged, always learning professional.

For All

Seth Godin offers sage advice via his books and blog we can apply to presenting ourselves as LIS professionals in the professional commons. In a time when anyone and everyone can have a blog, Godin (2009) urges those curious about participating in the online world to be authentic—stressing quality over quantity: "There's no limit now. No limit to how many clicks, readers, followers and friends you can acquire" (para. 2). "Instead of getting better, you focus obsessively on getting bigger" (Godin 2009, para. 3).

We would argue that the most important facet of participating in the professional commons is the careful refinement of the networks and contacts. Quality does usurp quantity. Look for those that inspire you, that make you think. Look for connections where you can share and learn. Cite the people you have connected to when they inspire you. Be authentic. Be honest. Be yourself.

A MAP THAT CAN BE FOLLOWED

In identifying the affordances of specific technologies that build the professional commons, we have started readers on a path that can be followed. Knowing the signs to look for on your journey will not help you entirely: you need to know what to do when you get there. What you do in the professional commons is up to you, but we suggest following this guide as you progress through its virtual space.

Presentation

Be personable, but be professional. Too much rhetoric in pre-professional LIS education has been bent on presenting a version of ourselves that is almost inhuman. A version so focused on presenting ourselves as flawless that it is nearly impossible to do. In the professional commons show your character in your writing or in how you share the content you create. You are human and you have a personality, but because the environment is filled by professionals and perhaps potential employers, it is important to keep your life private to some extent. Find the fine balance.

Place

As you explore the commons' disparate spaces for gathering and conversing with other members, reflect on your experiences and what you are getting out of the time you are there. Is it idle chatter? Is it too academic? Is the content focused on media instead of text? As you encounter these environments, begin to recognize the differences, what you appreciate about them, and if it is a good use of your time. You may find multiple networks that you find valuable; you may only find one. Explore and experiment with places as you work your way through the commons.

Engage Meaningfully

The commons has a lot of noise. Do not find yourself caught up in superfluous gossip or snarky comments. Beware those who promote themselves only for the sake of promoting themselves. Engage meaningfully in the commons with your own updates, conversations, and shared media by sparking thought and dialogue centered on issues and trends. This is not to say that criticism or opposing viewpoints are not valued. They are! But the best members of the commons take time to engage in constructive criticism not unfounded attacks. Remember the importance of true engagement and quality not quantity: "Showing up isn't sufficient. Friending ten or twenty or a thousand people in Facebook might be good for your ego, but it has zero to do with any useful measure of success" (Godin 2008, 59).

Create Connections

While the professional commons is built on social technologies, it would not exist without the individuals who use the sites and applications. Do not forget: The commons is about people and connections. Take time to listen and respond to individuals. Make connections with those you support; make connections with the heretics whose viewpoints make you think.

Develop Networks

Make individual connections with a wide variety of professionals, and as you do you will soon realize the breadth at which professional interests span. While your day job may define you as a reference librarian, the LISPC will have you exploring and participating in micro-networks whose discussions take you far beyond reference librarianship. These micro-networks will connect you to a broader network of ideas and individuals outside of your home professional position.

Pay it Forward

Eventually, you will not even think about participating in the LIS professional commons. It will become commonplace, a normal part of a day's routine. The relationships built in the commons may even be so ingrained in your being that you find yourself missing their insights and updates if you are not connected, and that is a sign of a successful interconnected community. As a permanent member of the professional commons, the onus is now on you to mentor new participants, get them acquainted with other members, and see that they have as successful experience as you did.

THE BENEFITS OF HIRING AN ACTIVE PRACTITIONER IN THE LIS PROFESSIONAL COMMONS

The benefits of hiring a professionally trained librarian who understands and uses the professional commons far outweigh employing those who may not participate. In fact, question paths concerning an applicant's knowledge and use of the LISPC are becoming a regular part of the interview process. A recent student just reported back on an interview saying that two questions were asked of him: What social networks do you engage with for professional development, and which ones for personal networking?

What if you already have librarians on staff who have not used the LISPC or know nothing about it? Administrators and other hiring bodies should fear not; there are mechanisms that enable the education a library can put into place to bring all employees up to speed.

The following section surveys those benefits and offers suggestions for educating all staff. The key to these benefits is experience and engagement within the LISPC. A librarian cannot simply set up a series of feeds in a reader or create a Twitter account but must commit time and attention to interacting within the LISPC. Hopefully, participation has begun during graduate school. Just as librarians seek to instill a desire for "lifelong learning" in their constituents, the professionally focused practitioner should do so as well. In fact, Roger Hiemstra (1976, 9–10) noted that three forces promote ongoing interest and need for lifelong learning in an early work highlighting the concept: constant change, occupational obsolescence, and an individual's desire for self-actualization.

The benefits are based on our experience, research, and interaction within the LISPC itself. Stephens (2008, 323–25) surveyed early adopters of one of the key elements of the commons, blogs, specifically library-focused bloggers, and found that 56 percent of those surveyed reported a "feeling of belonging to a larger group for informal discourse and connection" and 36 percent reported "that blogging keeps them up-to-date and involved with the profession." Early LIS bloggers used phrases such as "keeping current" and "essential part of my professional development" to describe why they blogged. Anecdotal evidence via discussions with active participants has yielded further evidence that other channels beyond blogs carry similar benefits. The online, networked professionals engaging in the commons reap the following rewards for themselves and their institutions.

Connected and Engaged

The librarian participating in the professional commons can be connected and engaged with peers, colleagues, and practitioners on a global scale. The power of conversation across distance and time as an enabler for learning and exchange leads to opportunities for finding things out and getting answers to questions. A survey of recent Twitter discussion from librarians in Europe, the United States, and Australia concerning e-book lending demonstrates the power of this exchange on a global scale.

Knowledgeable

Closely tied to being connected and engaged, participation in the LISPC affords the chance to be aware of trends and findings from various channels. Subscribing to various library, technology, and news sites for updates offers the connected librarian the chance to "be the first to know" about some new study or report. These insights can be communicated to others in meetings or the library's internal channels.

Skillful and Innovative

The LISPC promotes an understanding of online community engagement, the mechanisms for enabling conversation, and an enhanced degree of technical prowess. Understanding how to build successful communities of practice/working groups by participating in them can lead to further success building similar resources for a library's community. Other technical skills can be acquired as well as the means to get support and answers for various questions or problems via the LISPC. Librarians have reported learning how to design user communities with open source content systems such as Drupal or Wordpress via help from others engaged in the same practice. This continuum of learning, assistance, and knowledge creation only becomes richer and more useful as participation increases.

Potential for Leadership

A librarian linked into the LISPC may find pathways to leadership roles easy to navigate. Within the LISPC anyone can be a leader on a project or some other endeavor, as Seth Godin (2008) argues in Tribes, and those skills can also transfer into practice within the institution. Consider the grass roots efforts by librarians to gather donations to buy a library in India or the "#followalibrary Day" on Twitter organized via the social networks as two examples where individuals could demonstrate leadership qualities. Those skills translate to home institutions.

Suggestions for Administrators and Managers

To reap the benefits of the LISPC, administrators and managers must promote participation by staff. Allow time and resources for professional staff to continue participation. Also, create your own commons within the library if you haven't already. Intranet-based sharing and conversation brings the benefits of the LISPC to all staff.

Many libraries have utilized the Learning 2.0 model of employee education to acquaint all staff with many of the technologies that are part of the LISPC. Created at the Public Library of Charlotte and Mecklenburg County, the open source learning program has been replicated more than 1,000 times in libraries and nonprofits (Blowers 2009). This is another means to introduce your professional staff and all employees to the LISPC.

Recent research by one of the authors has yielded a promising picture of the benefits of Learning 2.0 in libraries, echoing many of the benefits noted previously. Using the program to introduce library staff to the LISPC yields results such as improved confidence and a willingness to explore emerging technologies first and foremost. These changes, however, can lead to improved sharing, communication, and visibility for libraries that continue the practice (Stephens and Cheetham 2011).

FINAL THOUGHTS

The LISPC is a vibrant and growing community of practitioners from all professional levels and areas of library and information studies. LISPC's continued evolution and open access to discussions, thought processes, and member-created media is a cornucopia of insight for library professionals of all types. The benefits of participation include engagement with discourse concerning issues and trends impacting LIS professionals globally, opportunities for learning, and enhancement of leadership potential for all who chose to participate. As such, its value cannot be denied.

REFERENCES

American Library Association. 2008. *Code of Ethics of the American Library Association.* Accessed January 22. http://www.ala.org/ala/issuesadvocacy/proethics/codeofethics/codeethics.cfm.

Blowers, Helene. 2009. "WJ Hosts 23 Things Summit." LibraryBytes (February 28). Accessed February 6, 2011. http://www.librarybytes.com/2009/02/wj-hosts-23-things-summit.html.

Godin, Seth. 2008. *Tribes: We Need You to Lead Us.* New York: Penguin.

Godin, Seth. 2009. "Infinity—They Keep Making More of It." Seth's Blog (blog). Accessed April 29. http://sethgodin.typepad.com/seths_blog/2009/04/infinitythey keep making-more-of-it.html.

Hiemstra, Roger. 1976. *Lifelong Learning.* The professional education series. Lincoln, NE: Professional Educators Pub.

Shirky, Clay. 2008. *Here Comes Everybody: The Power of Organizing without Organizations.* New York: Penguin.

Smith, Gene. 2007. "Social Software Building Blocks." nForm. Accessed April 4. http://nform.com/publications/social-software-building-block.

Stephens, Michael. 2008. "The Pragmatic Biblioblogger: Examining the Motivations and Observations of Early Adopter Librarian Bloggers." *Internet Reference Services Quarterly* 13(4): 311–45.

Stephens, Michael, and Warren Cheetham. 2011. "The Impact and Effect of Learning 2.0 Programs in Australian Academic Libraries." *New Review of Academic Librarianship* 17(1): 31–63.

Wenger, Etienne. 1999. *Communities of Practice.* Cambridge: Cambridge University Press.

12

THE POLITICAL CASE FOR SUPPORTING THE VALUE OF PROFESSIONALISM

Bill Crowley
Dominican University

A WESTERN AMERICAN STORY

While employed with the Alabama Public Library Service (APLS), I once attended a governor's conference on libraries and information services held in a western state. The conference had been well planned, and APLS Director Anthony (Tony) W. Miele wangled several invitations for his staff in hope of picking up useful ideas for his state's own conference. At the start of activities the conference planners ran into an unexpected and unwanted problem. The governor was not available to start the proceedings, and the lieutenant governor, a long-serving politician who had failed in his own efforts to be elected governor, arrived in his place.

It is a well-known political truism that governors will do everything possible to attend events sponsored by the influential people of their state. The absence of this governor from the conference confirmed for the participants that library and information concerns did not rank very high in the eyes of the head of state government. Before the opening remarks, while some at the conference clustered in small groups to complain about how unfair the governor was, a number of the state's leading librarians, trustees, friends, and other supporters took a different approach. They made a point of warmly welcoming the lieutenant governor. Possibly expecting the usual disappointment at his appearance as a gubernatorial substitute, the lieutenant governor seemed delighted at this positive reception, delivered his remarks with gusto, and then spent a considerable part of the day attending various conference activities. The lieutenant governor had been a teacher in his younger days and had an interest in the roles libraries could play in learning. Building on this commonality, his library escorts pointed out how a few million extra dollars might not make much of a difference with many state-assisted programs but could work a revolution with libraries, particularly public libraries serving communities and assisting teachers and students as part of their educational commitment.

Shortly thereafter, the state's voters surprised many and elected the often-overlooked lieutenant governor as their next governor. According to information later provided to me by library consultants at the state level, the new governor recalled what he learned while substituting at the library and information conference, increased the state's commitment to libraries in various ways, and went on to spend a considerable amount of time speaking to appreciative "library" audiences on various matters. Out of this fortuitous combination of an outgoing governor's absence, an underrated lieutenant governor with a teaching past, and professional and civic leaders able to demonstrate the importance of the library's educational role and its popularity with voters came an unexpected political momentum that benefited the state, its library and information community, and the new governor as well.

This study has several possible morals ranging from "never miss an opportunity to cultivate new friends" and "good manners never hurt" to "politicians can and do make unexpected comebacks," and most importantly, "people can be remarkably positive about supporting services that match their existing beliefs and advance their own goals." The last rule is absolutely crucial for librarians, information specialists, knowledge managers, and archivists who now encounter increased competition for limited resources.

Over the years I have found that effective extroverts usually learn early to pitch their programs to the priorities of their funding sources. Introverts may need a bit more coaching and support. However, a few successes can encourage them to prioritize services from the point of view of those who control the increasingly scarce but always necessary funds. While this rule certainly applies to corporations, schools, and universities, it is particularly relevant where the decisions are made by elected officials whose own performance is regularly judged by voters.

POLITICIANS, LIBRARIANS, AND BUREAUCRATS

Another way to understand the necessity of matching library, information, knowledge, or archival services to the priorities of funding sources is to look at the simple question that often consciously or unconsciously influences decisions made by those who control resources: What has this program or department done lately to help me solve my priority problems or advance my agendas? Trouble can arise when library and information directors, managers, and other professionals do not prioritize to the concerns of those who control the money and, instead, organize and provide services solely on the basis of their own "professional norms, ethics, and work procedures" (Ward 2007, 629).

In the public library environment, such unhelpfulness in solving the problems besetting funders and their agendas may even lead to boards of trustees and city government officials responding in ways that are particularly harmful to professionalism. In recent decades such drastic responses have even included the replacement of professional librarians as part of the outsourcing of a public library's management to commercial firms whose priority, as might be expected, is profit, not services.

The many negatives for professionalism resulting from outsourcing either the management of a library or its entire operations are addressed in the last chapter. At this point what needs discussion is the reason why library boards and city governments might make such a sweeping change. At least one "outside" analysis, surprisingly, found the decision to outsource all or part of a library's operations may be made for reasons other than saving money. Major negative decisions, such as outsourcing or disproportionately reducing library budgets, may actually reflect the perception of a library board or city government that its own priorities are being frustrated because of (a) the incompetence of library managers or (b) opposition to such priorities arising from the professional norms and values of library administrators and other professional librarians (Ward 2007).

WE ALL HAVE INVISIBLE CONTRACTS WITH OUR BOSSES—AND SOMETIMES PHILOSOPHICAL DIFFERENCES

In several decades of "doing" before "teaching" I learned as an administrator that private values and professional norms can have enormous impact on the work of professional and other employees in library, information, knowledge, and archival organizations. Each of us has our own idea of what we want to prioritize in our work and how much effort we will devote to its achievement.

On the individual level we tend to have what can be termed an invisible contract based on a "nuts and bolts" view of our relationship to our employer. This generally gets translated into something like, "for what you pay me, this is what you get from me." Such contracts tend to be evidenced through very specific actions, or nonactions, along the lines of, "This public library really doesn't pay me enough to spend my free time at home preparing to lead book discussions, so I will do everything possible to avoid it," or "I may work in a school library, but my priorities are elsewhere. My kids are home from middle school by four P.M., and I am not going to leave them alone to conduct after-school programs for other people's children, even if there is extra money in it for me."

An invisible contract related to employee work output does not necessary imply any philosophical differences over the purpose of the organization with the corporate CEOs, university presidents, library boards, or city councils who allocate funding and directly or indirectly set or influence policy. However, on a practical basis, whatever they might term it, invisible contracts are regularly encountered by managers who are often required to work with employees to adjust their views of the job in ways that better support the organization's needs and expectations.

At times, adjusting staff invisible contracts involves drastic action, particularly when an employee's unwillingness to alter her or his view of appropriate working circumstances can lead to the decision by senior managers that (a) the aims of the public library do not require so many professional librarians working as readers advisors or (b) the school's emphasis on keeping its students engaged after classes would be better served by eliminating the school library media specialist position and employing the enthusiastic, if part-time, library clerk on a full-time basis.

PHILOSOPHICAL DIFFERENCES OVER THE PURPOSES OF THE LIBRARY, INFORMATION CENTER, KNOWLEDGE CENTER, OR ARCHIVE

A second and larger area for disagreement lies in the philosophical differences over the purposes of the organization that can exist between professional librarians, information specialists, knowledge managers, and archivists and their funding sources. This is a conflict over fundamentals, over why a library, information center, knowledge management center, or archive exists and is worthy or not worthy of a certain level of support. Different philosophies of service can have important implications for funding and programs and, for example, reflect contrasting views on how libraries should influence a community's children. For example, a newly elected majority of a city council, reacting to voter concern that children are being pursued by online predators and are being "prematurely exposed" to adult concerns, might demand that the library board adopt policies providing for separate youth and adult library cards and the filtering of web access for anyone younger than 18 years of age.

Library directors and professional librarians adhering to the anti–age-discrimination portion of the American Library Association's (ALA) "Library Bill of Rights" (Rubin 2010, 389), and/or doubting the effectiveness of such limitations on the basis of previous experience, would likely oppose new restrictions on youth access to digital or hardcopy material. However, "professional norms, ethics, and work procedures" (Ward 2007, 629) can rank lower in the eyes of elected officials and judges than city ordinances or state laws. In this particular case, treating juveniles differently under the law has a long tradition in the United States. According to the State of Missouri's 16th Judicial Circuit of Jackson County,

> The British doctrine of *parens patriae* (the state as parent) was the rationale for the right of the state to intervene in the lives of children in a manner different from the way it intervenes in the lives of adults. The doctrine was interpreted to mean that, because children were not of full legal capacity, the state had the inherent power and responsibility to provide protection for children whose natural parents were not providing appropriate care or supervision. (16th Judicial Circuit of Jackson County 2011)

The preceding summary addresses the rationale for having juvenile courts. However, the underlying premise that young people can be treated differently because they are not of "full legal capacity" is as justified in American culture, if not more so, as the professional librarian's commitment to providing youth with access to all library resources, including unfiltered Internet access. This reality ought to be kept in mind should a library board acquiesce to the city council's stipulation that youth and adults have separate cards and be treated differently. Professional librarians, based on the ALA philosophy of service, may feel compelled to resist this decision in a number of ways, including broadly interpreting any "exceptions clause" in the new policy, or simply ignoring it. These sorts of action are traditional bureaucratic tactics used to thwart the instructions of legally constituted authority. The response of the city council to reports that professional librarians were undermining its expressed aim of "safeguarding the community's children" might well have an impact on future funding decisions and/or the employment status of the library director. It can come as a shock, particularly to newer professionals, that sometimes there are consequences for ignoring the stated objectives of one's paymaster. Determining in advance what price one is willing to pay for one's professional values requires the recognition that sometimes there really are prices to be paid.

Although it will usually conflict with their self images, when individual invisible contracts regarding working conditions are too self-serving or the standards of professionals are too divergent from expressed community or organizational priorities, there really is a risk that the librarians involved will be seen by many community members and governing officials not as professionals, but as nonre-sponsive bureaucrats. The word *bureaucrat* has particularly negative connotations in American popular culture. By definition, bureaucrats are considered to be peo-ple who place their own preferences above the legitimate demands of their employ-ers or the people they are hired to serve. Equally problematic in this devaluation of professionalism is the often-parallel perception that professionals frequently lack the willingness to change their behavior and must either be compelled to do so or be replaced in the interest of a greater good.

A CASE STUDY OF ACADEMIC BUREAUCRATS

The reality that professionals can be perceived as self-serving bureaucrats is not solely a phenomenon involving public libraries. I encountered a similar perception of librarian self-centeredness in a university environment while earning a second master's degree part time as I served as an upper-level library administrator in a state agency.

At times my day job required something that occasionally seemed to me like a periodic 24/7 commitment. Consequently, I only enrolled in evening courses where I could reasonably minimize my absences. After class one evening, the senior professor teaching the course, who knew I was a librarian, drew me aside with a complaint about the university's library services. This professor had grown tired of working with students or library assistants who staffed the desks at night after "all the librarians go home." Apparently, there were no librarians scheduled at service desks after the early evening. When this well-recognized professor complained to the library administration about the nightly absence of such professional help, he was informed that the librarians, who had faculty status and rank, needed to work during the day and not on weekends so that they could "be available for meetings."

This faculty member's response, repeated to me in a strongly irritated tone of voice, was that he had to attend daytime meetings even when he was teaching a night class on the very same day. He went on to make other points, all of which revolved around the issue of "what was it that gave librarians the right to demand special privileges?" By the time our post-class conversation ended, it was clear to me that this nationally respected academic perceived the librarians of his university to be stereotypically self-serving bureaucrats filling their days with meetings rather than providing professional service.

As a librarian I had done my own research. However, following this conversation I made a point of talking with the staff of several of the academic library's public service desks after evening classes. In these exchanges the professor's allegation that no reference librarians were available for consultation at night was apparently confirmed by the experience of these long-serving desk staff. If librarians were in-deed present, I was informed, they seemed to have carefully hidden their presence. In the end, the practical effect of the initial conversation and subsequent discus-sions was twofold. First, I decided not to follow up the matter with the library bureaucracy. I was a part-time short-timer at the university, and it was up to the professor and his colleagues to pressure the administration to direct the university librarians to make any necessary changes. Second, the apparent lack of interest by the university library administration in effective marketing enhanced my own inter-est in the approach, a commitment that was soon to involve helping to organize a statewide marketing effort (Cheski 1993, ii).

When a university's librarians are perceived, fairly or unfairly, as prizing their own comfort over the needs of their clientele, and the classroom and teaching faculty believe themselves to be much more responsive, a philosophical chasm clearly exists. Based on the information thus provided, I believe that this university's librarians had chosen to operate with the worst possible bureaucratic norms, thinly disguised as being required to carry out their professional responsibilities. These rules were significantly different from the "work day and night" values of the research and teaching faculty who had to meet much higher standards for tenure than the faculty librarians.

Displaying library values that are too different from the values of the research and teaching faculty is an inherently problematic course of action for academic librarians. On many campuses they are already seen as outliers whose faculty status, where it exists, may be viewed as difficult to defend. Most librarians lack the doctoral credential of most tenure track university faculty, and relatively few teach courses for credit or bring their university millions of dollars in grants. When labeled by faculty, and those administrators who came up through the faculty ranks, as "others—not us," academic librarians can easily be seen as targets for elimination in poor economic times.

If I were to revisit that university and again encounter the perception among the research and teaching faculty that librarians are dominated by negative bureaucratic norms, or if I were to encounter comparable perceptions of poor librarian customer relations at another higher education institution, I would have a real problem. It would be difficult not to write that any "professionals" who exhibit such self-serving behavior might (almost) deserve to be deprofessionalized.

WHAT DO FUNDING SOURCES ACTUALLY WANT FROM THEIR LIBRARIANS, INFORMATION SPECIALISTS, KNOWLEDGE MANAGERS, AND ARCHIVISTS?

"Correct" Answers

Ethical researchers usually are wary about offering "cookbook" solutions to problems in individual service contexts. If asked, "What does your research tell me about what the funding sources and customers of my library, information center, knowledge management center, or archive really want?" the correct response is seldom well-received. No one really wants to hear, "Who knows? It's your library, information center, knowledge management center, or archive. You really should be the one to do the marketing studies necessary to find the answer to that question!"

Obviously, the busy reader is going to take exception to such a response. Even so, each context for providing service is different, and the answers may even vary between adjacent public libraries or across neighboring school districts. Their residents may belong to different co-cultures that prioritize diverse library and information programs or even no services at all. Such divergence only adds to the complexity of solving problems and runs up against the reality that the craving for "simple answers to complex questions is a typical American response" (Holmes and Rhoads Holmes 2002, 14). This cultural bias toward less-complex answers needs to be kept in mind whenever library, information, knowledge, or archival professionals have to justify their actions to those who control the needed funds.

Experienced managers know that limitations in available resources virtually demand that problems or issues be simplified to the point where their solutions are seen as affordable and can actually be applied. Multifaceted issues, such as delivering the most effective service possible to the homeless children and their parents, often require a menu of solutions and the application of resources beyond those affordable within a library's limited budget or even justifiable as a library program. Resolving some issues might actually require changes in community values and multi-agency cooperation. In consequence, such issues can seldom be truly remedied. Sometimes the most effective solutions to complex problems involve not actual resolutions, but agreed-upon strategies to diminish their negative consequences.

Fortunately, finding out what library, information, knowledge, and archival funding sources and customers/patrons/users really want at any given time is a solvable problem in responsive marketing and effective personal communication. However, problem identification needs to be followed by a problem solution, and such solutions are usually dependent on the perception that one's agency is of value to those who control the necessary resources.

The Political and Values Nature of Allocating Resources

It is a cross-national phenomenon that in recent years, even preceding The Great Recession of 2007, a number of funders and recipients of library, information, knowledge, and archival services have become concerned about the quality and effectiveness of the assistance provided. This may be seen as part of a "value for money" or return on investment (ROI) movement that has migrated from the profit-making sector as the funding to provide public services has become more limited. Before addressing the expressed views of customers and funding sources for library and information programs of various types, it is necessary to offer a few words on the inevitably political nature of resource allocation.

Briefly, the reader needs to keep in mind the realities that

1. All decisions on allocating funds, extending from the national level exemplified by the British and Canadian Parliaments and the Congress of the United States to the elected board of trustees of the smallest Illinois public library district, are "political decisions." So too are the decisions made on allocating financial and other resources by private corporations, private and public school systems, as well as not-for-profit and for-profit colleges and universities. It is all political—defined as who gets what and how.

2. Facts, the basis of the usual arguments for funding of so many library and information professionals, only work when decision makers are already on one's side. Social and behavioral scientists, as well as the Committee on Science and Technology of the U.S. House of Representatives, have found that "*political decisionmaking is 'irrational'—or not based wholly on objective information—to the extent that political choices are based on a complex set of factors including facts, values, distributive effects and political judgments of the public good*" (U.S. Library of Congress 1986, 175, emphasis added).

3. To the degree that librarians, information specialists, knowledge managers, and archivists (a) are deficient in their understanding of the priority of emotional connections; (b) do not share the values of their funders or

are unable to establish the "worth" of their own values in the judgments of such decision makers; (c) lack understanding of the formal and informal rules of their government or organizational environments; (d) refuse to market their programs, both online and, more importantly, face to face; and (e) rely on objective facts to make their cases for funding and other forms of program support, they will too often fail ignominiously in preserving their professional status and positions.

The Irrational Value Choice to Eliminate School Librarians

In a June 24, 2011, article titled "In Lean Times, Schools Squeeze Out Librarians," *New York Times* reporter Fernanda Santos provided rare glimpses into the values and perceptions behind decisions that lead to the refusal of administrators to fill vacant librarian positions in defiance of state regulations and/or actual layoffs of school librarians. In this article, Shael Polakow-Suransky, chief academic officer of New York City's public schools, saw the issue as saving classroom teachers by cutting school librarians who may be teachers and required in state regulations but who work "in a support capacity." Polakow-Suransky also stressed that students "equipped with laptops, tablets, or e-readers" can do research from their classrooms ("the way of the future") and might no longer need to visit the library (Santos 2011).

The article also described the process through which the school superintendent of Lancaster, Pennsylvania, whose district is poor and substantially composed of immigrants, eliminated "15 of the district's 20 librarians" under the excuse of needing to do so in order to continue to offer full-day kindergarten classes. Superintendent Pedro Rivera dealt with a looming $10 million deficit by brainstorming with his senior staff members over the question, "if this budget is an expression of our values, what is it that we value the most?"

As the superintendent described his version of a value-driven planning process to the *New York Times,* limiting class size, preserving arts, music, and prekindergarten classes, even physical education, were determined to be priorities. Having thereby created an artificial forced choice between maintaining full-day kindergarten or keeping all school librarians and their services, this emotion-driven process concluded with the decision that three-quarters of the librarians had to go (Santos 2011). This clearly problematic and very subjective process for deciding on cutbacks brings to mind several immediate questions, including (1) "Was a professional school librarian among the superintendent's "senior staff?' "; (2) "If no, why not?"; and, (3) "If yes, did he or she sleep through the planning meeting?" Additionally, one might reasonably ask, "How could such a negative decision on the employment of school librarians be adopted in a Pennsylvania school system after a strong factual case for supporting the state's school libraries and librarians was made a decade before and published as *Measuring up to Standards: The Impact of School Library Programs and Information Literacy in Pennsylvania Schools* (Lance, Rodney, and Hamilton-Pennell 2000)?

To borrow and expand the words of Kathleen de la Peña McCook (2000), even if the Lancaster, Pennsylvania, school librarians had "a place at the table" during the superintendent's decision-making process on programs to save or cut, the obvious lack of appreciation for their work at the administrative level was demonstrated by the outcome of the review. A true emotional connection with school librarians and their valuable contributions to student learning, as emphasized in Pennsylvania's own study, would have eliminated such a drastic reduction from the list of available options. The "facts" were there, but, to the Lancaster superintendent and his "value" cutback process, they didn't seem to matter. Any time a connection to values and agendas is demanded, to provide a mere "factual" defense of school librarian professionalism is virtually a guaranteed recipe for failure.

How Could This Happen?

Those who seemingly cannot network with decision makers, who cling to the illusion that facts can be persuasive in defending the value of school librarianship, need to revisit the presentation "What's It Take?" by Gary Hartzell (2002), Professor of Educational Administration and Supervision, University of Nebraska, Omaha, at the June 4, 2002, White House Conference on School Libraries. As some readers may recall, this conference was hosted by then First Lady and former school librarian Laura Bush. According to Hartzell, school administrators do not understand the great potential of school librarians and school libraries for four "inter-related reasons."

1. A good number of present-day school administrators grew up with poor library service and stereotypically negative ("shush") images of the librarian. They have no personal experience of excellent service delivered by school library professionals.
2. Most teacher training and administrator preparation courses do not discuss the value of the school librarian/school library media specialist. Instructors in such programs usually do not appreciate and endorse the crucial role of the principal in encouraging teacher–librarian cooperation.
3. "Librarians deliver services that empower others, and their contributions get swallowed up in the activities of those people." In other words, the people behind the scenes do not automatically get recognition for their fine work.
4. School librarians do a miserable job of marketing the value of themselves and their programs. They will talk with other school librarians and deliver and attend valuable programs at school library conferences but will not routinely network with their supervisors or present on the value of school librarians for principals and superintendents at school administrator conferences. School librarians simply do not get the "value" message across to their bosses, the school principals and superintendents, on how effective school librarians and school libraries/school media programs can advance the principal's interests and the superintendent's agendas. (Hartzell 2002)

What Funding Sources and Customers Really Want—Approximate Inferences

It is to be recalled, depending on context, that the political case for generating support for library, information, knowledge, and archival professionalism has to be made within and without each library and information agency or department. Given such a reality, this section of the chapter addresses requested services and programs within these broad categories as well as within the major subdivisions traditionally categorized under the broad term *library.*

A UNIVERSAL TECHNOLOGY RULE FOR SERVING FUNDERS, CUSTOMERS, PATRONS, AND USERS

A critical point needs to be made that applies to all service contexts: library, information, knowledge, and archival professionals must develop and maintain levels of technological expertise, specifically including variations of web-enhanced marketing, which enhance personal networking and meet and preferably exceed the expertise levels of the individuals and communities they are tasked with helping. Because such proficiency rapidly evolves, and state-of-the-art quickly becomes outdated, no specific software will be endorsed at this point. Professionals are expected to keep current with their markets in the digital era, period. This rule should be envisioned as representing an eternal learning curve whose apex is going to be reached only by the truly technologically savant, and then only for a limited time.

LEARNING FROM THE CORPORATE WORLDS OF INFORMATION AND KNOWLEDGE MANAGEMENT PROFESSIONALS

Unlike so many of their counterparts in the library, school, and university sectors, information specialists, knowledge managers, and archivists in profit-making environments quickly learn how the organizational political or power game is played successfully. This reality was brought home to me one late afternoon in my fourth year as a Dominican University faculty member. A former student, who had taken several of my courses, dropped by my office to bring me up to date on her career while waiting to attend an evening program at the university. As she talked this student casually mentioned her salary, which was nearly 250 percent of what I was making at the time. As I tried to think only good thoughts and keep the smile on my face, I asked her what was the secret involved in earning that sort of income. She replied that she followed what she had learned during a meeting of the Special Libraries Association (SLA).

"I was sitting at the same table with an experienced information specialist who told me that my job, and the job of every information specialist, is to help solve the problems that are keeping our bosses up at night," she said.

The wisdom encapsulated in the instruction to help solve the boss's problems, and thereby let the boss get some rest, is known at the bone-deep level by effective corporate information, knowledge, and archival professionals. They comprehend that their work is actually evaluated both subjectively and objectively. Such professionals understand that it behooves them to possess the effective relationship skills necessary to find out what the boss's work problems really are, as well as the research, analysis, and communications abilities necessary to help solve them. Over the years, I have found that students who self-identify as would-be information and knowledge professionals in corporate environments tend to be more extroverted than their classmates. They appreciate that outgoing behavior is an asset in environments where long hours, job instability, and high salaries just seem to go together.

Slipping into my professor role, I asked this alum if in her work she had ever been pressured to get hold of either grey information (obtained through nonstandard, often questionable methods) or black information (obtained illegally). The topic of obtaining necessary information on competitors by any means necessary had generated a lot of discussion in one of our shared courses, and I was interested to find out if she had encountered the issue in her post-degree life. If memory serves, her response had been to sit back in the chair, smile, and reply, "My boss and I know where the line is. And we never cross it."

MONEY AND SUCCESS IN AN ENTREPRENEURIAL WORLD

In both established and emerging free-enterprise or capitalistic societies, making lots of money, regardless of the means, acquires a unique status. As the famed sociologist Robert K. Merton pointed out long ago, the concentration on building wealth without an equal emphasis on socially approved means for doing so, means that "money has been consecrated as a value in itself" (Merton 1968, 190). This concentration on moneymaking at all costs, whether for quarterly reports or for end-of-year bonuses, can set in motion situations of ethical conflict when demands to secure vital information for decision making may lead the information specialist or knowledge manager to seriously consider obtaining either grey information or black information to help develop a product or increase market share.

In the era of the Enron Corporation, the scandal-plagued energy firm, and Arthur Andersen LLP, its failed corporate auditor, political back-room deal making may not present the most extensive ethical challenges to library, information, knowledge, and archival professionals. Granted, there will always be the occasional city or county where elected or party officials arrange protected jobs for precinct leaders in public libraries or, more likely, school systems with their much larger budgets. However, ethical challenges of the "means and ends" type are more likely to arise in certain corporate offices on the uncommon occasions when information specialists, knowledge managers, or competitive data analysts are encouraged, by a wink or a nod from their bosses, to cross the line to secure necessary information for decision makers or product developers. Such activity may enhance their value with certain corporate leaders, but at what cost?

Several questions arise from this conversation with the successful information specialist that are fundamental to any discussion of the political case to encourage funding sources and customers to support the value of library, information, knowledge, and archival professionalism.

1. What kinds of assistance or services do funders, customers, and patrons ask for or could ask for from library and information professionals?
2. In what areas might the priorities of students, library and information professionals, and their professional associations conflict with the legitimate expectations of funders, customers, patrons, and users?

Because these fundamental questions cross jurisdictional boundaries, the relevance of each in power-based relationships to library, information, knowledge, and archival professionalism will be discussed en bloc.

ONCE AGAIN, WHAT ASSISTANCE DO FUNDERS, CUSTOMERS, AND PATRONS WANT FROM LIS PROFESSIONALS?

The reader is reminded that no general summary of the actual or potential assistance sought by funders, customers, and patrons can ever substitute for the individualized marketing approach necessary for effectively serving one's community or organization. It would be foolish for any professional to see the generalities provided in this chapter and throughout *Defending Professionalism* as anything more than a menu of effective possibilities to be explored in developing marketing approaches to one's own community, organization, school, or college/university. Nevertheless, anyone contemplating such an effort should consider the following.

In reviewing the suggestions for improvement that may be provided to library and information professionals from a variety of sources, including users and funders, it is important not to see any "negative points" as mere attacks on library, information, knowledge, or archival professionalism. It would be more productive to see such criticism as invitations to consider changing or offering reasonable justifications for current patterns of service. If they are truly representative of popular feeling or funder priorities, suggestions to change or invitations to defend programs, at a minimum, may be considered evidence that such programs are not being effectively marketed, advocated, or otherwise communicated.

Suggestions to Change or Invitations to Justify Professionalism

- In his 2004 *Who's In Charge?: Responsibility for the Public Library Service*, consultant Tim Coates (2004) asserted that public library users were most interested in a broad range of books and other reading material, extended hours including evenings and weekends, and library facilities that were "clean, welcoming places to visit and in which to study" (1). Coates, whose work experience prioritizes the for-profit sector and profit maximization rather than lifelong learning (29), also asserted that "the demarcation between professional and non-professional staff should cease" (20).

- In 2006, *Long Overdue: A Fresh Look at Public and Leadership Attitudes about Libraries in the 21st Century* reported on the perceptions of "many civic leaders" that the varied governance structures of American public libraries—such as departments of local governments, independent taxing districts, not-for-profit corporations, and so on—were "a major stumbling block" to cooperating at the local level. The report also stressed that public library "shortcomings" also included

  - Lack of library marketing,
  - Impassive advocacy, and
  - Isolation from the community (Public Agenda Foundation, Bill and Melinda Gates Foundation, and Americans for Libraries Council 2006, 13).

To the extent that the *Long Overdue* findings are accurate, operating a public library in a manner that so completely lacks adequate connections to its service community is a recipe for disaster. One could even wonder why funding cuts for public libraries, institutions that so often don't market, advocate, and are isolated, rank only as the second most popular way for mayors to slash budgets in poor economic times (American Library Association 2011, 12).

- During 2009, Great Britain's Department for Culture, Media, and Sport (DCMS), the cabinet agency responsible for public library matters, issued *Empower, Inform, Enrich: The Modernisation Review of Public Libraries: A Consultation Document*. The purpose of this document was to encourage a nationwide discussion of the roles and future of the British public library. In the opening section of the document, titled "The Challenge for Public Libraries: Introduction," the first noteworthy "challenge" was to demonstrate that public libraries were "still relevant and vital" to "citizens, commentators, and politicians" (Great Britain Department for Culture, Media and Sport 2009, 4). The implications for library professionals in the marketing requirements inherent in this "challenge" are substantial.

- In 2011, the International City/County Management Association (ICMA) published *Maximize the Potential of Your Public Library: A Report on the Innovative Ways Public Libraries Are Addressing Community Priorities*. This work, addressed to the ICMA membership, detailed the findings of the ICMA Public Library Innovations grant program, funded by the Bill & Melinda Gates Foundation. It stressed that local government managers may view library services as an amenity, not a necessity because these services are not generally associated with local "core needs, such as public safety, health, and economic development." Further, *Maximize the Potential* emphasized, "if the public library wants to be more engaged with community priorities, the library must adopt these priorities as its own and reach out to local government and community partners" (International City/County Management Association 2011, 2).

Discussion

An age-old saying relates that governments generally pass laws to limit behavior when people are already behaving in ways that such governments find disturbing. A similar, if inverse, relationship exists between behaviors governments want to encourage and what people are apparently not doing. At worst, it would be a pardonable exaggeration to assert that these American and British reports depict a world where too many public libraries, as well as professional librarians and other staff, (1) are out of touch with their communities; (2) operate for the convenience of the librarians and staff, not the needs of customers or patrons; (3) hire employees deficient in personal communication skills; (4) lack successful marketing programs; and (5) possess little or no effective leadership.

This list is a litany of managerial failure. As such, it is far from an effective defense of the professionalism of those who allowed the problems to develop on their watch.

WHERE MIGHT THE PRIORITIES OF STUDENTS, LIS PROFESSIONALS, AND PROFESSIONAL ASSOCIATIONS CONFLICT WITH THE EXPECTATIONS OF FUNDERS AND USERS?

- The 2010 publication *The Modernisation Review of Public Libraries: A Policy Statement* was issued by Great Britain's Department for Culture, Media and Sport as the culmination of the consultation process started the previous year with the challenge outlined (previously) in *Empower, Inform, Enrich* (2009).

In its recommendations regarding the education provided public librarians, the report argued for a new framework for "professional qualifications, founded on user driven policy and practices." Among the strongly advocated changes were demands for the instruction of students in

1. Customer service and people skills,
2. Community outreach,
3. Working with children,
4. Marketing, and
5. Leadership (Great Britain Department for Culture, Media and Sport 2010, 9).

• The previously discussed International City/County Management Association (ICMA) publication *Maximize the Potential of Your Public Library: A Report on the Innovative Ways Public Libraries Are Addressing Community Priorities* is particularly helpful in highlighting challenging perceptions of libraries held by American city and county managers. These perceptions include already observed problems arising from the fact that public libraries may be legally independent of city or county governments, as well as the view held by some managers that libraries are merely discretionary services, amenities, not necessities. Additionally, there is also the judgment by certain city and county managers that public libraries and librarians are too fixated on collections and circulation statistics and not sufficiently engaged with true community priorities. This perception inevitably has negative implications for funding (International City/County Management Association 2011, 2–3).

Maximize the Potential of Your Public Library and ICMA recommended a threefold approach for city and county managers to resolving the problem of relating to the local public library:

1. The librarian in the public library must understand the "local government's strategic and development plans and work to assist in accomplishing those plans,"
2. Local government leaders "need to recognize the potential of the library to support their priorities." and
3. There must be a local government-public library "joint assessment of what capabilities [the library] . . . has to contribute to community priorities and how to make the most of those priorities" (International City/County Management Association 2011, 4).

Discussion

The reader would not be out of line in considering the recommendations in both *The Modernisation Review of Public Libraries: A Policy Statement* and *Maximize the Potential of Your Public Library: A Report on the Innovative Ways Public Libraries Are Addressing Community Priorities* as, in fact if not law, approaches for generating support for public libraries and public librarians by tying their programs to the goals of the city or county governments. Many professionals would see such a development as a loss of library independence, however ill-funded such a "freedom" might be. However, inherent in improved collaboration is also a greater probability for the public library to influence the development and prioritization of municipal or county goals, particularly as they relate to meeting community needs for library services. In the words of former Speaker of the U.S. House of Representatives Sam Rayburn, closer relationships encapsulate the practical reality that "Sometimes, in order to get along, you have to go along" (Sam Rayburn House Museum 2011).

Problems in Professional Education

In the United States of America, variations of the remark "I'm from the government, and I'm here to help" are often used as punch lines in political jokes. That a government agency, Britain's Department for Culture, Media, and Sport, would insist that "providers of library and information sector courses" should teach "customer service and people skills, community outreach, working with children, marketing, and leadership" could be a bit of a cultural shock for certain ALA-accredited programs in North America, which have convinced ALA that the association had better let them teach what they want in the manner they choose to teach—or else (Crowley 2008).

These recommendations to British academics are fundamental to equipping their students in the processes of building an expanded base of "repeat customers" in market-oriented economies. However, they also define a critical problem. To the extent that required instruction in "customer service and people skills, community outreach, working with children, marketing, and leadership" is not already offered by Britain's providers of library and information education, it can be asserted that such education is irrelevant to the actual needs of the future professional public librarians (Great Britain Department for Culture, Media and Sport 2010, 9). Such an equation would be equally sustainable in Canadian and American programs accredited by the ALA.

Although the interests of faculty often cause higher education to be remarkably resistant to change, it is also likely that the public librarians of Britain are partially responsible for their own mal-education. If the directors of Britain's public libraries were marketing oriented, they would have observed the lack of preparedness of new professionals for determining needs and delivering services. Had they been true leaders, they would have pressured their university-level "education providers" to make the necessary changes before government "bureaucrats" had to step in to propose solutions.

Multiple reasons can be listed for a mismatch between higher education priorities and work requirements. In ALA-accredited programs such causes have included the dominance of the theoretical information model over more practical library education; the preferences of students as tuition-paying (and indebted) consumers to select their own classes, regardless of the relevance of such classes to the needs of potential employers and customers; and, most importantly, the unwillingness of the ALA bureaucracy and leadership to insist on nationally required courses out of fear that the structure of accreditation would be abandoned by major universities (Crowley 2008, 114–18). In consequence, ALA has operated a system of professional education without any effective way of ensuring that instruction is matched to the needs of the ultimate users.

Every year, numerous professionally educated academic, public, and school librarians enter the labor market without training in marketing and advocacy and possessing minimal abilities to communicate in a variety of contexts. The fact that the public library is viewed by city and county managers as obsessed on the circulation of fiction and DVDs (International City/County Management Association 2011, 2) is an example of the problematic consequences resulting from a lack of effective marketing. So too is the lack of official recognition that fiction reading actually has multiple educational benefits! When local city or county managers see reading fiction as a frivolity rather than a priority, it is most likely that professional librarians have not informed them of the research on how reading for pleasure and a simple rise in reading volume, a main concern of certain library reading programs, increases the literacy, vocabulary, and the "verbal intelligence" of children, teens, young adults, and senior citizens (Cunningham and Stanovich 1998, 7; see also, Roman, Carran, and Fiore 2010; Ross, McKechnie, and Rothbauer 2006). Worse yet, the professional librarians have doubtlessly neglected to provide decision makers with examples of how this research is validated locally through similar successes in their own communities and schools.

The envisioning of libraries as simply collections of resources measured by circulation figures suggests that educated professionals and other types of public librarians have not kept local government administrators up to date on their other vital functions. Too often those who control the resources have not been informed of the crucial roles of public libraries in support of job searches, formal schooling, adult basic education, English as a second language, and the many components that constitute lifelong learning.

In the State of Illinois, public libraries and public library districts are created "to provide local public institutions of general education for citizens of Illinois" (Illinois General Assembly, Public Library District Act of 1991). The broad mandate set forth in this legal rationale would be sufficient to support a wide spectrum of services offered by city or county governments, schools, and universities. That such potentially collaborating organizations remain largely ignorant of a public library's capabilities is a marketing, advocacy, and communications failure that reflects poorly on the professionals involved.

Helping the "Boss" in Schools and Universities

Schools

The range of cutbacks in the ranks of American and Canadian school librarians was extensively discussed in the first chapter of this work. British school librarians have suffered their own losses (Streatfield, Shaper, and Rae-Scott 2010). At a minimum, such cutbacks suggest that the affected professionals involved were not schooled in the "solve the boss's problems" approach that characterizes effective information and knowledge professionals in the private sector.

In Canadian and American schools communication problems arise when the bosses of school librarians, the principals and superintendents, do not appreciate, for example, how professional librarians encouraging youth to read what they enjoy reading can help increase student scores on standardized tests (Ontario Library Association, Queen's University, and People for Education 2006, 4–5). A successful marketing approach to administrators would likely be a one-on-one approach addressing how the combination of professional teacher-librarians/school librarians, student satisfaction, and increased standardized scores may contribute to enhancing an administrator's reputation and consequent professional longevity. This very real possibility seems to encapsulate a particularly notable conjunction of student, librarian, and administrator self-interest. If everybody involved is shown to benefit, a wise administrator thinks twice before breaking up the "team." To do otherwise, even in times of temporary financial distress, is classic short-term thinking.

Universities

Of late, concerns over the value of librarian professionalism in academic environments have reached the point where a Canadian university library head announced to web streamed and on-site Pennsylvania State University audiences that new hires at his university library would more likely be PhDs than professional librarians with the ALA-accredited master's degree (McMaster University Academic Librarians' Association 2011).

It is too often the case that many professionals who direct and staff academic libraries are short-term reactors who seldom ask the "What next?" question when considering certain actions. In consequence, such leaders too easily fall into the classic problem of applying a solution that becomes the next problem to be solved. The difficulty is even worse when administrators operate on the either–or approach, as seems to be the case in this master's degree–librarians versus PhDs issue in academic libraries. One wonders if such managers ever thought, in a very poor employment market for PhD-qualified academics, that it might be possible to hire master's degree librarians with PhDs or, in the rare cases where no qualified professionally educated librarian is available, appoint a PhD on an acting basis while he or she earns the library and information science degree. The fundamental value of creatively supporting the worth of the professional master's degree and the service culture it represents, so easily abandoned by some leading academic librarians (Neal 2006), is discussed in further detail in chapter 14, "Advancing Professionalsim in Library, Information, Knowledge, and Archival Services in the 'New Normal World.'"

Even when such school or university programs are subjected to rigorous state-level evaluations (Lance, Rodney, and Hamilton-Pennell 2000), the librarians who are not locally valued may find themselves expendable, as the Lancaster school librarians recently discovered (Santos 2011). Alternatively, they may be losing professional positions because of library heads afflicted by short-term, professionally destructive thinking (McMaster University Academic Librarians' Association 2011; Neal 2006). In a future marked by resource scarcity (Pew Center on the States and Public Policy Institute of California 2010), school librarians and academic librarians without effective marketing, advocacy, and leadership approaches to defending their professionalism may eventually find themselves a part of the accumulation of losses discussed in the "School Libraries" and "Academic Libraries" sections of future editions of ALA's annually issued *The State of America's Libraries: A Report from the American Library Association* (American Library Association 2011).

POLITICS, POWER, AND NETWORKING

The inevitable problem with making the "political case for supporting the value of professionalism" is that effective politics involves a give-and-take approach and a willingness to accept compromises. Historically, this flexibility has been countered by the American national culture's insistence on "absolute standards," something which researchers have found to be without peer in the "developed world" (Lipset 1997, 207). For example, it is worth considering the implications of the hard line stance taken by ALA on providing children with equal access to all library resources, including unfiltered web access. In certain library circles even a supporter of such access who acknowledges that those who oppose it have a legitimate case to make can be seen as betraying the central library concern of intellectual freedom. Nevertheless, something that is increasingly absent from the discussion of issues on the national level, the old political attitude of being able "to disagree without being disagreeable," is often found alive at local levels where police, fire protection, schools, and libraries can be nonpartisan issues. Combined with Rayburn's admonition that "Sometimes, in order to get along, you have to go along" (Sam Rayburn House Museum 2011), it raises the possibility that influential local leaders might feel comfortable supporting a professional librarian on some issues and disagreeing with her or him on others.

TALKING ABOUT CENSORSHIP
AND POLITE DISAGREEMENT

Back in the day, when print material was still the main arena for battles over censorship, I remember talking with a local politician who was enraged at library supporters calling him a censor and claiming that he was against the First Amendment to the U.S. Constitution for wanting certain books off local library shelves. After an extended discussion on the plusses (him) and minuses (me) of removing material from the library, this politician, while perhaps more knowledgeable, was still angry. "I fought for this country and I believe in the First Amendment, but you have to remember that the First Amendment does not prevent us from protecting our children."

Just before we parted, this army veteran turned politician observed, "I would have felt a lot less attacked and a lot more open to discussing matters if the librarian and her supporters had just said something like 'If you start taking things off the shelves, the librarian can't do a professional job of serving our community.'"

Shaking his head, he smiled. "I still might not have gone along with her. But a respectful disagreement over how best to serve the children of our town just seems to be a lot easier to solve when name calling doesn't get in the way."

CONCLUSION

It is doubtless the case that library directors fighting to preserve their budgets, or "making do" after budgets were already cut, might prefer deferring the discussion of how best to defend professionalism to another time. Times are indeed hard, and there is a commonsense view that "When you're up to your backside in alligators, it's hard to remember that your goal is to drain the swamp" (Hudson 2011). Nevertheless, the fundamental problem with deferring the necessary work to preserve library, information, knowledge, and archival professionalism is that inaction is likely to leave us with little or nothing to save.

Because chapter 14 will draw on the spirit of the other chapters and provide more detailed guidance on how best to preserve professionalism, this present chapter on community and organizational political effectiveness will conclude with one of my favorite stories about a shy librarian turned effective library advocate.

Quite some time ago, I conducted a series of workshops on lobbying, which was discretely termed "information provision to legislators," around the State of Indiana. In the process I learned several lessons about how the introvert–extrovert distinction can become relatively meaningless in successful library advocacy and marketing efforts. After being trained, a number of librarians, particularly public library directors, school librarians, and academic library heads, went on to coach others on what they had learned and, quite often, to successfully gain support for library programs from state and federal legislators. About a year after the workshops, one library director, who had learned how to lobby from a colleague who had attended one of the workshops, came over to talk to me at a state conference. This library director, who self-identified as a "truly extreme introvert," excitedly informed me how she had "turned one legislator around" and developed strong relationships with other political supporters. After her remarks I asked her how she did it.

"I always take a deep breath, remember what I learned about lobbying, and start making my case. I tell them about what we have done and what we can do for our communities and, in particular, what is happening for the good in their legislative districts," she explained. "Most of the time it works."

Smiling, she added. "After one of these discussions, no matter how I feel it went, I always reward myself with some of the first-rate chocolate that I keep for special occasions."

The moral of this story, of course, is that the chocolate one most enjoys may be the chocolate that professionals earn while successfully communicating the value of their professionalism in designing and delivering the responsive and valued services of their libraries, information centers, knowledge management centers, and archives.

REFERENCES

American Library Association. 2011. *The State of America's Libraries: A Report from the American Library Association*. Chicago, IL: American Library Association. Accessed June 19, 2011. http://www.ala.org/ala/newspresscenter/mediapresscenter/americaslibraries2011/index.cfm.

Cheski, Richard M. 1993. "Foreword." In *Marketing and Libraries Do Mix: A Handbook for Libraries and Information Centers*, ed. H. Baird Tenney, i–ii. Columbus: State Library of Ohio.

Coates, Tim. 2004. *Who's in Charge? Responsibility for the Public Library Service*. London: Libri Trust. Accessed July 22, 2011. http://www.rwevans.co.uk/libri/Who%27s%20in%20char_e_(as%20printed.pdf.

Crowley, Bill. 2008. *Renewing Professional Librarianship: A Fundamental Rethinking*. A Beta Phi Mu Monograph. Westport, CT: Libraries Unlimited.

Cunningham, Anne E., and Keith E. Stanovich. 1998. "What Reading Does for the Mind." *American Educator* 22(1–2): 1–8. Accessed July 28, 2011. http://www.aft.org/pdfs/americaneducator/springsummer1998/cunningham.pdf.

Great Britain Department for Culture, Media and Sport. 2009. *Empower, Inform, Enrich: The Modernisation Review of Public Libraries: A Consultation Document*. London: DCMS.. Accessed August 1, 2011. http://webarchive.nationalarchives.gov.uk/20110208165439/webarchive.nationalarchives.gov.uk/+/http://www.culture.gov.uk/images/consultations/librariesreview_consultation.pdf.

Great Britain Department for Culture, Media and Sport. 2010. *The Modernisation Review of Public Libraries: A Policy Statement*. London: DCMS. Accessed August 1, 2011. http://www.official-documents.gov.uk/document/cm78/7821/7821.pdf.

Hartzell, Gary. 2002. "What's It Take?" Paper presented at the White House Conference on School Libraries, Washington, DC, June 4. Accessed July 22, 2011. http://www.imls.gov/news/events/whitehouse_2.shtm#gh.

Holmes, Lowell D., and Ellen Rhoads Holmes. 2002. "The American Cultural Configuration." In *Distant Mirrors: America as a Foreign Culture*, 3rd ed., ed. Philip R. De Vita and James D. Armstrong, 4–26. Belmont, CA: Wadsworth/Thomson Learning.

Hudson, Michael. 2011. "Stay Out of the Weeds, Stop Fighting Fires, Focus on What Really Matters." *Credit Union Times* (July 19). Accessed July 28, 2011. http://www.cutimes.com/2011/07/19/stay-out-of-the-weeds-stop-fighting-fires-focus-on.

Illinois General Assembly, Public Library District Act of 1991, Illinois Compiled Statutes 75 ILCS 16/1–15. Accessed July 29, 2011. http://www.ilga.gov/legislation/ilcs/ilcs4.asp?DocName=007500160HArt.+1&ActID=993&ChapterID=16&SeqStart=100000&SeqEnd=1300000.

International City/County Management Association. 2011. *Maximize the Potential of Your Public Library: A Report on the Innovative Ways Public Libraries Are Addressing Community Priorities.* Washington, DC: ICMA International City/County Management Association.

Lance, Keith Curry, Marcia J. Rodney, and Christine Hamilton-Pennell. 2000. *Measuring Up to Standards: The Impact of School Library Programs and Information Literacy in Pennsylvania Schools.* Greensburg: Pennsylvania Citizens for Better Libraries.

Lipset, Seymour Martin. 1997. *American Exceptionalism: A Double-edged Sword.* New York: W.W. Norton.

McCook, Kathleen de la Peña. 2000. *A Place at the Table: Participating in Community building.* Chicago: American Library Association.

McMaster University Academic Librarians' Association (MUALA). 2011. "MUALA Review of University Librarian Jeffrey Trzeciak—Update of May 16, 2011 [4/4]." Accessed July 27, 2011. http://muala.ca/node/23.

Merton, Robert King. 1968. *Social Theory and Social Structure.* New York: Free Press.

Neal, James G. 2006. "Raised by Wolves: Integrating the New Generation of Feral Professionals into the Academic Library." *Library Journal* (February 15): 42–44. Accessed July 28, 2011. http://www.libraryjournal.com/article/CA6304405.html.

Ontario Library Association, Queen's University (Kingston, Ont.), and People for Education. 2006. *School Libraries and Student Achievement in Ontario a Study.* Toronto: Ontario Library Association. Accessed July 27, 2011. http://www.peopleforeducation.com/school-libraries/2006.

Pew Center on the States and Public Policy Institute of California. 2010. *Facing Facts Public Attitudes and Fiscal Realities in Five Stressed States.* Washington, DC: Pew Center on the States. Accessed July 28, 2011. http://www.pewcenteronthestates.org/uploadedFiles/PCS_PPIC.pdf.

Public Agenda Foundation, Bill and Melinda Gates Foundation, and Americans for Libraries Council. 2006. *Long Overdue: A Fresh Look at Public and Leadership Attitudes about Libraries in the 21st Century.* New York: Public Agenda.

Roman, Susan, Deborah T. Carran, and Carole D. Fiore. 2010. *The Dominican Study: Public Library Summer Reading Programs Close the Reading Gap.* River Forest, IL: Dominican University, Graduate School of Library and Information Science. Accessed August 1, 2011. http://www.dom.edu/academics/gslis/downloads/DOM_IMLS_book_2010_FINAL_web.pdf.

Ross, Catherine Sheldrick, Lynne (E.F.) McKechnie, and Paulette M. Rothbauer. 2006. *Reading Matters: What the Research Reveals about Reading, Libraries, and Community.* Westport, CT: Libraries Unlimited.

Rubin, Richard E. 2010. *Foundations of Library and Information Science.* 3rd ed. New York: Neal-Schuman.

Sam Rayburn House Museum. 2011. "Bits of Wit and Wisdom." Accessed July 28. http://www.visitsamrayburnhouse.com/index.aspx?page=797.

Santos, Fernanda. 2011. "In Lean Times, Schools Squeeze Out Librarians." *New York Times*, June 24. Accessed July 23, 2011. http://www.nytimes.com/2011/06/25/nyregion/schools-eliminating-librarians-as-budgets-shrink.html?_r=1&pagewanted=all.

16th Judicial Circuit of Jackson County [Missouri]. 2011. "Juvenile Court History." Accessed July 28. http://www.family-court.org/history.htm.

Streatfield, David, Sue Shaper, and Simon Rae-Scott. 2010. *School Libraries in the UK a Worthwhile Past, a Difficult Present—and a Transformed Future?: Main Report of the UK National Survey*. London: CILIP. Accessed July 29, 2011. http://www.cilip.org.uk/get-involved/special-interest-groups/school/Documents/full-school-libraries-report.pdf.

U.S. Library of Congress. 1986. *Research Policies for the Social and Behavioral Sciences: Report*. Washington, DC: U.S. GPO. Accessed July 20, 2011. http://www.eric.ed.gov/PDFS/ED289725.pdf.

Ward, Robert C. 2007. "The Outsourcing of Public Library Management: An Analysis of the Application of New Public Management Theories from the Principal-Agent Perspective." *Administration and Society* 38(6): 627–48.

13

AN OBSTACLE: THE DIFFICULTY OF CONVINCING OTHERS TO CHANGE THEIR THINKING AND BEHAVIOR

Robert F. Moran Jr.
Librarian Emeritus, Indiana University Northwest, and Columnist
Library Leadership and Management

ANOTHER WASTED PLANNING EFFORT?

What! They didn't take any of our recommendations? The recommendations were consistent with the guidelines! We answered every question raised in the initial review of our draft, which they judged as well done. Our logic was impeccable!

How often has this been said or heard? Perhaps this was the response to a planning committee's rejection of a department's recommendations for its space in a new building? Or, was it the refusal for funding for a new public relations effort? Sometimes an ad hoc committee will spend weeks researching the issue to which it was assigned, consult with involved personnel, proceed through several drafts with the result being a logical, and well-founded report. Then, when the report is submitted, the committee is told that the report was well done and its arguments compelling, but it will not be implemented. When the committee chair asks where the report was lacking, what is not logical and well founded, the response is similar to: "There's nothing wrong with the report. That change is just not going to be made." Logic does not always carry the day. Even in the rationally oriented world of libraries, having the best argument is frequently not enough to move decision makers to accept a recommendation.

The authors of the chapters in this volume have made detailed, step-by-step arguments for the need for professionally educated librarians. They argue well for the critical importance of a professional education, whether for those who will offer traditional activities such as the story hour in a public library and the choice of books for a college library or the newer technology-assisted activities such as academic research and content organization and management. If logic were sufficient to persuade others, we could be certain to see in the months after publication an increase in overall support for the need for professionally educated librarians. However, given our experiences alluded to previously, we should expect that logic will not be enough by itself to move others to change their thinking or behavior. Unless otherwise indicated by sentence context, the term *library* should be understood as including information center, knowledge management center, and archives, and the term *librarian* as including information specialist, knowledge manager, and archivist.

AN IN-DEPTH LOOK AT CHANGE

Because more than good arguments are needed to change the thinking of others and lead them to the desired behavior, it will be helpful to take an in-depth look at how change in people occurs. We all know that change is difficult, especially changing how someone else thinks and behaves. Yet, few are equally aware of the depth of the difficulties faced by those who seek to change others. A consideration of some of the research on change will help us understand why changing others is so difficult. This understanding should help when seeking to motivate others to recognize the value of a professionally educated librarian as well as a willingness to commit resources needed to employee fully qualified staff.

While studying people who had been told that they needed to change their behavior, Kurt Lewin (1947) found that they were able to do so only after they understood fully that their current behavior was inadequate, learned new, more effective behavior and then used this new behavior long enough for it to become ingrained. Lewin conceived of a person's current pattern of behavior as being in a state of equilibrium with forces for maintaining in the current state of an individual's behavior equal and opposite to forces toward change. With this characterization in mind, he identified three stages of behavioral change. He described these as unfreezing, moving, and refreezing. Unfreezing involves a change in the forces either for or against the current behavior, either less force for maintenance or greater force for something new. Once the need for change is felt, a new equilibrium is sought. Then, once this new equilibrium is reached it needs to be maintained. It needs to be frozen (Lewin 1947).

One of the benefits of this research lies in its recognition that change in a person's behavior is a multistep process that takes time. Anyone who wants to change the behavior of others needs to understand that an order from a superior or even a well-developed argument is not likely to result that day or even that week in new and permanent behavior change. Perhaps in the military this can happen, but not in most other organizations. Changing others takes time.

Edgar Schein (1968) looked at change within organizations from the point of view of interpersonal relationships. He explained Lewin's stages in less technical terms. If people are to change their behavior permanently, as change in organizations requires, they need to be adequately motivated to change, to find and adopt a new, more effective behavior, and then to practice the new behavior long enough for it to become ingrained. Here, too, change is shown to be a lengthy process. In addition, there is a recognition that the people who are expected to change need to be involved. People need to be motivated to change, and this means that they need to understand the inadequacy of current behavior as well as the value of the new behavior. A person wishing to change the behavior of others needs not only to accept that it will take time before the change occurs, but also be willing to invest the attention and energy required so that the others can understand the value of the new behavior and then accept the need to change; that is, be motivated to change (Schein 1968).

The results of these studies and analyses bring to mind the adage, people don't resist change; they resist being changed. Habitual behavior of others can be changed, but only through the involvement of the person who needs to change. To expect people to change their behavior because a logical argument is presented or a command is issued is simplistic. They need time to absorb the argument, relate it to their current personal situation, and weigh the consequences of the change. Librarians wishing to convince others to support and fund a fully professional staff will have to accept that special attention and effort needs to be given to the dynamics of behavior change.

A more recent and extensive study reported in the online journal *Fast Company* (Deutschman 2005) dramatically reinforces the results of these earlier studies and, consequently, reinforces the realization of the need for this special attention and effort from anyone wishing to change others. The description of the study begins by asking whether the readers would change their behavior if they found out that they were going to die if they did not change. Specifically, what if the reader was told by someone who was well informed and trusted that without a change in habitual ways of acting, death in the near future was a certainty? Faced with the likelihood of death in the near future, would harmful activities be stopped and new beneficial ways of acting adopted?

This study investigated the response of seriously ill heart patients to the need to change their lifestyles. After having been told by their physicians that they had to change the way they lived in significant ways, only 10 percent did so. Two years after coronary-artery bypass surgery, 90 percent of those studied continued the harmful behavior they had been warned to change. To reinforce the applicability of their results beyond their sample, the authors note that in study after study of people needing to change their behavior, the same inability to change in the face of serious consequences was found. The authors conclude, "Whether the need for change within an organization is due to the need to respond to external changes, or we wish to change our own approach to management, more often than not, we can't" (Deutschman 2005).

Here again research demonstrates that people will not change habitual behavior just because they had been given a logical argument for doing so. A statement, though objectively true, will influence other people only if those people can take it in a way that is meaningful to them.

A consideration of how our minds work provides additional support for this contention. Our minds are not just a long list of facts to which we add other facts. Rather, the information and observations we make are taken in and then related to what we already know and organized with this previous data to allow effective thinking. When, while driving, we see a fire truck, our minds respond with more than "red truck." Rather, this observation is immediately related to fast moving vehicle: "move to the side of the road, something bad is happening somewhere, etc." Cognitive researchers refer to these related and organized sets of facts as frames—mental structures that shape the way we see the world. We may be presented with facts, but for us to make sense of them, they have to fit the mental structures that are already there. If they don't, the new facts are rejected; they are perceived as false.

For example, suppose that, during a meeting of senior staff, the door of the room suddenly flew open and a shabbily dressed man stumbled into the room and shouted, "Wow, am I glad you don't start meetings any earlier," flopped down in a chair and continued, "OK, let's get at it!" Immediately, the person in charge of the meeting stood up and said, "Wonderful to see you, Ted. Staff please welcome our new assistant director." Those at the meeting are unlikely to accept immediately the statement that this person is the new assistant director. Unspoken responses might include, "Is this some kind of a joke?" or "Is there something going on here that I haven't been told about?" Some might respond with a blank stare. No one would stand up immediately, walk over to the new person, and welcome him to the staff.

Why might the kind of responses described be more likely than a casual acceptance of the chairperson's statement? An authority figure who is in a position to know who this person is has presented the group with an objective fact, "Here is a new member of the administration." The problem is that this fact does not fit the understanding of assistant director in a professional organization that most people have, their mental structure, their frame for a person who holds authority in a library.

This example is clearly contrived. Here is another, perhaps not as striking but more likely. New management arrived in a business that for years has been run as a strict hierarchy. Decisions were all made at the top and passed down with no opportunity to comment or question. When staff members dared to raise a question or concern, they were told with no uncertainty to do what they had been told and leave decision making to the decision makers! Infrequent requests from management for ideas and suggestions produced responses that were never used and often not even acknowledged.

Soon after the management transition, a member of the new management team began a meeting by saying that everyone's opinion would be welcomed, and each member of the staff was encouraged to raise any concern or question that he or she might have. At the end of the meeting, the new manager asked the assembled group for ideas on changes they believed were required. How likely is it that those gathered for the meeting enthusiastically and without hesitation began to outline those changes they have wished for years? Experience suggests that it is unlikely. There could be several reasons for this lack of response. Among them would be the lack of congruence with the request for advice from management and the understanding that the staff had learned over previous years of what upper level management does with advice offered by staff. Several, if not all, at the meeting would have said nothing because of the inability to take the request seriously, even though it came from someone in authority able to make the request. The objective fact: a request for advice did not fit with their perception of a manager. Not only is it unlikely that the staff would have offered suggestions that day, it is unlikely that they would do so for quite some time. They won't until they have learned that there can be a different kind of management than that which they have experienced. They need time to experience a new set of facts about the new managers and incorporate them into a new perception, a new frame, for what a manager is and does.

The way our minds are constructed and function requires time to process something we have been told, especially if this something requires new behavior. The time required often needs to be of sufficient duration to allow a change in the way we perceive reality, to change our frames. Those who want to influence others to accept the value of a fully professional library staff need to understand this. Also, they need to assume that those not intimately involved in the practice of librarianship will have to change the way they think about libraries and librarians before the logic of their arguments will be meaningful.

But, this is not all. As explained previously, logic alone cannot lead others to change behavior. Motivation, one's feelings, must be evoked. A second study reported in the same *Fast Company* article used a holistic strategy to assist seriously ill people. They were provided psychologist-led group support sessions, access to personal improvement programs, and they were helped to frame the need to change in a positive manner. In other words, they were treated like people, that is, individuals with the need to think through what they had been told to do and individuals with feelings that influence their actions, rather than machines with buttons to push for different operations. After a period of time, 70 percent of these people replaced harmful behavior with beneficial behavior (Deutschman 2005).

People are not just minds. Emotions are an equally important part of who we are. In fact, in everyday living, our emotions play an equal if not greater part in what we do. Upon consideration, the necessity to address the emotions of those who need to change is not surprising. When we purchase a new car or make a similar purchase, do we make our choice just on the item's qualities, or just as much on how we feel about it? "I just fell in love with the style and comfort!" How frequently does someone undertake a rigorous exercise to determine a new course of action and then make a choice as soon as the comparison of benefits and costs is completed? Isn't the change made only after the person begins to feel that to do so is a good idea? If we interact with others without recognizing the important part emotions play in their lives, our interactions will likely not meet our expectations.

Change in the behavior of people is a complex, lengthy process that needs to be understood and taken into account, whether wanting to change another's behavior or mind. Briefly put, people will change only when they thoroughly understand the value to themselves of new behavior and feel that they should change, that is, are emotionally inclined to change. With regard to understanding, the new behavior must make sense, not only logically, but also personally, to each person as an individual with a particular view of the world. With regard to emotions, people need to have sufficient sense of the positive relation between the change they are expected to make and their personal wants and desires before they will be adequately motivated to undertake the new behavior.

STRATEGIES FOR IMPROVING ADVOCATES' SUCCESS

Get to Know Those on Whom You Depend

Arguments in favor of professionally educated librarians will in most cases be made to those with whom advocates have infrequent and short involvement. Generally, a hearing with a board of trustees, an accrediting agency, or legislators will be brief and the opportunity for arguments often will be limited to a written report. Finding ways to influence these people's mental context (frames) within which libraries fit and at the same time convey the importance of professional librarians in a way that will be emotionally meaningful to them will be quite difficult. But it seems a necessity. While it may be difficult to follow the various steps to winning the hearts and minds of decision makers, the alternative is worse. Not doing so has historically resulted in failure.

Once one accepts the need to do more than prepare an argument in order to lead such a group to change its members' habitual thinking on an issue, some ideas come rather easily to mind. Looking at lobbyists and their activities gives the opportunity to learn from those who are successful in changing the minds of decision makers. Lobbyists are never satisfied with sending a legislator a report or meeting with him or her in an office for 10 minutes. What is known about lobbyists that can be copied? The fabled over and under the table gifts might not be attractive, but there are other lobbyist behaviors that are acceptable and available.

The time spent getting to know those who need to be influenced will be time well spent. Getting to know a little of who they are, how they look at their world, and what is of most importance to them will provide more of an opportunity to change their perceptions of libraries and librarians. They often have opportunities to visit with them in their offices. Don't do so only when bringing a request but also to say hello and to ask how they can be assisted in their work. Also, look for them at formal and informal functions. Show up for board meetings early; stay late. Invite key individuals to give a talk or introduce a speaker or present an award. An invitation to someone interested in public appearances will be appreciated. Even better, find a way to give an award to them, not only to increase their appreciation of your library but also to spend some quality time with them. Will all this take a lot of planning and time from other duties? Yes. But when weighing the activities you have to give up to make time for this effort against the increased likelihood that a crucial request will be supported, which is more important?

If personal time with them is not possible, we are librarians! How much can be learned about these people by just putting in some time researching? What can be learned about their interests, their preferences, and specifically about the importance of libraries and librarians in their lives? How best can their perception of libraries and librarians be influenced?

Finally, identify the opinion leaders in the group. Who in the group to which the presentation is to be made has swung this group's opinions in the past? What kinds of activities and behavior have influenced them in the past, and what kind are sure to lead to a negative reaction? Focus the efforts on these people.

In summary, one strategy for improving the likelihood that a proposal will be approved is finding ways to get to know and be known by those who will make the decision. Both experience and research on what influences people to change show that rational arguments are often insufficient by themselves to move others to make favorable decisions. The research described argues for the need to change their intellectual construct, as well as for the need to influence the decision-makers' emotions. Their full personalities need to be engaged. How they view and feel about the world needs to be understood. Being able to influence them in favor of a proposal won't happen without the capability of interacting with them fully as people.

Requiring a Fully Professional Staff Must Be Something Funders Feel Strongly About

A second strategy for improving chances for support of professionally trained librarians, and funding to staff libraries with such, is to fully convey the context of the request, that is, what libraries are and why libraries are important to those to whom the request is being made. Any belief that funders already understand and appreciate libraries is short-sighted. It can't be assumed that they understand adequately what libraries do now-a-days and, of more importance, why what they do is vitally important to those to whom a funding request is made and to their constituents. Ensuring that those on whom we depend have a developed and accurate awareness of what libraries do and why what they do is important for them can make the difference between support or nonsupport. This full awareness of the value of libraries is needed to increase the likelihood that a request is properly understood. It is needed as a means to connect with the feelings of those being asked for support. Actually, the time spent conveying the benefits of the library with regard to the community of which it is a part is as beneficial as the well-crafted argument for professionally trained librarians. It is not likely that the need for professionally trained librarians will touch the feelings of these people, but an argument based on the importance of libraries can succeed where the former fails.

It has to be recognized that the usefulness of statements such as the following time-worn contentions has long passed. Assertions such as, "Libraries are essential for a democracy," and certainly, "The library is the heart of the university (or the community)," have little value. In addition, it is unlikely that those who need to be influenced will be moved by more recently developed arguments based on the library's importance as a center for the community, or a location where everyone can *learn* to use and then *use* technology. None of these will touch decision makers as people.

As Richard Martin (2003) asserted at the 2002 ALA Library Leadership and Management Conference, people will be moved to support and use libraries when libraries clearly identify and offer those services and programs within their scope of expertise that are directly beneficial in significant ways to current and potential users. Using the ideas of Mark Moore and Jo Rodgers, he spoke about creating public value. For libraries to be successful when seeking funding, they first need to understand what they can do better than other institutions. They need to understand what their core competence, their core business, is. If they choose to offer services that other institutions can offer just as well, the likelihood of support is cut in half, at best. The core competence of libraries, the capability unique to libraries, is the creation and dissemination of knowledge (not information) for anyone in the community. In other words, libraries stimulate and facilitate learning by all learners at all times (Martin 2003).

Second, for librarians to be successful when seeking funding, they need to identify and offer services that make the lives of current and potential users better in truly significant ways.

> We need to . . . listen to the communities we seek to serve. We need to ask them not about what we do that they like and don't like. We need to pursue truly deep inquiries into what they want and need to make their lives better. And then we need to fashion programs and services that meet those needs and desires. (Martin 2003, 72)

"To make their lives better" is the phrase that needs to be fully understood. When seeking to convey the importance of libraries, the arguments must focus on how libraries, and especially local libraries, make a real and felt difference in the daily lives of users, that is, how they make their lives *better* (Martin 2003, 72). Organization theorist Peter Scholtes makes the same point. An organization's purpose and the activities toward this purpose must provide real and tangible benefits and capabilities to their clientele if they expect support for their work (Scholtes 1988).

When seeking support, library administrators must know what users deeply value about their library and incorporate these values in their arguments. If they can't identify such, they need to find out what new services can be introduced that will touch the lives of their users before they ask for additional support. People may support institutions with long-term presence in their lives even if these institutions only provide marginal current benefit in making their lives better. However, if the desire is to receive more support or to avert a cut in support, the service or activity in question needs to be seen as worth it. It must be perceived as making user lives better in a clear, emotionally felt way.

When preparing a request for funding for a fully professional staff, find out what there is in the library's array of services that are of personal value to those upon whom the decision depends or to their constituents. Then see that your argument includes a description of the effect of this funding request on the related important service. For instance, the story hour in public libraries is an example of a highly valued service in many communities. The introduction of children to reading and help toward a love of reading is highly valued by many parents. The opportunity to spend time hearing a story and then to learn and practice personal access through reading is priceless. This service can be especially valuable to parents today when the requirement of two wage earners reduces time parents can spend with their children in these activities. In this age of expanding access to information through digital means, many parents are even more concerned about instilling a love of reading in their children. In a community that values the library story hour, an argument that focuses on the importance of professionally trained, graduate-degreed librarians who have studied the range of children's literature as well as means for engaging children in listening and reading is likely to impress both the minds and feelings of funders. For these people, the library story hour truly makes their lives better to the extent that they don't want to be without it. The possibility of being without it, or even of having its quality affected negatively, will touch their feelings! Here, as elsewhere, value of consistently marketing the importance of professional librarians, this time to even the smallest "customers" and their parents, needs to be kept in mind.

Here is another example of a library service making a vital difference in the lives of users. At a medium-size college library the annual book budget was sufficient only to provide books for the students' studies, with little money to purchase books and journals to support faculty research, even though the faculty were required to publish at levels similar to those for faculty at large research libraries. Recognizing this, the library staff put special emphasis on interlibrary loan to the extent that every request was given personal attention and every faculty researcher known personally. The interlibrary loan staff kept in close communication with the faculty, reporting delays and immediately responding to requests to find other sources as needed. No request was denied. The interlibrary loan librarian would do anything as evidenced by phone calls to the British Museum in a successful attempt to obtain material not usually loaned across the Atlantic. Faculty was quoted as saying that the service at this library was better than that received at much larger universities. It is not hard to imagine the response of the faculty if there was a threat to the competence of the interlibrary loan staff, for instance, staffing with clerks rather than professionals.

One more example demonstrates the development of a new service discovered through close monitoring of the user community for needs the library could meet. In the 2003 article in *Library Administration and Management*, Martin described a library in a large metropolitan area that discovered that most people eligible for the Earned Income Tax Credit (EITC) were failing to apply. Either they did not know about it or did not know how to apply. The librarians set up training sessions in the branches serving the city populations most likely eligible for the EITC. It was estimated that as a result of this library education program $86 million was returned to applicants and, of great significance to and appreciation from city leaders, to the city's economy. Again, it is not hard to imagine the responses of both local residents and city fathers to a suggestion that the city library needs only clerical staff (Martin 2003).

These examples demonstrate the meaning of making a significant difference in the lives of current and potential library users. Research on how people respond to being asked to change habitual ways of thinking and acting concludes that they will do so only if they feel the change will be good for them. Those developing a request for funding for professionally trained librarians, or for the maintenance of funding for a professional staff, have to do more than prepare a rational argument. They need to identify and incorporate related library services of felt importance to the decision makers. This will meet a requirement for inducing approval of the request; it will touch them as more than minds, that is, as people.

NOT JUST A TASK BUT AN ONGOING BEHAVIOR

This analysis of what is needed to change the habitual thinking and behavior of others argues that much more is needed than effort over a few days or even weeks. Both the way people think and what moves them to act are embedded qualities. An effort to change the way they think, and motivate them to new behavior, needs both time and a developed understanding of the decision makers as thinking and feeling people. In fact, the descriptions and examples in this chapter suggest that preparations for submitting an argument for avoiding significant decreases to funding or for a substantial increase with respect to funding for professionally trained librarians are ongoing activities. People do not change the way they perceive things in a few days. One doesn't find ways to get to know board members a week before the submission of an important proposal. While it is possible for library administrators to quickly identify services that are, from their point of view, of special importance to funders and their constituents, there needs to be a means for verifying the continuing truth to these perceptions. The likelihood of success in funding requests requires a continuing effort to know funders, to know on an ongoing basis whether the library continues to be truly important to them, and, if not, to do what is needed to make it so.

Most successful administrators do this. One of the elements in the list describing the duties of a successful administrator is that of interacting with those outside the library on whom the library depends. Successful library administrators find ways of getting to know those on whom they are dependent and those whom they serve and learning what the library can do that is important to these people. A developed understanding of why and how people change as presented here will remind them that knowledge gained about funders and users needs to be incorporated in the preparation and presentation of funding requests. For newly appointed administrators and those who do not spend a good deal of time addressing the community environment outside the library, this chapter provides ample reason to do so.

LOOKING BEYOND THE OBVIOUS

Finally, a discussion of change and the difficulty people have in changing long-held understandings and attitudes ought to include a consideration of the study of obstacles to change on a societal level. Why do humans struggle so long and so unsuccessfully to change customary ways of behaving even when there is broad agreement that how they are acting must change or there will be dire consequences? The concern for the environment comes immediately to mind. Policymakers and people in general have expressed great concern for the future of our world and the quality of life for future inhabitants, but it seems impossible to make the changes this concern demands.

In an attempt to answer this question, several organizational development scholars interviewed in-depth renowned inventors and successful entrepreneurs asking them about their learning methods and thought processes. The result of this effort was the book *Presence* (Senge et al. 2005). The authors begin by noting that learning is at the core of change, of development. Learning happens through thinking and doing. In other words, to change, especially in the sense of to develop, or to grow, we need to learn why it will be good for us to change and then determine what needs to be done to move forward. Because learning results from interaction with our world, of seeing and responding to our reality, how we see the world then influences our learning; a limited understanding of reality will limit what we learn and how we respond, and a broader understanding will lead to a more realistic and therefore effective learning and response.

The interviews the authors conducted revealed a difference between the learning most of us develop and learning of those people who were able to introduce extraordinarily successful techniques and products. This difference is a depth of awareness of reality so much deeper as to be different in kind and quality. The world of those interviewed is so much broader and deeper than the world most of us habitually access that we miss a good amount of what influences our actions and offers opportunities. People like Bill Gates see opportunities to which almost everyone else was oblivious.

Presence, which led the participants to delve more deeply into their work world, provides an example of both what is meant by a deeper awareness and what is there at this deeper level. A group of doctors practicing in hospitals in a health care district in Germany wanted to innovate and improve emergency care in the hospitals in this district. They were under enormous pressure to manage costs and quality. They contracted with outside consultants to assist them identify helpful changes to existing processes and procedures.

The investigation began with interviews of doctors and patients; the interviews focused on doctor/patient relationships. Four relationships were identified. Two of the relationships were expected. The first of these was transactional; the patient had a broken part, and the doctor is expected to fix it today. The next level of relationship has to do with a prescription to avoid a reoccurrence, medicine, or a change of habit. The other two doctor/patient relationships found are less frequent but were chosen as more desired by both the doctors and patients. The first of these less frequent relationships can be expressed by the statement, "Help me understand why I act in the way that led to this problem." Finally, an even deeper relationship was identified, "Help me learn what it is about my perception of the world and myself, who I am, that leads me to live in a way that is harmful. In other words, what is really at the base of what ultimately causes my health problem?"

As the participant group discussed these results, a member who was a local mayor noted that the description of the health care system was similar to the government of his town. He said that all that was happening was fixing broken parts at levels one and two. Never was there an attempt to move to levels three and four where cures, not bandages, could be found. For example, a water leak might be plugged (level one), and a replacement pipe ordered (level 2), but no attention was given to the pressure in the water distribution system (level 3) or the entire distribution system in relation to geologic and demographic changes since its installation (level 4). Then a teacher in the group reacted, saying that in education teachers' awareness seemed to get no further than level two, and so they were unable to help their students move their learning to include the broader world and their relation to it.

Next, a farmer said that the same could be said of farming where focus stopped on identifying problems and fixing them. He characterized the conventional approach to farming as industrial with concentration on inputs and outputs. He contended that an appreciation of the earth and the need to work with it was lacking. In summary, involvement in this project about health care helped the participants realize how much more there is of their world than they habitually have in mind. The assumptions learned as one grows, the habitual way of thinking developed over one's life, the business of daily life, the prejudices and biases everyone has, and, for many, the need to move, to act quickly, all serve as blinders limiting what is seen of the world in which they live.

If people learn by experiencing their world and reacting to it, to the extent that their habitual view of reality is limited, the learning that occurs as they experience the world they see will also be limited. If their perception misses part of the totality of the world they live in, their learning, especially in terms of the need for development, for change, will be limited to reactions to the incomplete world they see rather than the full world they live in.

The authors of *Presence* posit a broadened model for learning in which people need to go beyond reliance on past personal experience and develop an awareness of the world outside daily experience; the world as it is, not the world as they see it. Once this awareness is attained, then it is to this fuller understanding of reality that they can react and learn what needs to change and how to change. Specifically, the authors suggest that when faced with a problem, those involved enhance the well practiced actions of (1) analysis of the problem, (2) consideration of the problem as now defined in the light of our experience, and (3) choice of a response that past success suggests. This enhancement is taking the time to develop a broader awareness of their life context than that of which they are immediately aware. They need to take time to think beyond their workplace, their community, and the people and institutions with which they regularly interact. They need to develop an awareness of culture as it restrains them, of ingrained socially approved ways of acting that only seem unchangeable and of the loci of the power to make real and permanent change (Senge et al. 2005).

For those wishing to influence decision makers to accept the necessity of professionally trained librarians, the ideas of the authors of *Presence* can lead to previously unseen obstacles and opportunities. This awareness of a world much larger than that of most people's daily perception and even larger than the broadened view developed during planning sessions can provide previously unseen opportunities for influencing these people. Undoubtedly, the practice of thinking in this manner will need to be developed over time; it won't happen during the week before a funding request is due but probably will take months if not longer. Still, for those wishing to influence the people with the purse strings, the awareness of a broader reality than that ordinarily accessed can lead to new strategies to influence these people in ways beneficial to the library and the administrator's efforts to hire and retain effective librarians.

CONCLUSION

The research described in this chapter, corroborated by the personal experience of many library administrators, provides a firm basis for accepting that rational arguments alone are not sufficient to move those who fund libraries to be amenable to ongoing funding for professionally trained librarians. Among the obstacles not addressed by reasoning is the resistance to change inherent in most people. Library administrators need to understand that this general tendency to resist change in both one's thinking and one's behavior is as much of an obstacle to a successful proposal as the criticisms and objections brought up by those to whom the proposal is submitted. The need to address this inherent resistance to change is as important as the need to present relevant facts and well-stated explanations and arguments. The need to spend as much time addressing this obstacle is as important as putting together the rational argument.

Some Suggestions

Besides the need to be aware as planning proceeds that people's inherent difficulty to change can be an obstacle to their acceptance of a well-presented, rational proposal, there are some additional actions that can address this obstacle. As noted previously, most successful administrators develop personal relationships with outside individuals who are important to the library, and also, these administrators know which of the libraries' services are of special value to users. Keeping this knowledge in mind and having it ready to bring to bear when seeking approval of a proposal may not be as common.

Don't assume that every criticism or rationale for rejecting a proposal is based on reason and so needs a reasoned answer. A criticism that seems unreasonable or perhaps unexpectedly antagonistic may be motivated by feelings related to the difficulty of change rather than opposition to the content of the proposal. It may be that a response to the stated opposition different from restating the objective benefits of the proposal will be more effective. For instance, asking for a more detailed explanation of a criticism of the proposal may reveal a misunderstanding, or a response of an assuring nature might be better to a person known to be having difficulty giving up the traditional perception of the library as a place for books and quiet.

Don't limit interactions with boards and legislators to formal instances. Find ways to get them to the library frequently enough that they can experience the library and in doing so change their perception of what a library is (their "frame").

When seeking funding for something new, find a way to relate it to an existing service that is successful and important to those receiving the proposal. An argument stating that the new service will provide specific benefits similar to the benefits of the existing service will be better than an abstract rationale.

One benefit from broadening one's awareness of reality, as suggested by the authors of *Presence*, is a recognition of the inherent interdependency of everyone and everything in our world. This realization counters the perception so prevalent in the United States that we are independent people who don't need help to achieve our goals. In reality, we need help all the time, so looking for partners is always helpful. When putting together a proposal, take some time to look for organizations or people with whom you can partner. For instance, as many have learned, the staff collective bargaining union can be much more than an advocate for higher salaries. In closing, remember that proposals are presented to people, not computers. People have set ways of looking at things (frames) that may be different from those presenting a funding proposal. Also, people are moved by feelings more than they are by reason. Recognition of this will increase the probability of success when seeking funding for professional educated employees.

REFERENCES

Deutschman, Alan. 2005. "Making Change." *Fast Company* 94: 52–56, 59–60, 62. Accessed Dec. 31, 2010. http://www.fastcompany.com/magazine/94.

Lewin, Kurt. 1947. "Frontiers in Group Dynamics: Concepts, Methods, and Reality in Social Sciences; Social Equilibria and Social Change." *Human Relations* 1(1): 5–41.

Martin, Richard. 2003. "Keynote Address: What Is Our Leading Edge?" *Library Administration and Management* 17(2): 71–73.

Schein, Edgar. 1968. "Personal Change through Interpersonal Relationships." In *Interpersonal Dynamics: Essays and Readings on Human Interaction,* rev. ed., ed. Warren G. Bennis, Edgar H. Schein, Fred I. Steele, and David E. Berlew, 333–69. Homewood, IL: Dorsey.

Scholtes, Peter R. R. 1988. *The Leader's Handbook.* New York: McGraw-Hill.

Senge, Peter C., C. Otto Scharmer, Joseph Jaworski, and Betty Sue Flowers. 2005. *Presence: Exploring Profound Change in People, Organizations, and Society.* New York: Doubleday.

14

⊷•⊶

ADVANCING PROFESSIONALISM IN LIBRARY, INFORMATION, KNOWLEDGE, AND ARCHIVAL SERVICES IN THE "NEW NORMAL WORLD"

Bill Crowley
Dominican University

DEVELOPING AND SUSTAINING A CULTURE OF PROFESSIONAL SUPPORT

Timeless Advice from John Mackenzie Cory

When this author was quite young, he was privileged to work in several capacities with John Mackenzie Cory, Director of the New York Public Library (NYPL). For a semester, I was a student in John Cory's Library Administration class at Columbia University's School of Library Service. During the period of my Columbia graduate education, I also worked in NYPL's public relations office where I would occasionally sit in at a meeting of administrators and reporters as a glorified "gofer." My role at such times was to take notes, look attentive, and be ready to obtain any additional material needed while Cory or another library administrator discussed library matters with a reporter. In one such session, during a period of funding cutbacks, the reporter tried repeatedly and unsuccessfully to lure Director Cory into directly attacking New York City's government for its inadequate support of the library. After the session, once he had walked his visitor to the door, Cory gestured for me to wait. When the reporter was safely out of range, he told me he had another bit of management advice to convey.

"In your career you will be associating with a great variety of people, some of whom will be supportive of what you are trying to do for a library. Others, like this reporter, will be pursuing their own interests," he stressed in his barrel-deep voice. "What you need to remember is that you have to work with people as they really are. If you expect more than they are willing to give, you are going to be seriously disappointed."

This final chapter is written in the spirit of Director John Mackenzie Cory's advice. It is hoped that the reader will find it so.

Facts Are OK, but it Really Is All About Values and Perceptions

In chapter 12, "The Political Case for Supporting the Value of Professionalism," the author drew on the classic study produced by the Congressional Research

Service of the Library of Congress for the Committee on Science and Technology of the U.S. House of Representatives and issued as *Research Policies for the Social and Behavioral Sciences*. This report addresses why research findings on public issues are seldom used in policy decision making, presumably including policies made on the employment of professional librarians, information specialists, knowledge managers, and archivists, because

> Policymaking is a process that uses many inputs—values, advocacy or interest group pressures, and scientific information—to name but a few. Often the validity of behavioral and social information is measured against standards embodied in the consensus of prevailing social and political values. Verified, or even non-verified behavioral and social information will be used in policymaking if it coincides with these values . . . Other factors which impede utilization are: behavioral and social science information may be counterintuitive, irrelevant, politically naïve in that it challenges existing bureaucratic authority, too late, overly quantitative and jargon-laden, and inaccurate or unverified. (U.S. Library of Congress 1986, 221)

I do not believe that it was mere coincidence that the Congressional Research Service listed "scientific information" after "values, advocacy or interest group pressures" in the *Research Policies'* list of inputs for policymaking. If "*verified, or even non-verified behavioral and social information will be used in policymaking if it coincides with these values*" (emphasis added), then any reader who actually believes that "facts" constitute the primary basis for decision making in any community, corporation, school, university, or organization is a prime candidate for purchasing the famous bridge that stretches between my native Borough of Brooklyn and the Borough of Manhattan, an historic structure that I would be willing to part with for a reasonable fee. In reality, facts are so often "after the fact" justifications for decisions made primarily on values, emotions, and perceptions.

In the real world, values, emotions, and perceptions trump everything. As editor, I am fully aware that no research or series of recommendations for supporting or advancing professionalism contained in this book will become near to being accepted by readers unless the research and recommendations

1. Match the existing values of readers or
2. Reach readers who are already questioning their dissimilar values, often because they perceive that such values are not supported by significant others, including funders, or have otherwise proven ineffective in sustaining a priority area such as preserving professionalism.

If they have been progressing through *Defending Professionalism* to this final chapter, some readers may have found themselves rejecting what certain chapter authors view as valid findings and recommendations, even if they seem to be based on something close to irrefutable research or arguments. In reflecting on such disagreements, readers might benefit by searching their personal and professional value systems to determine which strongly held beliefs the authors are challenging. Loyalty to values is not evil; it is simply human. Indeed, Richard Rubin and Rachel Rubin most effectively stressed the role of values in determining professionalism in chapter 2, "Justifying Professional Education in a Self-Service World." Brenda Roberts skillfully demonstrated a similar approach in chapter 4, "We Build Communities through Knowledge: Demonstrating the Value of the Professional Public Librarian." This author also sought to highlight the functions of values in chapter 10, "A Culturally Pragmatic and Feminist-Influenced Approach to Defending Professionalism."

The identification of prized values is the necessary first step for readers to consider their continued significance. The second step is for readers to perceive whether accepting the arguments presented in this work, and the values they represent, are in their long-term interest. As editor, I urge the reflective reader to avoid the common reaction to proposed innovations described by the often-quoted Garrett Hardin, who observed that a "double-standard" exists in evaluating proposals for change. New proposals can be rejected over a single flaw, while the status quo will continue to be accepted despite numerous problems "while we wait for a perfect proposal" (Hardin 1968, 1247).

No perfect proposals for defending library, information, knowledge, and archival professionalism are in existence. There are promising approaches and recommendations for a better future than the current reality where professionalism can and is so easily disregarded.

A Note on the Contemporary Context

This closing chapter is being written in the midst of an extended period of cutbacks in response to the still-powerful effects of the world financial crisis. In the current need to counter the still active wave of reductions in the numbers of library, information, knowledge management, and archival professionals, one must tread carefully to avoid blaming the victims. Nevertheless, from one point of view, the sometimes disproportionate layoffs of library, information, knowledge, and archival professionals (American Library Association 2011) represent a collective failure in effective networking.

As Herbert White, Distinguished Professor and Dean Emeritus at Indiana University, pointed out to a December 1996 audience of federal librarians at the "Getting the Word Out: Marketing Your Library's Information Services" symposium, "People do not fire friends" (quoted in Federal Library and Information Center Committee 1997). Unfortunately, library, information, knowledge, and archival professionals who presently lack "decision-maker friends" cannot return to the past and change their existing relationships with those who control their funding. In the short term the situation may be even more complicated. Depending on context, efforts to establish stronger relationships with decision makers, and thereby earn the "friend" designation, may encounter the reality that these same funding sources are even now planning to impose deeper cuts.

To adapt and extend the observations of Canadian advocacy supporters in *Library Advocacy Now! A Training Program for Public Library Staff and Trustees*, constructing and maintaining solid relationships with funders may be emotionally challenging. It is so "because so many librarians [information specialists, knowledge managers, and archivists] consider themselves to be victims of irrational, unfair budget cutting, their attitudes towards those who had to make those decisions is often not one of respect but anger. They feel betrayed" (Canadian Association of Public Libraries 2011, 9).

The understandable reality of justified (or unjustified) outrage aside, the fundamental purpose of *Defending Professionalism* is not to stoke resentment over past wrongs. Rather, it is to promote more effective approaches in the present to help to build the professional future. In this context, borrowing additional advice from Canada's *Library Advocacy Now!*, it is vital to "learn genuine respect for the role of decision-makers, the challenges facing them on a daily basis, their own needs, priorities and ambitions for society. When we appeal to them on that level, they are much more likely to listen and act" (Canadian Association of Public Libraries 2011, 10).

NATIONAL DIFFERENCES

National political customs are not totally transferable, and it's probably for the better. To some in the United States, following the Canadian advice to develop respect for those who may have inordinately impacted one's program and directly or indirectly eliminated the jobs of one's colleagues and friends (American Library Association 2011) is almost "un-American." North, south, east, and west, significant components of American culture are just more comfortable with what President John F. Kennedy termed the "wonderful law of the Boston Irish political jungle," a precept that has resonated over the years as "Don't get mad; get even" ("Don't Get Mad; Get Even" 2011).

Canadian advice, although immensely valuable, has to be taken by Americans with the understanding that America is "the country of the revolution [and] Canada of the counterrevolution" (Lipset 1991, 1). In consequence, there are times when Canadians appear to have a greater respect for government officials and other authority figures than do Americans (Lipset 1991, 3). Presumably, they are also less inclined to apply to such authority figures the political tools of persuasion found necessary to reverse—or prevent—negative political decisions.

In America, our political game is hardball, broadly understood, not slow-pitch softball. This is the spirit underlying Janice Del Negro's revolutionary chapter 3, "Youth Services in Public Libraries: A Return to Belligerence" and Don Hamerly's inspirational chapter 5, "Strategies and Aspirations for Defending School Library Professionalism."

Within the U.S. electoral context, politicians learn early how to count votes, or they have short runs in office. With such rules in play, these same politicians can develop a genuine respect, if a bit grudging, for those who show they can lead a successful struggle to regain what was lost, if they "disagree without being disagreeable." It helps quite a bit, for example, if public or school library advocates who are successful in persuading decision makers to restore funding, jobs, and services know enough to swallow hard and invite the very same people who cut their support in the first place to make celebratory speeches at the library when money and services are ultimately restored, personnel are rehired, or branches reopened. It is how the game is played. After suffering a few such calculations of the value placed on professional librarians in schools and communities, the funders involved, if only out of self-defense, might begin to see definite advantages in enrolling successful advocates for such library and information programs as a part of their own professional networks.

Alternatively, those who simply take the cuts, the management doormats who have not marketed their services, who lack advocacy ability or even interest, and who have not demonstrated their value to decision makers, simply get cut again. Because the top manager's job is usually safe, it is others, front line professionals, support staff, and customers/users/patrons, who suffer while the manager goes off to yet another meeting to plan further service reductions.

THE VIEW FROM THE GALLERY
OF THE INDIANA HOUSE OF REPRESENTATIVES

This author was once sufficiently fortunate to play a role in an Indiana library struggle against a powerful Speaker of the House over control of local library budgets. This was a dispute that climaxed with the defeat of the Speaker's bill to control library funding in his own house during one remarkable legislative evening. Because the library community, while lobbying hard in the best Indiana tradition, had resolved "to argue philosophies and not to personalize the issue," the struggle became a populist fight over the value of public libraries, which, after concluding with a memorable library victory, did not result in the Speaker launching an anti-library reign of terror (Crowley 1994, 96–98). Knowing that Hoosiers really did like their public libraries, the Speaker's "punishment" simply consisted of transferring money from one pot of library assistance to another, in effect, providing to all a relatively gentle reminder of who actually controlled Indiana's state aid budgets (Crowley 1994, 96–98). We library supporters had won, but we had played by the accepted political rules, although admittedly the rules in play resembled more the "Chicago way" than the "Ottawa option."

Because it is likely that this work may be read by English speakers in a number of contexts, it is important to again stress that local rules trump general advice from *Defending Professionalism* in the struggles for funding and defenses of professionalism in American, British, Canadian, and other national communities, schools, universities, corporations, and additional organizations. Briefly put, it is usually best to observe what achieves success for others in one's own context and do much the same, if legally and ethically possible.

While values reign in decisions, facts are not to be disregarded. Once shared values are established with funders, and the value of professional performance is demonstrated for their benefit; facts can suddenly be interpreted to the benefit of library, information, knowledge, and archival professionals. This approach was particularly well demonstrated through the fine analyses of Lenora Berendt and Maria Otero-Boisvert in chapter 6, "Future Proofing the Academic Librarian" and Cleo Pappas in chapter 7, "Understanding the Worth of the Professional Librarian in the Research University or Institution." Not surprisingly, information theorist Michael Koenig once again effectively demonstrated his quantitative/qualitative approach to justifying professionalism in chapter 8, "Valuing the Return on Investment of the Information Professional in Specialized Institutions (Corporations, Government Agencies, NGOs, etc.)."

When library, information, knowledge, or archival professionals are valued members of the professional networks of decision makers and funders, when they help make their bosses' lives easier, their explanations of how their professional education and experience made them so effective tend to be accepted as a straightforward reality. Success in assisting decision makers simply creates or reinforces their perceptions of the clear worth of the professionals involved. It is worth repeating: decision makers who benefit significantly from professionals' expertise in helping to solve their problems will often accept their explanations for how it was developed as a matter of course.

Issue 1: Advocacy, Marketing, and Short-Term Survival

It is likely, at least in the government and not-for-profit sectors, that the "New Normal" environment for library and information professionals and other personnel created by The Great Recession will continue in the United States into the near future, regardless of the nation's credit rating. In a joint analysis, the Pew Center on the States and the Public Policy Institute of California pointed out that most U.S. federal stimulus funds provided to the states were scheduled to "run out by July 2011" and discerned that even a revived national economy would not soon bring back healthy state budgets. Consequently, the organizations predicted additional "cuts, new taxes, or other remedies" (Pew Center on the States and the Public Policy Institute of California 2010, 5) at the state level, a looming reality that has implications for funding for libraries, schools, and universities for at least several more years.

Recalling the chapter 12 analogy regarding dealing with threatening alligators (short-term thinking) versus draining the swamp (long-term thinking), beleaguered readers may need to proceed along two fronts. If facing pressing cutbacks, readers should immediately secure and use a copy of the excellent *Library Advocacy Now! A Training Program for Public Library Staff and Trustees* developed by the Canadian Association of Public Libraries (2011). While more deferential than American tradition prefers, it is a practical resource that otherwise demands honest responses, not evasions, from its readers.

Others may be more comfortable employing the intense advocacy approaches compiled by the American Library Association's (ALA) Office for Library Advocacy and its online Advocacy University and "Resources" links (American Library Association, Office for Library Advocacy 2012). Valuable state level advocacy tools, such as those provided by the New York Library Association (New York Library Association 2011) or the Texas Library Association's Save Our Texas Libraries! web page (Texas Library Association 2011), can also be of assistance. On the cross-Atlantic level, the Campaigning Resources web page of Britain's Chartered Institute of Library and Information Professionals (2011) or CILIP (Chartered Institute) can be similarly useful in fighting pressing battles over funding and staffing issues.

As discussed in chapter 10, professionalism often lacks strong support in state, provincial, or national law and has no guarantees in the corporate world. It is thus pragmatically established and maintained at the level of the individual institution or community. A clear demonstration of how archivists have developed and marketed their own expertise in such circumstances can be found in Cecilia Salvatore's chapter 9, "Defending the Professional Archivist." Such local connections can inspire creativity and may even be more effective because state regulations and data-supported state studies, as discussed in chapter 12, can be and are ignored by school administrators looking for places to cut (Santos 2011).

Issue 2: Building the Long-Term Structure of Sustaining Professionalism

Another Indiana Political Story

After conducting the Indiana lobbying workshops described in chapter 12, the author was elected chair of the statewide committee that coordinated campaigns to convey the value of the services of librarians and libraries to legislators and other elected officials in both Indianapolis and Washington. This position involved facilitating the planning for library political platforms and sustaining the lobbying network necessary to encourage beneficial legislation and discourage that which was detrimental to library interests. As might be expected, even with a first-rate lobbyist handling the day-to-day work, serving as legislative committee chair occasionally required a rather intense interaction with elected officials.

One such interaction took place while eating lunch with a state legislator in the massive cafeteria that formed part of the capitol complex in Indianapolis. For a significant part of the meal the author amused his audience of one with a detailed statistical justification for increasing Indiana's financial aid to libraries. After glancing at the document, the legislator finally laughed aloud and explained that he did not need such data to be convinced. He would, however, save the information to share with his colleagues if he was asked at some point to explain his long record of pro-library votes.

"I support libraries because I like libraries," he said. "I've always liked libraries."

After this admission the legislator, entirely unprompted, went on to explain in depth how he had become a lifelong reader and library user, benefiting from the efforts of first-rate librarians who first introduced him to the magic of pre-school library storytelling and later supported his reading interests in a wide variety of ways. Many years later, this self-description of how a legislator became a library supporter, presented so enthusiastically that it almost caused him to be late for a crucial vote on another matter, seems to be another clear example of chapter 10's "Return On Emotional Investment" (ROEI), defined as "*a continuing emotional connection between users and the libraries and professional librarians who provide the library services and programs that people deem to be vital to their lives*" (Crowley 2010, emphasis added).

Lifecycle Librarianship and ROEI

Throughout this legislator's formative years, librarians had been present to foster his interest in reading and lifelong learning. In essence, they helped developed his ROEI for public libraries. As a result of the extended efforts of professional librarians and other staff, a young Hoosier boy grew up to become an influential legislator while remaining a dedicated library enthusiast. It was yet another example of how " 'passionate librarians' involved in their communities can make a difference" (De Rosa and Johnson 2008, 1-6) through the development of "super supporters" (De Rosa and Johnson 2008, 2-88) who become the dedicated activists working to make good things happen for libraries, librarians, and the people they serve. Because the operation of ROEI was extensively reviewed in several contexts in chapter 10, readers are directed to that chapter for further analysis of its operation.

THE FACTS ABOUT VALUES, EMOTIONS, AND PERCEPTIONS

In 2008 OCLC and Leo Burnett issued a report titled *From Awareness to Funding: A Study of Library Support in America*. This analysis of the attributes characterizing library supporters and nonsupporters, encapsulated in its chapter 4 title, "Library Funding Support Is an Attitude, Not a Demographic," found that

> Library funding behavior is drive by attitudes and beliefs, not by demographics. Voters' perceptions of the role the library plays in their lives and in their

communities are more important determinants of their willingness to increase funding than their age, gender, race, political affiliation, life state or
income level. (De Rosa and Johnson 2008, 4–1)

In a way this report codified the common knowledge of library advocates that
the willingness to strongly commit to libraries represents an emotional, not a rational connection. Data can help, of course, but tends to play a secondary role,
serving as a justification to others for actions based on an emotional connection.

While information, knowledge, and archival contexts are more highly rooted in
information provision and analysis, both the OCLC/Leo Burnett findings and the
experience of long-serving librarians reinforce an essential truth. While corporate
information and knowledge centers are "information intensive," any discussion
of the future of professionalism in academic, public, and school libraries must be
based on the reality that the field is grounded in the value of continuing efforts to
assist users in their reading, lifelong learning, and information-seeking activities.
The most effective techniques in such educational, informational, and recreational
efforts have always involved emotional contacts on levels ranging from children's
storytelling to online safety instruction and reader's advisory and reference in-
person or online interviews.

As stressed by Kyle Jones and Michael Stephens' in chapter 11, "The LIS Professional Commons and the Online Networked Practitioner," social networks and
other e-communication will increasingly play powerful and complementary roles
with face-to-face communication in providing avenues to positively and emotionally
impact our various clienteles. Overall, the constructive results of both face-to-face
and electronic communications must be seen as representing library, information,
knowledge, and archival *emotional labor*, defined as "work performed by those
whose jobs involve a high degree of personal contact and who are expected to produce an emotional state, such as pleasure, gratitude, or self-esteem in the people
with whom they deal" (Shockley-Zalabak 2006, 311).

When professional assistance is seen as a continuum spanning the human lifecycle, librarians, information specialists, knowledge managers, and archivists can
more easily perceive the times and circumstances for applying their professionalism.
Whether involving assistance to children, teens, adults, parents, educators, corporate professionals, or senior citizens, all such arenas for service inevitably involve
sustaining values and developing emotional connections that are crucial for supporting professionalism.

As was described in chapter 10, "A Culturally Pragmatic and Feminist-Influenced
Approach to Defending Professionalism," support for professionalism is ultimately
dependent on how effectively a professional's education and experience help solve
the pressing problems or concerns of funders, voters, clients, customers, patrons,
or users. The determination of success in such efforts is ultimately subjective. At
bottom, it reflects either a positive or negative ROEI by those who expect to see
themselves benefiting from the professional's efforts.

ADVOCACY, MARKETING, COMMUNICATION, AND REINVENTION

Whether managers, professionals, and other staff actually know the full details,
each library or information organization does have a marketing plan for service

delivery, if only by virtue of providing services in some manner to some customer base. When the marketing plan is so unorganized, it is most likely a poor plan that can be written down as a compilation of the accumulated details of day-to-day services. An unwritten marketing plan deals with the immediate. It is unlikely to mention, let alone emphasize, the long-term necessity to shore-up library and information professionalism. Given the financial problems of the next several years facing many government units, including libraries and schools, it will be difficult but essential to focus on the value of professionalism even where intense advocacy is needed just to keep the doors open.

Bob Moran's chapter 13, "An Obstacle: The Difficulty of Convincing Others to Change Their Thinking and Behavior," effectively addresses the issue of resistance to change. As he thoughtfully demonstrates, the reality that restructuring the marketing of library, information, knowledge, and archival programs to focus on the value of educated professionalism in meeting priority funder and user needs can be extraordinarily difficult, particularly when organizational survival is already in jeopardy. To be effective and appreciated, professionalism has to be interwoven with responsiveness in the delivery of quality services: one has to be seen as part of the other. As the reader will have already noted, many of the chapters of this work provide accounts of how professionals of all types are in the midst of campaigns to save their jobs or, worse, may be suffering through the effects of job loss.

In mounting the short-term effort to keep the doors open and the longer-term campaign needed to emphasize the value of the educated professional, it is well to remember and stress that others, including professional city managers, have seen the emotional connections that citizens can develop with institutions that meet their needs. In regard to public libraries, as pointed out a dozen years ago by Roger L. Kemp, experienced public administrator, scholar of government policies and operations, and objective critic of library operations, "one of the few municipal services that helps citizens personally satisfy their service demands in a positive way is through the programs provided by local public libraries. For this reason, many citizens increasingly support the services provided by their community library" (Kemp 1997, 225).

GENERAL AND SPECIFIC
RECOMMENDATIONS FOR CHANGE

In the first chapter, the developments that undermined or ill-supported library, information, knowledge, and archival professionalism were considered through a review of the relevant categories. For comparable ease in discussion the suggestions for change, which consist largely as elaborations on the explicit and tacit recommendations offered by the chapter authors, will be similarly addressed by category. As the reader will recall, these categories include

  I. Professional associations, which often helped bring about the initial availability of appropriate professional education;
 II. Universities providing such professional education;
III. Professionals and students seeking to become professionals;
 IV. Employers who hire, in part, on the basis of an appropriate education, defined in law, regulation, or policy, often adding the further requirement of relevant experience; and

V. Funders, customers, patrons, users and other decision makers within geographical or organizational (academic, corporate, government, school) communities who accord professional recognition and/or support only to those they see as acting "professionally" to advance their interests.

I. PROFESSIONAL ASSOCIATIONS

What ALA Can Do

It is to be recalled, while other library, information, and knowledge associations provide first-rate continuing education for their membership, it is only the ALA that operates something close to full-spectrum program accreditation at the master's degree level (American Library Association 2008). Because the association's bureaucracy is unlikely to promote changing the definition of "library and information studies" to include more library-friendly components, positive action by the ALA in the future is likely to be limited to (a) supporting the system of accreditation, (b) advocating for the ALA-accredited master's degree as the appropriate terminal degree for academic librarians, and (c) participation in the National Council for Accreditation of Teacher Education (NCATE) accreditation of programs to educate school librarians.

One can always hope, but it would represent an optimistic disregard of John Cory's sage advice regarding accepting the limits of people and institutions to base any effort to defend professionalism on the remote possibility that ALA will endorse an employment standard for professional librarians, information specialists, knowledge managers, or archivists that requires a master's degree from its own accredited programs.

These realities aside, in the proverbial ideal world, ALA would

1. Mandate, without exception, that all students in ALA-accredited master's degree programs take courses in

   a. Marketing and leadership;
   b. Advocacy; and
   c. Customer service and people skills.

2. Strongly encourage all students intending to work in academic, public, or school libraries to take additional courses, with appropriate modifications by specialty areas, in

   d. outreach;
   e. working with children, teens, and adults;
   f. reading; and
   g. lifelong learning.

3. Reword the definition of "library and information studies" to include direct references to lifelong learning, reading, community building, etc. (Crowley 2008b).

4. Publicize a definition of librarian, information specialist, knowledge manager, and archivist that requires a master's degree from an ALA-accredited program.

In this same ideal world, ALA would also

5. Hire as its own senior managers only individuals with a master's degree from an ALA-accredited program or, lacking individuals with this non-negotiable qualification, require new hires to obtain an ALA-accredited master's degree at the association's expense in a reasonable period of time.
6. Develop a marketing campaign aimed at funding sources to promote the value of hiring professionals with degrees from ALA-accredited programs.

The previous listing of required courses is largely derived from the research and recommendations contained in documents reporting on studies and approaches developed in three nations: (a) Britain: *The Modernisation Review of Public Libraries: A Policy Statement* (Great Britain Department for Culture, Media and Sport 2010); (b) Canada: *Library Advocacy Now! A Training Program for Public Library Staff and Trustees* (Canadian Association of Public Libraries 2011); and (c) United States: *Long Overdue: A Fresh Look At Public and Leadership Attitudes about Libraries in the 21st Century* (Public Agenda Foundation, Bill and Melinda Gates Foundation, and Americans for Libraries Council 2006); as well as the practical experience and related theory behind the author's "lifecycle librarianship" (Crowley 2008a).

II. UNIVERSITIES PROVIDING PROFESSIONAL EDUCATION

General Observations on ALA-Accredited Program Responsiveness

In addressing how ALA-accredited programs may contribute to safeguarding the future of library, information, knowledge, and archival professionalism, it is necessary to face the realities that (a) programs have gotten used to teaching what they will and may resist the imposition of any required courses by the ALA (Crowley 2008b, 114–18), and (b) the same technological and educational approaches that support professionalism through bringing online degrees to students without local ALA-accredited programs inevitably complicate the teaching of personal marketing, advocacy, and other skills with heavy face-to-face components.

Self–Interest and Change

Change is possible, but it is an unfortunate reality that negative circumstances can sometimes be required in order to generate needed transformations. If the economy worsens, there is the possibility that the number of unemployed graduates of ALA-accredited programs will reach a critical mass, and potential new students will become less attracted to library and information studies. A loss of students and a subsequent program income could lead to a possible reduction in faculty numbers. Such an equation might lead universities with ALA-accredited programs to implement limited change. These programs could accept a few "noncontroversial" required courses, such as marketing and advocacy, and might even develop and offer supplementary workshops and other forms of nondegree instruction designed to increase the skills necessary for success in contemporary professional positions, which could maintain or increase employment opportunities for new program graduates.

The possible or actual loss of faculty positions is a powerful motivator in problematic economic times. It was a primary reason why a number of years ago at least one British university library school transformed itself into a corporate-oriented information program, albeit possibly to the detriment of educating public and other librarians. This transformation was discussed in *Renewing Professional Librarianship: A Fundamental Rethinking* (Crowley 2008b, 1–3).

Educating the Extroverted and Introverted

It is likely that both extroverted and introverted students will benefit from the rationales and techniques taught in marketing, advocacy, and communication courses, preferably at the level of one area covered per course. One assumes that marketing would be accepted as a required full course, as would communication, which is actually an entire academic field. Advocacy deserves the same level of commitment. Here it will be noted that the School of Interpersonal Communication of the author's doctoral alma mater Ohio University offers a graduate course titled "Communication and the Campaign," which addresses the "processes of communication as applied in a campaign, defined as any organizational goal-oriented effort designed to influence behaviors of [an] identifiable population" (Ohio University 2011). This is clearly advocacy by another name and deserves more than a single session on the topic in a management or marketing course. Educated expertise and experience in advocacy is required because the potential stakes are so large, up to and including the continued employment of library, information, knowledge, and archival professionals.

ALA-accredited programs are now facing a profound ethical and moral choice. They can continue to recruit and educate introverted students and send them emotionally unprepared into work environments that increasingly demand either extroverted personalities or the ability to adopt extroverted personas. Alternatively, in addition to the usual content and technology courses, these programs can provide the schooling and training necessary for introverted students to break out of their "zones of silence" or their Internet-only, no face-to-face, communication styles. Competency in face-to-face communication is a non-negotiable requirement for future success in many workplaces. Here it is worth noting that a former student of the author, self-admittedly shy and hesitant to start a conversation, forced herself to take an "improv" or improvisation acting workshop offered in downtown Chicago (The Second City 2011). While she noted that her basic personality remained shy, she now feels comfortable taking about the value of libraries in virtually any situation.

In this author's estimation, the primary values of marketing, advocacy, and communication courses, as well as improvisation or other acting workshops for future library, information, knowledge, or archival professionalism, is (1) to help introverts break free of their personal, as opposed to electronic, communication chains and (2) to provide both introverts and extroverts with guidance and experience in expanding and communicating with their professional circles, broadly understood. The availability of instructors should not be a problem. Most universities have business schools with marketing expertise, as well as independent or combined schools of communication and theater. Even community colleges have theater courses, often found in their communication departments. In major metropolitan areas the presence of skilled practitioners in all such areas will be an added bonus.

Additional Courses

As already noted, this author recommends that all ALA-accredited programs require that students intending to work in academic, public, or school libraries take such additional, preferably required, courses as: community outreach; working with children, teens, and adults; reading; and lifelong learning. Long-term survival of professionals in libraries, information centers, knowledge management centers, and archives often requires a variant of "relationship marketing" and an emphasis on providing service through all or critical parts of a customer-patron-user's life (Crowley 2007). Courses such as community outreach; working with children, teens, and adults; reading; and lifelong learning, adapted for context, will increasingly become more important when seen as vehicles for focusing on the needs of particular aspects of the academic, public, or school library's onsite and offsite clienteles in the information self-service age.

When joined to the previously discussed and priority courses in marketing, advocacy, and communication, as well as to the courses in technology and technology instruction already offered by most programs, these classes will help the professionals heading or working in academic, public, and school libraries to regularly reorient their services as required by changing circumstances. Undoubtedly, corporate information and knowledge students wishing to prepare themselves to work in a variety of contexts will also find such "library" courses attractive, if only as a "back up."

Complications of Online Education

Canada's *Library Advocacy Now! A Training Program for Public Library Staff and Trustees* (Canadian Association of Public Libraries 2011) is persuasive regarding the importance of ongoing face-to-face contact with influential people. Even in the electronic age, "face time" still counts in efforts to influence decision makers, particularly senior decision makers. This reality practically demands that online advocacy education by ALA-accredited programs (a) use every conceivable video and audio medium and (b) be supplemented by some sort of internship requiring extensive face-to-face contact with advocacy experts.

It is likely that online classes or workshops in improv or other theater and communication courses will need to be accompanied by substantial on-the-ground experiences. Successful Internet communication is possible, in part, because it has a psychologically freeing effect that allows the introverted to communicate more effectively. While this is a plus, the value of the old-fashioned handshake followed by several valuable minutes of face time can be immense, particularly if the face time is so important that it is rationed.

III. PROFESSIONALS AND STUDENTS SEEKING TO BECOME PROFESSIONALS

"They Changed My Job, and I Resent It"

About two years ago I received an unexpected phone call from an experienced academic librarian who had read *Renewing Professional Librarianship* (Crowley

2008b) and wanted to vent to the author. The caller asked to be called "Annie," which I believed then and now was a pseudonym, and she chose not to provide a last name or identify her academic library for fear of the consequences. Basically, her complaint was that she was being forced to shoulder her bosses' marketing responsibilities and really resented it.

"My job used to be divided into working the public service desk, helping faculty and students with their research, supporting online instruction, teaching the use of all types of library resources, creating online and print pathfinders for various courses, and building up certain parts of our collection in my off-desk time. I really enjoyed that," she explained.

"Now my boss was told by the administration that the library is behind in marketing, and she decided that I was the one who was going to do the work. She and her assistant will go to the occasional meeting but that's about it. Most of the time they just sit in their offices playing with their computers and doing stuff that really doesn't require actual human contact."

The irritation rising in her tone, the librarian continued: "When I am not at the desk I am out meeting with our central PR people, faculty, administrators, or other campus groups and otherwise going out to personally market the library. That's the sort of thing that is in my bosses' job descriptions. When I complained, they told me that my job's requirement for interpersonal and customer service skills covered any marketing assignments they wanted to give me."

Reacting to the Unexpected Complaint—or Opportunity?

I sympathized with the telephoning librarian and easily agreed with her that, if everything was as she described, it certainly did represent a dereliction of duty for her well-paid senior managers to "play with the computer all day" (her words) while she had to do the in-person library marketing across and off campus. During much of the conversation, I found myself wondering at the nature of a profession where bureaucratically inclined administrators preferred to hide in their offices and force their far-less-well-paid subordinates to do upper management advocacy work. Unlike the case of the professor I cited in chapter 12, "The Political Case for Supporting the Value of Professionalism," I have no personal knowledge about Annie on which to accept or reject her story. In truth, while I was accustomed to getting similar calls from distressed professionals while working at the Alabama Public Library Service and State Library of Ohio, they are rarely received, except from the occasional alum, in my current capacity as a professor with Dominican University's Graduate School of Library and Information Science. Because even a semi-anonymous phone call to complain can take a bit of nerve when believing that being found out could cost one's job, I tend to feel that Annie was being truthful in her version of the events.

However, Annie and the author came to a parting of the ways toward the end of our conversation. As politic as possible, I reminded this academic librarian that her boss and assistant boss are who they are. No matter how competent they may be technologically, they were obviously far behind her in the vital communication areas of face-to-face advocacy and marketing. I urged Annie, both for her long-term career prospects and the reputation of her current employer, to do what she could to make her marketing efforts a success. From her reply, I doubt if she agreed. Her state of mind was not entrepreneurial but resembled more the betrayed feelings expressed by certain Canadian librarians toward those funding sources that had undervalued their contributions (Canadian Association of Public Libraries 2011, 9).

What Students and Professionals Can Do

The first thing that students and professionals need to understand about the New Normal World of restricted funding and greater demands for effectiveness in delivering services is that many senior administrators rose to their library, information, knowledge, or archival leadership positions at a time when they were not required to have marketing and advocacy skills. Although perceptive leaders, whether introverted or extroverted, made a point of developing such skills, too many "bosses" used the need to gain or maintain technological expertise as an excuse to avoid regular face-to-face communication with their funding sources. In consequence, it is highly doubtful if many such "office-bound" administrators are members of the professional network of their mayor, university president, corporate CEO, or school superintendent. It is equally unlikely that they use effective marketing techniques to identify and meet the needs of their users and potential users.

Too many of these administrators were promoted without the ability to meet the present, radically changing needs of their organizations through effective advocacy and marketing. Consequently, as they march off to yet another meeting on what next to cut, a number of such senior administrators embody a new definition of AWOL—leaving their librarians and other staff *Adrift WithOut Leadership*.

In addition to embracing the professional values taught in ALA-accredited programs and developing the subject and technology competencies required in the workplace, students need to demand that their ALA-accredited programs

1. Provide education in advocacy, marketing, and communication;
2. Facilitate effective outgoing and networking behavior, whether by equipping extroverted and introverted students with group facilitation skills, or by encouraging introverted students to develop the capacity for outgoing personas through improvisation (improv), other acting, or similar communications workshops; and
3. Ensure that program alums may (a) audit marketing and advocacy classes on a space available basis for a small fee and (b) attend student-oriented workshops on these and related topics on the same basis as current students.

IV. EMPLOYERS

To adapt a management axiom to a time when advocacy and marketing are coming to the fore, "All senior managers who do not personally lead the advocacy and marketing efforts of their library, information, knowledge, or archival organizations, are stealing their salaries and ought to be offered a generous retirement package."

Employer and Managerial "Sins" in Undermining Professionalism

Both chapter 4, "We Build Communities through Knowledge: Demonstrating the Value of the Professional Public Librarian," by Brenda Roberts and chapter 2,

"Justifying Professional Education in a Self-Service World," by Rachel Rubin and Richard Rubin address the reality that many threats to professionalism are internal to the professions. Such threats are often generated by employers seeking to reduce costs with insufficient regard for how their short-term actions affect the perceptions of their organizations' own professionalism or impact perceptions of the professionalism of the library, information, knowledge, or archival field as a whole.

As seen in chapter 1, "Why Are We Trashing the Professionalism of Librarians, Information Specialists, Knowledge Managers, and Archivists?", chapter 10, "A Culturally Pragmatic and Feminist-Influenced Approach to Defending Professionalism," and chapter 12, "The Political Case for Supporting the Value of Professionalism," political decisions or the "who gets what and how" choices for organizations and communities are often quite subjective and usually biased to the interests of those who control the resources. The results can be more or less effective in achieving the ends of officials and managers and are inevitably symbolic of a community, corporation, school, or university's priorities. It can hardly be otherwise because politics, as a system of choices, "is expressed through symbolism" (Kertzer 1988, 2) when one understands that the allocation of funds and other resources has both practical and symbolic effects.

The importance of symbolism in both political and library and information contexts cannot be overstated. In the political sphere, elected officials will sport American flag lapel pins while appearing on camera or stand at podiums with the Canadian Maple Leaf flag or the British Union Jack visible in the background. In these instances, they are attempting to use valued national symbols to generate in their audiences an otherwise inexpressible sense of common purpose. This emotional connection can break down, particularly in a mixed or "nonpartisan" audience, when politicians reveal their visions of how to address such incendiary topics as appropriate tax rates for the wealthy or the intrinsic value of supporting social programs for the poor.

In his working life the author has regularly seen the symbolic nature of the library at work. When library funding is not a priority, a university president may "pay the library off" in accepted rhetoric, reminding the campus that the "library is the heart of the university." In private, when library requests for support become overly burdensome, the same university president can term the academic library "the black hole" that will swallow all dollars provided and demand yet more.

In the area of public libraries, I once heard a mayor declare in all sincerity that he did not believe his community was a "true city until it had built its own public library." Down in south Alabama, in a variant of the national aphorism, I once heard a county commissioner describe his values as "God, country, family, motherhood, pecan pie, and the public library."

In that lofty enumeration of community values, placing sixth still put the public library in rather exalted company.

Key Questions

The reader is asked to consider what sort of practical and symbolic messages are being sent to community or organizational decision makers when

1. Public library boards and directors replace librarians with the MLIS degree with social workers with the MSW;

2. Academic library deans have job descriptions changed to allow them to replace librarians with the MLIS with PhDs who served an apprenticeship in an academic library in lieu of the MLIS degree;
3. School librarians are replaced by library aides;
4. Archivists are replaced by student assistants; and
5. Corporate knowledge managers are replaced by employee self-service.

Answers and Analyses

Librarians and Social Workers

The values of library, information, knowledge, and archival professionalism are critically important, as evidenced by the chapters of this work, and library expertise should be a part of every professional job description in a public, academic, or school library. No exceptions. If necessary, the organization should pay for the head of IT and head of the business office to earn a degree from the local ALA-accredited program or, lacking such, online. When public library boards and directors replace MLIS-holding librarians with MSW social workers, they send the message that library professionalism—and the culture it represents—is of secondary importance for contemporary library work.

It is appropriate to view social work expertise as an additional knowledge that is of value to library service, along with such expertise as multiple language competencies, marketing, and knowledge of adult basic education techniques. If local circumstances demand, hiring a librarian with both the MLIS and a social work degree or, at worst, employing a social worker on the condition that she or he secures the library and information science degree within a reasonable amount of time is defensible. If feasible, scholarship funds could even be made available for this purpose.

Nevertheless, if public libraries are being stressed by their default role as the last chance agency for dealing with many social issues, the preferred approach to addressing homeless and other traditional "social work" issues in public and other libraries is to provide basic social work training for a range of librarians and other staff in order to schedule individuals with "social work know-how" during all hours of library operation. This could be secured through workshops or even on-site courses. Any thoughtful administrator knows that a library social worker cannot be on site 24/7/365. Other staff would inevitably need to be responsible for social work–like activities—as is the case with readers advisory expertise or any other such specialized activity—during all library hours (Crowley 2005, 41).

PhD Academic Librarians

Changing job descriptions to employ PhDs as *librarians,* lately including individuals lacking a master's degree from an ALA-accredited program but having an apprenticeship experience in another academic library, represents an ignorance of history. Clearly college library deans or directors are forgetting that it has not been that long since the university library dean or university librarian was a subject specialist with a PhD who did not make it as a teaching or research professor and needed a job. He (usually a male) supervised the professionally educated librarians (usually female) who toiled as lowly handmaidens and did the actual work. If library deans and directors continue to so devalue library culture and expertise, what is to prevent their own replacement with a PhD-only academic who can more easily be seen on the campus as "part of the academic club"?

If subject expertise were truly lacking among the ranks of MLIS-holding librarians, hiring a PhD with the stipulation that she or he would need to earn the MLIS, perhaps with academic library support, is a reasonable second choice. Given the fact that the job market for tenure-seeking academics is best described as "miserable" in many fields and disciplines, it can expected that many doctorate-holding individuals will jump at the chance to earn the professional degree necessary to join the library culture if that was the requirement for a reasonably secure academic job.

School Librarians and Library Aides

School superintendents and principals replacing school librarians with library aides or parent volunteers generally make the switch on the theory that limited resources could be better used in ways more attuned to advancing their professional agendas. In the process, if the change enhances their own job security, so much the better.

State aid is seldom allocated to support school librarians, and their salaries must come from local tax dollars. When superintendents choose to replace school librarians with clerks, library aides, or parent volunteers, it generally indicates that the librarians have not made themselves valuable members of the administrators' personal networks. Don Hamerly addresses how such tragedies can be turned around or avoided in chapter 5, "Strategies and Aspirations for Defending School Library Professionalism.".

When Archivists Are Replaced by Student Assistants

When archivists are replaced by student assistants in academic environments or by clerks or assistants in corporate circles, it generally represents a determination that their services were not seen as vital by funders. In academic environments, the absence of protesting historians, political scientists, or popular culture faculty may suggest that the now-missing archivists were poor marketers and unsuccessful program advocates. Cecilia Salvatore's chapter 9, "Defending the Professional Archivist" well outlines what is lost—and will need to be reclaimed—when professionalism is missing from archival services.

Corporate Knowledge Managers Being Replaced by Employee Self-Service

Given the need for corporate knowledge managers and information specialists to constantly market their services, their replacement by a requirement that employees will henceforth need to conduct their own research indicates either (a) unusually poor marketing by the knowledge managers and information specialists or (b) senior corporate executives have attended another workshop emphasizing self-service as a way to cut costs. Almost inevitably some sort of information or knowledge professional will be hired at some point when it is revealed that information quality has fallen off, costs are not contained, and the self-service experiment is clearly a failure. Michael Koenig's chapter 8, "Valuing the Return on Investment of the Information Professional in Specialized Institutions (Corporations, Government Agencies, NGOs, etc.)," so well documents the actual financial value of the information professional that readers in corporate environments may choose to share his findings with their funding sources.

V. FUNDERS, CUSTOMERS, PATRONS, USERS, AND OTHER DECISION MAKERS

A Really Bad Idea

The occasional demand to "run the library like a business," particularly the public library, occasionally leads to contracting out library service to for-profit corporations. In the "Introduction" to this work, early 2011 reports on the looming disaster facing British public libraries helped outline the challenges facing library in American, British, and Canadian contexts. Reducing the number of public libraries and replacing salaried professional librarians and other staff with volunteers was advanced as part of the "Big Society" vision of Prime Minister David Cameron. This quixotic notion assumes that Great Britain possesses a culture where a massive number of local residents aspire to run community libraries and deliver other public services without financial compensation. As an ideal of disinterested public service, it was quickly undermined when the *Independent* newspaper blew away the political smoke screen to reveal that certain politicians and their friends were interested in converting public libraries from agencies of public service to sources of private profit (Dutta 2011; Grice and Dutta 2011).

According to the *Independent*, the American company Library Systems and Services (LSSI) saw considerable profit to be made in Britain by managing the public libraries of eight local governments by the end of 2011. It further envisioned running about 15 percent of the total British public library market within half a decade (Dutta 2011; Grice and Dutta 2011). North Americans familiar with the actual operating approach of LSSI, as opposed to its self-serving declarations issued for public consumption, are aware that raising profits through the employment of less qualified and less expensive staff in place of professional librarians happens so often that it may be seen as a LSSI corporate priority (Oder 2004, 2010).

The fundamental problem with contracting out library services is that priorities of service will no longer be centered on educated understandings of the needs of the child, teen, adult, or senior user. The ideal of the public library as a center of lifelong learning, what has been rightly termed its "transformational force" (De Rosa and Johnson. 2008, 1–6), will be discarded or drastically redefined. Public libraries will operate increasingly on such narrowed definitions of success as patron counts, circulation statistics, and total customers using library computers, quantitative measures that easily can be manipulated to rationalize dismantling programs that do not inflate a corporation's bottom line but that might be a local government priority. Support for the professionally educated librarians, whose values sustain the worth of meeting customer lifelong learning aspirations, often via well-received yet sometimes labor-intensive programs, will either be nonexistent or, at best, severely diminished.

In the end, privatization of library service can and does limit the capability of librarians to develop and sustain vital educational programs in the areas of literacy, lifelong learning, reading readiness, and community and cultural activities. It also reduces a community's appeal to managers of 21st-century corporations who need to operate with a well-educated workforce. Right now it is the British shortsighted use of a negative American model that is likely to help undermine that nation's public library community development and lifelong learning efforts. Why would Canadians want to travel down the same path? Or we Americans compound our initial error?

What Do Funders, Customers, Patrons, Users, and Other Decision Makers Want from Their Libraries?

When I was thinking about this final chapter, it occurred to me that I would be again facing a particularly tempting trap—giving a general laundry list of what could and should be done by readers to defend professionalism in their own work cultures. Throughout this and the other chapters of *Defending Professionalism,* readers have been provided with examples of what has worked and what could work to improve responsiveness and support in library, information, knowledge, and archival environments. Such suggestions are positive examples that should not be allowed to overshadow the central reality of this volume—the readers of this work, through ongoing marketing, advocacy, and communications efforts, are themselves responsible for developing the services necessary to (a) help solve the problems that are keeping their bosses awake at night; (b) meet the service needs of their customers, users, patrons, faculty, students, and/or community members; and (c) do it in ways that support, not undermine, relevant library, information, knowledge, and archival professional education from ALA-accredited institutions. While these items are simple to list, they involve a continuing commitment to an ongoing process involving appropriate education, knowledge, and employment that cannot be avoided.

Once again it is necessary to return to the observation of Lowell D. Holmes and Ellen Rhoads Holmes (2002) that "Americans traditionally are content with simple answers to complex questions" (15). In frenzied times such as the present, this author would not be surprised to learn that the British and Canadians are being tempted to take the same approach. However, a bit more thoughtfulness is in order. While the answers to defending professionalism might be complex because they differ by the contexts of individual libraries, information centers, knowledge management centers, and archives, the processes for securing those answers—effective marketing, advocacy, and communication—are fairly simple and well established, even in Internet environments.

Although it does not specifically involve securing the positions of professional librarians, I would like to end this chapter, and this book, with a political achievement that is well within the reach of many library and information science professionals. It is an anecdote detailing how a library director, with an unshakable belief in the fundamental value of a revived library service, used the political process to reshape his elected library board. In the process he cemented support for what he saw as an absolutely necessary library program.

The Practical Wisdom of Ted Balcom

Since 1997 students in the author's LIS 763 Readers Advisory Services course at Dominican University's Graduate School of Library and Information Science have been taught to lead book discussions by a uniquely qualified guest instructor, Readers Advisory (RA) legend Ted Balcom (1992), author of the groundbreaking

Book Discussions for Adults: A Leader's Guide and a proud Dominican alum. Prior to retiring from full-time librarianship to concentrate on RA consulting, teaching, and leading book and media discussions, Ted served as the longtime chief administrator of the Villa Park Public Library. In this capacity he demonstrated a particularly positive approach to combining a community's appreciation of effective RA with shoring up essential support for responsive services. On several occasions Ted talked with students about a welcome and deliberate byproduct of his library's sponsorship of engaging book discussions, the identification and cultivation of strong supporters of library programs who proved willing, even eager, to stand for election to the library board.

As with most Illinois public libraries, the Villa Park Public Library is governed by an elected board of trustees. This means that fervent believers in the library, those staunch advocates who have been termed *super supporters* in the fundamentally important Leo Burnett study for OCLC (De Rosa and Johnson 2008, 2-88), need to gain the votes of their fellow citizens in order to participate in making decisions on library services. Over the years, the combination of leadership in the promotion of reading by the professional library director, first-rate book discussions, and elected trustees who saw a program successfully addressing what they valued most in the library caused the governing body of the Villa Park Public Library to be regularly refreshed with reading enthusiasts.

A Library Can Grow Its Own Market

Ted Balcom's years-long cultivation of the support of those who love reading, libraries, and professional librarians represents a particularly striking example of the encouragement of *Return On Emotional Investment* (ROEI) (Crowley 2008b, 3). As the reader will recall from the author's earlier discussion, ROEI is an essential component of *lifecycle librarianship*, an approach to securing the future of libraries and professional librarians that is rooted in identifying and meeting priority community needs for responsive services from "the lapsit to the nursing home." To restate its definition, ROEI can be envisioned as a continuing emotional connection between users and the libraries and professional librarians who provide the library services and programs that people deem to be vital to their lives.

It is important to distinguish ROEI from BOI, the classic business concept of return on investment. ROI, a standard approach to corporate evaluation, can be fundamentally important to information specialists and knowledge managers in the corporate environment. However, when it is applied to academic, public, and school libraries, usually through demands to "run the library like a business," ROI often means sacrificing quality and the public library's fundamentally important role in the promotion of various aspects of lifelong learning. The result can be poorly supported institutions that are increasingly staffed by nonprofessional and less costly staff hired at minimal expense to circulate materials in the least costly way.

ENVOI

Fundamentally, the chapters of *Defending Professionalism* have sought to equip librarians, information specialists, knowledge managers, and archivists with the understanding that generating and sustaining support for their professionalism requires sustained effort. It demands an appropriate professional education, one that equips graduates with the effective marketing, advocacy, and communication approaches to devising, delivering, and defending programs that are prized by their funding sources, specifically including elected officials, school administrators, higher education leaders, and voters. Such a commitment by library, information, knowledge, and archival professionals, well-educated extroverts and introverts alike, requires using effective advocacy, marketing, and communication approaches that support professionalism even as they deliver the valued services that meet critically important needs of the funding authorities, communities, and institutions whose problems they were employed to help solve and whose interests they were hired to advance.

REFERENCES

American Library Association. 2008. *Standards for Accreditation of Master's Programs in Library and Information Studies.* Chicago: Office for Accreditation, American Library Association. Accessed August 1, 2011. http://www.ala.org/ala/educationcareers/education/accreditedprograms/standards/standards_2008.pdf.

American Library Association. 2011. *The State of America's Libraries: A Report from the American Library Association.* Chicago: American Library Association. Accessed June 19, 2011. http://www.ala.org/ala/newspresscenter/mediapresscenter/americaslibraries2011/index.cfm.

American Library Association, Office for Library Advocacy. 2012. Advocacy University, Resources. Accessed March 6, 2012. http://www.ala.org/advocacy/advleg/advocacyuniversity.

Balcom, Ted. 1992. *Book Discussions for Adults: A Leader's Guide.* Chicago: American Library Association.

Canadian Association of Public Libraries (CAPL). 2011. *Library Advocacy Now! A Training Program for Public Library Staff and Trustees.* Ottawa, ON: Canadian Library Association. Accessed July 31, 2011. http://www.cla.ca/divisions/capl/Library AdvocacyNow.pdf.

Chartered Institute of Library and Information Professionals (CILIP). 2011. "Campaigning Resources." Accessed July 31. http://www.cilip.org.uk/get-involved/campaigning-toolkit/Pages/resources.aspx.

Crowley, Bill. 1994. "Library Lobbying as a Way of Life." *Public Libraries* 33(2): 96–98.

Crowley, Bill. 2005. "Rediscovering the History of Readers Advisory Service." *Public Libraries* 44(1): 37–41. Accessed August 11, 2011. http://www.ala.org/ala/mgrps/divs/pla/publications/publiclibraries/pastissues/janfeb2005.pdf.

Crowley, Bill. 2007. "Don't Let Google and the Pennypinchers Get You Down: Defending (or Redefining) Libraries and Librarianship in the Age of Technology." In *British Columbia Library Association Conference 2007: Beyond 20/20: Envisioning the Future, Burnaby, British Columbia (Canada),* April 19–21, 2007. Unpublished presentation. Accessed August 6, 2011. http://eprints.rclis.org/bitstream/10760/9373/1/Crowley_2007.pdf.

Crowley, Bill. 2008a. "Lifecycle Librarianship." *Library Journal* (April 1): 46–48. Accessed August 1, 2011. http://www.libraryjournal.com/article/CA6542287.html.

Crowley, Bill. 2008b. *Renewing Professional Librarianship: A Fundamental Rethinking.* A Beta Phi Mu Monograph. Westport, CT. Libraries Unlimited.

Crowley, Bill. 2010. "Know Your ROEI: Emotional Investment in Service Delivery Can Return Lifelong Benefits." *Library Journal* (February 15): 34–35. Accessed March 6, 2012. http://www.libraryjournal.com/lj/ljinprint/currentissue/853644-403/know_your_roei.html.csp.

De Rosa, Cathy, and Jenny Johnson. 2008. *From Awareness to Funding: A Study of Library Support in America*. Dublin, OH: OCLC. Accessed March 17, 2009. http://www.oclc.org/reports/funding/fullreport.pdf.

"Don't Get Mad; Get Even." 2011. Answers.com. Accessed August 7. http://www.answers.com/topic/don-t-get-mad-get-even-1.

Dutta, Kumal. 2011. "Ssshhh! The Noisy US Revolution Coming to British Libraries." *Independent* (March 7). Accessed August 11, 2011. http://www.independent.co.uk/arts-entertainment/books/news/ssshhh-the-noisy-us-revolution-coming-to-british-libraries-2234236.html.

Federal Library and Information Center Committee. 1997. Getting the Word Out: Marketing Your Library's Information Services—Librarians as Knowledge Workers." *FEDLINK Technical Notes* 15(1). Accessed July 31, 2011. http://www.loc.gov/flicc/tn/97/01/tn9701.html#getting%20the%20word%20out.

Great Britain Department for Culture, Media and Sport. 2010. *The Modernisation Review of Public Libraries: A Policy Statement*. London: DCMS Department for Culture, Media and Sport. Accessed August 1, 2011. http://www.official-documents.gov.uk/document/cm78/7821/7821.pdf.

Grice, Andrew, and Kunal Dutta. 2011. "Cameron's Big Society Relaunch Runs into Big Trouble: Libraries May be Run by US Private Firms / Non-dom to Head up Big Society Bank." *Independent* (February 15). Accessed August 11, 2011. http://www.independent.co.uk/news/uk/politics/camerons-big-society-relaunch-runs into-big-trouble-2215053.html.

Hardin, Garrett. 1968. "The Tragedy of the Commons." *Science* 162(3859): 1243–48. Accessed July 16, 2011. http://www.sciencemag.org/site/feature/misc/webfeat/sotp/pdfs/162-3859-1243.pdf.

Holmes, Lowell D., and Ellen Rhoads Holmes. 2002. "The American Cultural Configuration." In *Distant Mirrors: America as a Foreign Culture*. 3rd ed., ed. Philip R. De Vita and James D. Armstrong, 4–26. Belmont, CA: Wadsworth/Thomson Learning.

Kemp, Roger L. 1997. *Managing America's Cities: A Handbook for Local Government Productivity*. Jefferson, NC: McFarland.

Kertzer, David I. 1988. *Ritual, Politics and Power*. New Haven, CT: Yale University Press.

Lipset, Seymour Martin. 1991. *Continental Divide: The Values and Institutions of the United States and Canada*. New York: Routledge.

New York Library Association. 2011. "Advocacy Tools." Accessed July 31. http://www.nyla.org/page/advocacy-tools-65.html.

Oder, Norman. 2004. "When LSSI Comes to Town." *Library Journal* (October 1). Accessed August 11, 2011. http://www.libraryjournal.com/article/CA456252.html.

Oder. Norman. 2010. "LSSI Controversy in Santa Clarita, CA, Makes New York Times Front Page (Updated)." *LJ Insider* (September 28). Accessed August 11, 2011. http://blog.libraryjournal.com/ljinsider/2010/09/28/lssi-controversy-in-santa-clarita-ca-makes-new-york-times-front-page-but-much-is-missing/.

Ohio University. 2011. *Graduate Catalog* Interpersonal Communication. Accessed August 6. http://www.ohio.edu/gcatalog/95–97/AREAS/inco.html.

Pew Center on the States and Public Policy Institute of California. 2010. *Facing Facts Public Attitudes and Fiscal Realities in Five Stressed States*. Washington, DC: Pew Center on the States. Accessed July 28, 2011. http://www.pewcenteronthestates.org/uploadedFiles/PCS_PPIC.pdf.

Public Agenda Foundation, Bill and Melinda Gates Foundation, and Americans for Libraries Council. 2006. *Long Overdue: A Fresh Look at Public and Leadership Attitudes about Libraries in the 21st Century*. New York: Public Agenda. Accessed August 6, 2011. http://www.publicagenda.org/files/pdf/Long_Overdue.pdf.

Santos, Fernanda. 2011. "In Lean Times, Schools Squeeze Out Librarians." *New York Times*, June 24. Accessed July 23, 2011. http://www.nytimes.com/2011/06/25/nyregion/schools-eliminating-librarians-as-budgets-shrink.html?_r=1&pagewanted=all.

The Second City. 2011. "Second City Chicago Courses." Accessed August 6. http://www.
    secondcity.com/training/chicago/coursecatalog/.
Shockley-Zalabak, Pamela S. 2006. *Fundamentals of Organizational Communication:
    Knowledge, Sensitivity, Skills, Values*. Boston: Pearson.
Texas Library Association. 2011. "Save Our Texas Libraries!" Accessed July 31, 2011.
    http://www.txla.org/save-my-library.
U.S. Library of Congress. 1986. *Research Policies for the Social and Behavioral Sciences:
    Report*. Washington, DC: U.S. GPO Accessed July 20, 2011. http://www.eric.
    ed.gov/PDFS/ED289725.pdf.

INDEX

ABOUT THE EDITOR AND CONTRIBUTORS

LENORA BERENDT has spent over 20 years working in academic, public, and corporate libraries. She spent much of her library career in the University Libraries at Loyola University Chicago, where she focused on teaching and promoting library user instruction, and was active in the *Chicago Area Instruction Librarians Group*, which she chaired from 1996–2003. Lenora is currently *Career Services Coordinator* and *Adjunct Faculty* in the School of Library and Information Science at Dominican University in River Forest, IL.

BILL CROWLEY (Editor) worked for 23 years in New York, Alabama, Indiana, and Ohio libraries and library organizations in capacities ranging from part-time clerk to deputy state librarian. As of this writing Bill has authored 41 articles and book chapters in the library science, information science, higher education, and other literatures, as well as 2 books. The first, *Spanning the Theory-Practice Divide in Library and Information Science*, was published by Scarecrow Press in 2005. The second, *Renewing Professional Librarianship. A Fundamental Rethinking*, was issued as a Beta Phi Mu Monograph by Libraries Unlimited in March 2008. Bill earned a BA in history from Hunter College of the City University of New York, an MS in library service from Columbia University, an MA in English from Ohio State University with a thesis in occupational folklore, and completed a PhD in higher education at Ohio University in Athens, Ohio, with a dissertation on the research university library. Since 1996 he has been a faculty member at Dominican University's Graduate School of Library and Information Science where he is a tenured full professor. Bill regularly presents on professionalism and management topics, as well as issues involving conceptualizing the roles of the library and librarian. He welcomes e-mail to crowbill@dom.edu.

JANICE M. DEL NEGRO, PhD, is an assistant professor at the Graduate School of Library and Information Science at Dominican University in River Forest, Illinois, where she teaches Foundations of Library and Information Science, Children's Literature, Storytelling, Young Adult Literature, and the doctoral seminar on reading.

Professor Del Negro also serves on the advisory board for the Butler Center for Children's Literature at Dominican University. She recently collaborated with Ellin Greene on the fourth edition of the classic storytelling textbook *Storytelling: Art and Technique*, released in January, 2010. Professor Del Negro has served on the Newbery, Caldecott, and Lee Bennett Hopkins Poetry Award committees, served as chair of the American Library Association's 2005 Laura Ingalls Wilder Award committee, and subsequently chaired the 2007 Caldecott Award Committee. Del Negro's first picture book, *Lucy Dove* (1998), won the Anne Izard Storytelling Award; her second picture book, *Willa and the Wind* (2005), was an ALA Notable Book and an Honor Book for the Irma Simonton Black and James H. Black Award for Excellence in Children's Literature from the Bank Street College of Education in New York City. Her collection of supernatural tales for young adults, *Passion and Poison* (2007), received starred reviews in both *Horn Book* and *School Library Journal*. She has spoken and conducted workshops on book reviewing, publishing, storytelling, and reading motivation for teachers, librarians, parents, and other educators in a variety of settings, including the University of Chicago, the University of Illinois, the North Carolina State Library, and the University of San Diego. Del Negro has been a featured speaker, storyteller, and workshop leader at the National Storytelling Festival, the Illinois Library Association, the Society for Children's Book Writers and Illustrators, the Illinois Storytelling Festival, the University of Illinois Youth Literature Festival, and many other celebratory events.

DON HAMERLY is assistant professor and director of the School Library Media Program in the Graduate School of Library and Information Science at Dominican University in River Forest, Illinois. Before completing his PhD at The University of Texas at Austin, Dr. Hamerly served for 20 years in Texas public schools, capturing kids' hearts and feeding their heads as a teacher of English and French, as an Academic Decathlon coach, as a club sponsor, and as a teacher librarian. As a Texas native and recent transplant to Chicagoland, Dr. Hamerly has only recently come to fully comprehend the meaning of "four seasons" and welcomes e-mail to dhamerly@dom.edu.

KYLE M. L. JONES began his library career at a small, private liberal arts college as an information technology specialist before taking a public librarianship position on the East Coast. He is now a doctoral student in the School of Library and Information Studies at the University of Wisconsin-Madison. His research interests include knowledge management and subjects within e-Learning informatics such as the organization, access, and dissemination of information in traditional and nontraditional learning management systems.

MICHAEL E. D. KOENIG is a professor of knowledge management at the C.W. Post Campus of Long Island University, where he was the founding dean of the College of Information and Computer Science at Long Island University. His career has included senior management positions in the information industry, including manager of research information services at Pfizer Inc., director of development at the Institute for Scientific Information, vice president—North America at Swets and Zeitlinger and vice president data management at Tradenet, as well as academic positions such as associate professor at Columbia University, and dean and professor at Dominican University. Prof. Koenig holds a PhD in information science from Drexel University; an MBA in mathematical methods and computers, and an MA in library and information science from the University of Chicago; and an undergraduate degree from Yale University. A Fulbright Scholar in Argentina, he is the author of more than one hundred professional and scholarly publications, and he is the co-editor of *Knowledge Management for the Information Professional* (2000), *Knowledge Management—Lessons Learned: What Works and What Doesn't* (2003), and *Knowledge Management in Practice: Connections and Context* (2008), all published by Information Today for the American Society for Information Science and Technology. A member of the editorial board of more than a dozen journals, Prof. Koenig is also the past president of the International Society for Scientometrics and Informetrics. In 2005, he was awarded the Jason Farradane Award "in recognition of outstanding work in the information field."

ROBERT F. MORAN JR. is Librarian Emeritus at Indiana University Northwest where he directed the library for 22 years. In addition to a MSLS from Catholic University, Washington, he earned an MBA at the University of Chicago. A student of organizational structure and change for his entire career, his articles have been published in *College and Research Libraries,* and *The Journal of Library Administration,* and he writes a column on organization and change for *Library Leadership and Management.* As chair of the Comparative Library Organization Committee of the Library Leadership and Management Association of the American Library Association, he developed and oversaw programs on organizational structure at ALA conventions.

MARIA OTERO-BOISVERT is a doctoral student in the San Jose State University / Queensland University of Technology Gateway PhD program. She has a Bachelor's degree from Barnard College, a Master's in Romance Languages and Literature from Princeton University, and an MLS from the University of Michigan (1985). Maria has had a 20-plus-year career as an academic librarian. She has worked in collection development as a bibliographer, in management as a department head, and in administration as an associate dean and a consortium director. She has had a parallel career in publishing as editor of *Library Administration and Management* (ALA; 1996–2000) and as one of the editors of *Criticas Magazine* (Reed Business Info.; 2001–2004). Her list of published works goes back to 1988 and spans local, national, and international publications. She is currently the Editor-in-Chief for the SJSU, School of Library and Information Studies–based *Student Research Journal (SRJ).* Her doctoral work will investigate library advocacy, theories of influence and how they impact funding decisions in the academic library environment.

CLEO PAPPAS is an assistant information services librarian and assistant professor at the Library of the Health Sciences at the University of Illinois at Chicago (UIC). A graduate of Dominican University, Professor Pappas is also adjunct faculty in the Department of Medical Education (DME) of UIC's College of Medicine (COM). She is a senior member of the Academy of Health Information Professionals (AHIP) in the Medical Library Association and was recipient of a 2009 Fellowship to the Medical Informatics MBL/NLM Course Sponsored by the National Library of Medicine. In 2010, Professor Pappas received the first UIC Library Achievement Award. Her research interests include evidence-based healthcare (EBHC), evidence-based library and information practice (EBL), health information literacy—the effective change of consumer behavior through health information, and health literacy—the study of offering health information at an appropriate reading level or medium for the consumer involved.

BRENDA ROBERTS is coordinator of Adult Collections at the Ottawa Public Library (OPL) in Ontario, Canada. In addition to her MLIS from McGill University, she holds an undergraduate honours degree in Philosophy and a master's degree in Science Policy from Montreal's Concordia University. Brenda has spearheaded a number of projects related to professionalism during her career. She is a member of her union's collective bargaining committee as well as one of two founding library representatives on OPL's Joint Professional Development Committee. Her research interests include pragmatism and public policy and evidence-based librarianship.

RACHEL RUBIN is the director of the Bexley (OH) Public Library. Previously, she was the assistant manager in the Humanities, Fine Arts, and Recreation division at the Columbus (OH) Metropolitan Library and was the library manager of the Old Worthington branch of the Worthington (OH) Libraries. Rachel is active in the Ohio Library Council (OLC), served on the Program Committee for the 2011 OLC Convention and Expo, and has been a member of the OLC Diversity Awareness and Resources Committee and the Outreach and Special Services Action Council. She was a member of the inaugural class of ALA Emerging Leaders in 2007 and served as an intern on the ALA Council Committee on Organization. Rachel was also a trainer for the OCLC Webjunction Spanish Language Outreach Program. Rachel received her MLIS from Kent State University, her BA from Carleton College, and is currently pursuing a PhD in Managerial Leadership in the Information Professions through Simmons College in Boston.

RICHARD RUBIN is associate provost for Extended Education at Kent State University. Prior to his appointment as Associate Provost, he served for more than 10 years as Director of the School of Library and Information Science at Kent State University. He has been a faculty member there since 1988. Dr. Rubin previously worked as a reference librarian and Personnel Director at the Akron-Summit County (OH) Public Library. Dr. Rubin has published numerous books and articles including *Foundations of Library and Information Science*, 3rd Edition (Neal-Schuman 2010); *Hiring Library Employees* (Neal-Schuman 1993); and *Human Resource Management in Libraries* (Neal-Schuman 1991). He has been active in the American Library Association most recently serving as Chair of the ALA Committee on Accreditation. Dr. Rubin received his doctorate in Library and Information Science from the University of Illinois at Urbana-Champaign, his MLS from Kent State University, and his AB from Oberlin College.

CECILIA LIZAMA SALVATORE, MLS, PhD is associate professor at Dominican University in River Forest, Illinois, where she is expanding the archives and cultural heritage institutions curriculum and program. Previously, she developed the archives curriculum and program at Emporia State University in Emporia, Kansas, for which she received the annual "Award for Excellence" by the Kansas City Area Archivists (KCAA) in 2006. Dr. Salvatore is a Certified Archivist who has collaborated with and consulted for various archives and cultural heritage institutions, most recently in the Western Pacific Islands. Her area of research is on the place of indigenous and "other" knowledge and cultural heritage resources in mainstream archival institutions and education.

MICHAEL STEPHENS, after working for 15 years in public libraries, is currently an assistant professor in the School of Library and Information Science at San Jose State University. His research focuses on the use of emerging technologies in libraries and technology learning programs. He currently writes the monthly column "Office Hours" in *Library Journal,* exploring issues, ideas, and emerging trends in library and information science education. Stephens has spoken about emerging technologies, innovation, and libraries to audiences nationally and internationally, including a 2009 speaking/research tour of Australia. He is fascinated by library buildings and virtual spaces that center around users, content, digital creation, and encouraging the heart. He also believes in the power of the professional commons to help librarians move forward with services and stewardship.